STANDARDS AND
ETHICS FOR
COUNSELLING

TIM BOND

SAGE Publications
London • Thousand Oaks • New Delhi

To Jan

© Tim Bond

First published 1993
Reprinted 1994, 1995, 1997, 1998

SAGE Publications Ltd
6 Bonhill Street
London EC2A 4PU

SAGE Publications Inc
2455 Teller Road
Thousand Oaks, California 91320

SAGE Publications India Pvt Ltd
32, M-Block Market
Greater Kailash – I
New Delhi 110 048

British Library Cataloguing in Publication Data

Bond, Tim
  Standards and Ethics for Counselling in
  Action. – (Counselling in Action Series)
  I. Title   II. Series
  361.3

  ISBN 0–8039–8645–9
  ISBN 0–8039–8646–7 (pbk)

Library of Congress catalog card number 93–085416

Typeset by Mayhew Typesetting, Rhayader, Powys
Printed and bound in Great Britain by
Biddles Ltd, Guildford and King's Lynn

Contents

Foreword by *Professor Douglas Hooper*

As we move into the last years of this century it is clear that counselling and being counselled are likely to involve more and more people. In the complex and often difficult worlds which people inhabit in their families and at work, it seems that a person outside these worlds is often best placed to give personal help in times of stress and difficulty. Formerly people often received this kind of help from a family doctor, a social worker or from a priest. Although these individuals may still offer valuable help, counsellors are now increasingly used by people in trouble. There are two reasons for this increasing use of counselling. First, the necessary time and space for a troubled person has become very difficult to find. The demands on doctors and social workers have increased considerably so that less time is available for the counselling process, which needs to be unhurried to be effective. Next, and of equal importance, counselling theory and technique have improved markedly over the last decade, and it is now recognized that effective counselling requires someone properly trained to fulfil the role of counsellor. Doctors, social workers, priests, lawyers, and others may well be sensitive to a person's need for counselling, but have not often had time to undertake the training themselves.

But as well as the continuing demand within health, welfare, and education services, the very success of counselling leads more and more people to seek out a counsellor for help in these settings as well as in counselling agencies such as Relate. Private practice counselling has also markedly increased as lack of provision and long waiting lists lead people to seek out a counsellor.

This much increased demand for counselling has led to a proliferation of training opportunities for would-be counsellors, which raises a number of problems concerned with competence and standards. In this growing and fast-moving context, practitioners, clients and employers need support and guidance over the proper exercise of the counselling role to ensure good practice. Articles in the press over the last year have given prominence to these issues and have highlighted some troubled and dissatisfied clients for whom apparently the counselling process was very unsatisfactory.

Fortunately, the British Association for Counselling has been very active over the past few years in putting into place a series of codes of ethics and practice to protect clients by helping its members to work to good standards. This has been a co-operative exercise by a number of people but one in which Tim Bond has played a very prominent part. As he considered these issues, he became more and more aware of some of the complex practice issues which codes seek to regulate. These issues were not only those of counselling practice but also deeper ethical and moral concerns shared by all members of the caring professions.

The result of much of Tim Bond's thought is now available in this volume, and it is probably the first time in this country that these issues have been thoroughly discussed. This is, therefore, a timely book. Because it arises directly from the author's experience of dealing with real issues, it has a directness and a freshness which is helpful and stimulating. The emphasis is very much on the responsibility which a counsellor undertakes when he or she meets a frightened, anxious, depressed and often damaged person and this emphasis is exactly right. This book highlights the need for would-be counsellors as well as experienced practitioners to understand this responsibility very fully in their work – both to give as good a service as they can, but also to help themselves understand the ethical puzzles and confusions with which they can be presented by some clients.

Codes of professional standards are the crucial framework for practice, but they are also necessarily terse summaries of the complex matters involved. Again, the author provides valuable guidance here by teasing out the issues lying behind the published standards. He emphasizes that being a counsellor involves layers of responsibility which go beyond the client to colleagues, other professionals and (very important) the counsellor. He discusses, too, the mechanics of counselling such as records, supervision, quality assurance and so on. This is both helpful and important because these issues relate the counselling process to its structure and enable counsellors to feel confident in their practice.

But the core of the book is, rightly, about helping counsellors to deal more effectively with the key issues of confidentiality, exploitation, and the responsibility for the trust by the client in the counsellor's practice. This trust lies at the heart of the counselling process and Tim Bond helps the reader to develop it in the proper context of personal and professional ethical behaviour.

There is now an active and important debate about the need to regulate the training and practice of counsellors more closely than in the past. The British Association and many skilled counsellors will need to tease out these matters with others not involved in the counselling world. This book is going to be of considerable help to both these important matters, as well as to the training of the would-be counsellor and the daily work of the practitioner.

Acknowledgements

I am extremely grateful to Jan, my partner, to whom this book is dedicated. She has been encouraging and offered advice and ideas during its gestation and showed great patience as piles of papers tended to flood out of my office into the rest of our home. Simultaneous with the writing of this book, Jan was gestating 'Malachi' our pet name for the bump which has become our daughter, Zoe. I have enjoyed Zoe's company on the occasions she has been perched on my lap or shoulder as I have been writing. I am not sure that I have done justice to her suggestions. I am still a novice at interpreting the noises of babes and sucklings but I am learning fast.

I could not have become involved in a project as large as this, were it not for the support of Dr Bill Williamson, the Director of the Department of Adult and Continuing Education, and my friends and colleagues in our department and elsewhere at the University of Durham. Many have helped by contributing ideas or directing me towards articles. They include: Judith Baron, General Manager of BAC; Dr John Paterson, Associate Dean, University of Alberta (for the origins of 'counselling'); Nicola Barden; David Cliff; June Richardson; Linda Garbutt; and Janice Russell. Many useful ideas and comments on early drafts were received from some members of the Standards and Ethics Sub-committee, in particular Paul Carney, Alan Jamieson, Caroline Jones, Fiona Palmer-Barnes, Maggie Smith and Gabrielle Syme. Students on the current MA in Counselling course helped me to develop my line of argument in several chapters.

The staff and officers of the British Association for Counselling have been generous in their assistance in obtaining information for this book. I have really appreciated their encouragement.

I am particularly grateful to Kenneth Cohen, a solicitor with a particular interest in counselling and psychotherapy. He has given freely of his time and made many helpful suggestions during the writing of this book, as well as permitting me to quote from his pioneering article on 'Some Legal Issues in Counselling and Psychotherapy' with the consent of the *British Journal of Guidance and Counselling*.

Once again Alpha Word Power in Durham have performed magnificently in converting my dictation and written manuscript into type. I am particularly grateful to Terry Dobson, and to

Peter Hughes the proprietor. Professor Windy Dryden has made many useful suggestions as the series editor. The staff of Sage have provided very practical help.

I am grateful for all the help I have received from the people mentioned and many others. I hope they will feel that I have used their assistance appropriately. I take sole responsibility for the contents of this book.

Tim Bond

The author is grateful for permission to use copyright material granted by the American Counseling Association for extracts from Barbara Herlihy and Gerald Corey, *Dual Relationships* (1992), and *Ethical Standards of the American Association for Counseling and Development* (1988); the Association for Student Counselling for extracts from *HMI Inspection of Counselling Services* (1991), and *Requirements of Accreditation* (1992); British Association for Counselling for the *Code of Ethics and Practice for Counsellors* (1992) in its entirety, and the summary of the legal opinion of John Friel, 'In the Matter of the Powers of Her Majesty's Inspector of Schools to Inspect Counselling in Polytechnics, Colleges of Further Education etc.' (1993); *British Journal of Guidance and Counselling* for extracts from Kenneth Cohen, 'Some Legal Issues in Counselling and Psychotherapy' (1992), 20(1): 10–26; Children's Legal Centre for extracts from 'A Child's Right to Confidentiality?' (1989) in *Childright*, 57: 7–10; the Consumers' Association for an extract from 'Psychotherapy' (1991) in *Which? way to Health*, December: 212–15; Graham Dexter for an extract from *Counselling Network*, York and Scarborough College of Midwifery and Nursing Counselling Network (1991); *The Guardian* for an extract from 'Re. J. (a minor) (Medical Treatment)' in *Guardian Law Reports* (1992); Her Majesty's Stationery Office for Extracts from Her Majesty's Inspectorate, *Careers Education and Guidance from 5 to 16* (1988) and the Law Commission, *Breach of Confidence* (1981); Anne Hayman for extracts from 'Psychoanalyst Subpoenaed' (1965), *The Lancet*, 16 October: 785–6; Gaie Houston and The Rochester Foundation for extracts from *Supervision and Counselling* (1990); Hans Hoxter and the International Round Table for the Advancement of Counselling for extracts from *The Nature of Counselling* (1991); *Independent on Sunday* for extracts from Linda Grant, 'Counselling: a solution or a problem?' (1992), 19 April: 22–3 and 26 April: 20; Institute for Personnel Management for an extract from Michael Megranahan,

Counselling – A Practical Guide for Employers (1989); International Thompson Publishing Ltd. for extracts from John Rowan, *The Reality Game – A guide to humanistic counselling and therapy* (1983); National Youth Bureau and the author for Brigid Proctor, 'Supervision: A Co-operative Exercise in Accountability', in Mary Marken and Malcolm Payne (eds), *Enabling and Ensuring Supervision in Practice* (1988); Open University Press for extracts from Windy Dryden, *Therapists' Dilemmas* (1985), and Peter Hawkins and Robin Shohet, *Supervision in the Helping Professions* (1989); Oxford University Press for extracts from R.E. Allen, *The Concise Oxford Dictionary of Current English* (1990), Raanon Gillon, 'Autonomy and Consent' in Michael Lockwood (ed.), *Moral Dilemmas in Modern Medicine* (1985), and David Heyd and Sidney Bloch, 'The ethics of suicide' in Sidney Bloch and Paul Chodoff (eds), *Psychiatric Ethics* (1991), Jeremy Holmes and Richard Lindley, *The Values of Psychotherapy* (1989), and J.B. Sykes (ed.), *The Concise Oxford Dictionary of Current English* (1982); National Association for Citizens Advice Bureaux for extracts from 'Quality of Advice: NACAB Membership Scheme Requirements', in *National Homelessness Advice Service – Guidance on CAB Minimum Housing Advice Standards* (1990); Pluto Publishing for an extract from Alice Miller, *Thou Shalt Not be Aware – Society's Betrayal of the Child* (1990); John Rowan for an extract from 'Counselling and the Psychology of Furniture' in *Breakthroughs and Integration in Psychotherapy* (1992), Whurr; Sage Publications for extracts from Kenneth M. Austin, Mary E. Moline and George T. Williams, *Confronting Malpractice – Legal and Ethical Dilemmas in Psychotherapy* (1990), Windy Dryden, *Rational–Emotive Counselling in Action* (1990), Brian Thorne and David Mearns, *Person–Centred Counselling in Action* (1988), and Michael Jacobs, *Psychodynamic Counselling in Action* (1988); Simon and Schuster International Group for extracts from Laurence M. Brammer and Everatt L. Shostrum, *Therapeutic Psychology – Fundamentals of Counselling and Psychotherapy* (1982), Prentice Hall; United Kingdom Council for Nursing, Midwifery and Health Visiting for extracts from *Code of Professional Conduct* (1992); Youth Access for extracts from Arthur Musgrave, *What is Good Advice Work?*, a NAYPCAS discussion paper (1991).

These extracts have been reprinted with permission. No further reproduction is authorized without written consent of the original copyright holder.

PART I THE BACKGROUND

1 Introduction

My interest in ethical issues and the identification of standards of practice, like that of many other counsellors, has grown out of first-hand practical experience of counselling. What should I do when a client confides that she was sexually abused as a child and she fears the perpetrator is still abusing other children? How should I respond to a colleague at work who asks me for counselling, bearing in mind that we work together regularly and attend the same meetings? In my experience, issues of confidentiality and managing the boundaries between different kinds of relationships, or overlapping roles, often throw up the most acute dilemmas about standards and ethics for counsellors. This makes it all the more surprising that relatively little has been written about these issues to date. When I visit a library or book shop well stocked with counselling books, I am presented with a choice of several books on each of the well known methods of counselling, and sometimes the less well known. Similarly, I have no difficulty in finding a choice of books about eating disorders, depression, assertiveness, bereavement and a whole range of different problems and issues. Yet there appear to be no British books specifically about the standards and ethics of counselling to help me manage this aspect of my work with clients. I am left to consult a few texts from the USA, where the development of counselling has taken place in a different cultural and legal setting, or to look at books about the ethics of roles such as psychotherapy or social work which may, or may not, be compatible with counselling.

I probably would have been content to continue doing no more than grumbling about this unsatisfactory state of affairs if Windy Dryden had not asked me to write a book which addressed the needs of both trainee counsellors and experienced practitioners.

How to use this book

This book is intended to be practical, and I hope that many people will want to read it from cover to cover. I have structured the contents so that the logical structure of counselling ethics and standards of practice becomes apparent progressively through the book. However, when I am working with clients I do not always have time for extensive reading at the time when I most need information or inspiration. In these circumstances I tend to dip into books looking for specific topics. I have tried to bear this in mind by grouping related issues together into chapters. Sometimes I need quicker access to a shorter passage on a specific topic. The quickest way to find relevant passages is using the index at the end of the book.

For both the reader who wants to work from cover to cover and the one who wants to dip in and out, it may be helpful if I explain how I have organized the contents.

This book is divided into four parts. Chapter 1 in Part 1 considers some fundamental issues. Why are standards and ethics important to counsellors? What has been the role of the British Association for Counselling? Chapter 2 considers the question 'What is counselling?' The answer to this question is important to decisions about which matters are included within the ethical standards of counselling and which, more properly, belong to other roles with their separate systems of ethics and practice. In Chapter 3 I outline the main components in a framework of ethical standards. In Part 2, I consider a wide range of issues concerning responsibilities to the client. Is it important to have legal liability insurance? What are the implications of respect for a client's autonomy? How should a counsellor respond to a suicidal client? Clients are entitled to a competent counsellor but what does this mean in actual practice? How should counsellors avoid exploiting their clients? In my experience, the management of confidentiality often poses the most difficulties for counsellors. This issue concludes Part 2. In Part 3, I explore ethical standards which revolve primarily around the interface between the counsellor and people other than the client. I start with consideration of a counsellor's responsibilities to colleagues and the community. Counselling-supervision provides a means of considering many different responsibilities and is considered in Chapter 11. Record-keeping is an issue that is becoming increasingly important. Should all counsellors keep records? The final issue considered in this section concerns the monitoring of counselling. Should counsellors monitor their provision of counselling? To what extent can counsellors who are required to monitor counselling provided in organizational settings do so without compromising their ethical requirements, in particular confidentiality? In Part 4, I draw together all the different topics considered in the book by proposing a model for ethical problem-solving, and in the Epilogue I identify the main features of ethical standards for counsellors. The Appendices contain the, *Code of Ethics and Practice for Counsellors* (1992) issued by the British Association for Counselling and a list of useful addresses.

Concerns about standards and ethics

In writing this book, I have drawn heavily on my experience as a member of the Standards and Ethics Sub-committee of BAC since 1985, and more recently as the Chairperson of that committee. I have also reflected on my experience of conducting studies to identify good practice in HIV counselling, a joint project of BAC and the Department of Health (Bond, 1991b); and the project on role differentiation between advice, guidance, befriending, counselling skills and counselling for BAC and the Department of Employment (Russell et al., 1992). These different aspects of my work have brought me into contact with an enormous variety of counsellors working in very different settings, but often encountering quite similar issues. Some of the issues which are currently causing counsellors most concern are misunderstandings about:

What counselling is or is not
- inappropriate referrals, for example, 'I want you to counsel Brian off this course', 'Would you see Beryl and counsel her to take early retirement because we need to reorganize the distribution of work in her office';
- inappropriate expectations of the counsellor, 'I wouldn't have asked John to see you if I had realized you wouldn't tell me what he said to you.'

Counselling-supervision
- confusion between counselling-supervision and accountability to line-management, 'As your line manager I am accountable for your work. I don't want someone else confusing matters', or 'No other staff get independent supervision and support so I find it difficult to see why counsellors should be any different';
- suspicion of the need for on-going long term supervision, 'Surely you must be out of your probationary period by now. I can't see why you still need supervision.'

The need for training
- confusion over levels of competence requiring corresponding levels of training, 'We all counsel don't we? Surely three days' training is more than enough';

- expectations of creating instant experts in counselling, 'Here are two books on counselling. I want you to read them this weekend and become the counsellor on Monday'.

I have had comments like these reported to me from counsellors in schools, colleges, hospitals, social services, employee welfare, pastoral care, voluntary organizations and private practice.

These and many other issues are the subject matter of this book.

The importance of standards and ethics

Over the past few years I have become acutely aware that the public image of the usefulness, or the dangers, of counselling depends on how effectively counsellors maintain satisfactory standards of practice. Although, so far as I can tell, it is only in a minority of cases that standards are so low that they bring counselling into disrepute, the damage that results is serious both for the client and ultimately for the reputation of counselling as a whole.

Examples of the potential risks to clients of malpractice by counsellors were provided by several clients who wrote to me about their own experiences while I was working on the report on HIV counselling. One person wrote about his experience of being offered counselling for himself and his partner to help them with the consequences of a recent diagnosis of HIV infection. From the outset there was potential for difficulties arising from overlapping roles because the counsellor was also the manager of one of the people involved. These difficulties were compounded by the development of a social relationship when the counsellor would go out drinking with him and his partner and eventually would stay with them overnight. Towards the end of the counselling relationship, the counsellor declared that she had always disliked the author of the letter because of his racial origins and that, had the situation been different, she and his partner could have ended up in bed together. His letter concluded with an observation which is not only relevant to HIV counselling but can be applied to many other circumstances.

> I do not believe for a moment that our experience was typical. Indeed, it was bizarre to the extreme. But this does not mean that such a peculiar and dangerous situation could not develop again.

> As the number of people with HIV has increased so has the number of people coming forward to offer 'counselling'. Whilst many of these people are no doubt extremely competent, caring and professional in their approach to their clients, others may not be so. I refer to the

situation that developed between my counsellor, my partner and myself as 'dangerous' because I believe it had the potential to cause far more damage than it actually did. I was fortunate to have a partner and a family that were able to offer support. Others may not have had such support available. I also feel that although many people offering 'counselling' to people with HIV may do so with the best of intentions, this does not mean that what they actually provide is bound to be beneficial. A good intent does not necessarily produce a good result.

It is difficult to imagine how the counsellor's lack of any standards of practice about maintenance of boundaries in relationships, particularly when overlapping roles are involved, could have caused much more damage. The tone of the letter suggests that the counsellor set out intending to be helpful but lost her way due to lack of training and insufficient personal awareness of her own needs and prejudices. The author of the letter rightly observed that 'a good intent does not necessarily produce a good result'. Good intentions are insufficient in counselling and are dangerous unless the counsellor is also competent as a practitioner and working to a satisfactory level of standards and ethics.

In another situation, a young person with HIV felt he had suffered real harm when his counsellor had reduced his choice about whether to tell his parents about his health status to one of how they were to be told: either telling them himself or letting the counsellor tell them. The response of his parents to the news was so negative and blaming that, much as he had feared, he felt obliged to leave home. The rights of young people to confidentiality in counselling are complicated (they are considered in Chapter 9), but in this instance I believe the counsellor was ill informed about the standards of practice required in these circumstances and may have emotionally over-identified, as a parent herself, with the parents and what she assumed was their right to know. Regardless of her intention, the counsellor caused her client unnecessary suffering and harmed the reputation of counselling amongst young people in her geographical area.

The potential dangers of counselling, and particularly malpractice by counsellors, have become an increasing source of comment in the media. During the time I have been writing this book, the *Independent on Sunday* ran a two-part series on 'Counselling: a solution or a problem?' In the leading article, Linda Grant commented,

> Counselling has helped many thousands of people in Britain. It has rightfully taken its place alongside traditional medicine, and GPs are increasingly referring depressed or troubled patients to counsellors

rather than prescribing them drugs. But serious problems about counselling are emerging, as yet relatively unreported.

A rising tide of expectation is creating a demand for counselling which voluntary bodies, in particular, can have no hope of meeting. The industry is completely unregulated and there is no standard form of qualification, which makes it difficult for the public to know if it is getting a quality service. And complaints are beginning to emerge, as dissatisfied customers struggle to find recognition for their bad experiences at the hands of a profession with no mechanism for dealing with complaints of malpractice. (Grant, 1992)

The series included seven personal accounts from clients of situations in which they felt counselling had damaged them.

Three described situations in which they questioned the counsellor's basic competence. One stated that an experience of marriage counselling had been like a boxing match in which

the counsellor said very little. He was like a silent referee just occasionally asking a question which seemed designed to spur us on to new revelations . . . I can see the point of getting people to talk and their resentments and anger, if it can be looked at, discussed, dealt with, but it seems to me it is the counsellor's job to facilitate this, to use the information coming up to help people progress. I assumed that this was what marriage guidance training is designed to do. But there was none of that.

One felt deeply distressed by a counsellor who would sit opposite her, often with her hands in fists, and stare. After six months the counsellor suddenly said, 'I don't understand you. I don't know how your mind works. You're not like my other patients', which left her feeling devastated and a fraud.

In another client's account, the counsellor said that the client had no right to disagree with him and then after eight months of attending twice a week,

Quite out of the blue he announced he didn't want to go on working with me, that I was not working properly and he did not think there was much hope that my mental state would improve. I was shattered. . . . It was terrible and with hindsight, I think my therapist treated me in a grossly inappropriate and damaging way.

Another cause for complaint was the difficulties experienced in getting to see a counsellor and the overall disrespect for the client's needs. The difficulties concerned getting to see a counsellor who was part of a counselling group practice. The initial assessment of the client's suitability for counselling took place over the telephone and was followed by several months' waiting before she saw one counsellor for what seems to have been further assessment and negotiation over the fees. The next session was with a different woman who was to be the personal counsellor. The client found her to be full of the jargon, '"I hear what you're saying", "How does that make you feel?", "You sound a very angry young woman". It was like a parody of a counselling session. I wanted to say: "Don't use those words on me. Don't patronise me."' She cancelled her appointments and found better help by having a fortnightly lunch with a friend whom she had selected as being a bit older, more practical and sensible than herself.

The fifth complaint resulted from the counsellor kissing a nineteen-year-old woman on the lips and saying, 'I have been wanting to do that for a very long time.' The therapy had been going on three times a week for five years up to that point. This incident resulted in the client breaking off the relationship because she realized that it was a potentially very dangerous situation. She felt devastated and betrayed by someone she had learnt to trust.

The sixth reported case involved a mother and daughter who had been to see an eminent psychotherapist privately and had paid £105 for a 50-minute session. They were shocked when a friend pointed out to them an article written by the therapist which contained a full account of the session. Although the article did not include the clients' names, sufficient details of their background had been included to enable a friend to identify them. The daughter phoned to complain and had a half-hour conversation in which she pointed out

> that at least he could have asked our permission to see if we would mind, but he would not concede that he had done anything wrong. He was adamant that we could not be identified. But the point is not whether or not other people could identify us, but that my mother and I recognised that this was our story, and it has harmed my mother greatly. I feel furious and betrayed.

The seventh account was a complaint written not by the client but by someone affected by the outcome of the counselling. A mother wrote of her pain at watching her son distance himself from his family and eventually lose contact for over five years because, on the basis of what he had told his friends, she believes 'his counsellor had advised him to give up all contact with his family, who were the root of all his troubles and to start a new life which excluded them'. She would have liked to know the basis for such advice and whether the counsellor is still offering the same advice.

The articles and personal accounts of people dissatisfied with their experience of counsellors and therapists had a considerable impact when they were published by the *Independent on Sunday*. My own post bag grew as people wrote to me to draw attention to the articles and asked for my opinions as Chair of the Standards and Ethics Sub-committee of BAC. I think for many counsellors it was the first time they had seen such a catalogue of potential causes for grievance experienced by clients. As a result many counsellors who read the article reviewed their own standards of practice. I did. Some of the situations mentioned also caused me to revise some passages in this book because dangers were highlighted which had not been considered previously. For example, the possibility that clients might identify themselves in an account of a case from which names had been excluded and background details given in fairly impersonal and abstract terms seems not to have been considered before. Knowledge of the identity of the therapist seen by clients is a crucial factor. It was this knowledge that had helped the clients' friend to identify them in the sixth case, even in an account without names. The obvious conclusion is that greater safeguards are needed if any account of counselling could result in clients identifying themselves, or in someone else who knows the identity of the counsellor they have seen identifying them. Some of the other examples of dissatisfaction appear all too familiar. Poor standards of practice and unethical behaviour do occur from time to time. I hope this book will enable conscientious counsellors to avoid some of the pitfalls mentioned in this salutary and useful series of articles.

So far as I know, there has been no systematic survey of causes of dissatisfaction amongst clients of counsellors, so it is not possible to say whether these cases are typical. However, the same series of feature articles also contained references to the Prevention of Professional Abuse Network (POPAN), an organization established by psychotherapists Mary Edwardes and Jenny Fasal. They are reported as stating that between 50 and 70 per cent of all the complaints received by them, which are not restricted to complaints against counsellors, refer to sexual abuse. Others complain of financial abuse and being kept on as fee-paying clients much longer than necessary.

The experience of formal complaints made using BAC's Complaints Procedure has some similarities to that reported by POPAN. Although the number of complaints are relatively small, involving about 0.25 per cent of the total membership of over 9,000 people, a substantial proportion relate to sexual misconduct. The next largest category relates to students dissatisfied with train- ing courses and thereafter there is a wide spread of issues concerning counsellor competence or attitude.

It seems highly appropriate that there should be both media interest in examining cases of malpractice and attempts by professional organizations to regulate themselves. In some states in the USA, where counselling is more widespread than in Britain, these measures alone have been found to be inadequate. In the last resort, the greatest penalty any self-regulated scheme can achieve is a degree of professional and personal humiliation of counsellors who are guilty of malpractice by expelling them from the professional organization. However, there is nothing to stop the person from continuing to practice. Indeed, there is nothing to stop someone leaving imprisonment for fraud or serious sexual offences from putting up a brass plaque outside an office and setting up as a counsellor. This has led some observers to argue that before too long it will be necessary to regulate counselling in Britain by legislation so that counsellors guilty of malpractice would be committing a criminal offence if they continued to practise. It is also envisaged that such a scheme would set minimum requirements before someone would be eligible to offer themselves as a counsellor. Personally, I am doubtful that a legally enforceable scheme will come into operation in the near future. What I think is much more likely is the development of voluntary schemes of national registration for counsellors and systems for self-regulation. The idea of these schemes is that the public will be able to have a greater degree of certainty about the level of service they can expect of a registered counsellor and what to do if they are dissatisfied. Registration would be a sign of quality assurance. Psychotherapists are in the process of establishing a parallel scheme.

Even if a system of voluntary registration is introduced, there will still be nothing to stop unregistered counsellors from offering their services. This raises the question, why should counsellors be concerned to act ethically and maintain standards of practice? After all, a counsellor could argue, 'The worst that can happen to me as a counsellor, if I act unethically, will be my expulsion from any counselling organizations I belong to. They cannot stop me from continuing to take clients.' I believe this kind of response misunderstands the nature of counselling and also the interdependence of personal and professional ethical integrity. It is useful to ask the fundamental question: why be ethical?

Why be ethical?

Unless counselling is provided on an ethical basis, it ceases to serve any useful purpose. Clients usually seek counselling because they are troubled or vulnerable and they wish to be sure that the primary concern of the counselling is to help them to achieve a greater sense of well-being and is not to serve some other purpose. This means that counselling, by its very nature, needs to be a principled relationship. Even where there are actual differences in practice and theory between counsellors, the client's fundamental concern is likely to be that the principles which guide the relationship are directed towards his well-being.

However, clients are not usually well informed about what the standards of ethics and practice of counselling are, so they are more likely to base their assessment of the principled nature of counselling on a personal assessment of the ethical integrity of the counsellor. This is much more familiar ground. Every day, all of us are engaged in assessing the trustworthiness of the people we meet. One of the first concerns of a client at the start of counselling is 'How far can I trust this person to be my counsellor?' It is assumed that if the counsellor appears to have personal integrity then the standards and ethics she applies to her counselling will be of a similar level. From the client's point of view, the personal ethics of the counsellor are inseparable from the standards and ethics of counselling because one is the foundation of the other. If the counsellor lacks ethical principles, how can the client trust such a person to maintain a principled relationship directed towards the client's well-being? Without sufficient trust, the whole purpose of counselling is doomed to failure. Counselling is possible only when sufficient trust is established to encourage the active participation of the client, who has to be willing to take risks in exploring and often disclosing personally identifiable information. There is no way that counselling can be effective with merely passive compliance and low risk-taking by the client. Counselling is not like a medical procedure which can take place under anaesthetic on a passive or even unconscious patient.

The trust that enables the active participation of the client is founded equally on the client's sense of the counsellor's personal ethical integrity and her level of standards and practice as a counsellor. Issues of trust and ethics are inseparable and both are required to make counselling possible.

The role of the British Association for Counselling

In the United Kingdom, the British Association for Counselling (BAC) has been the major forum for debate about standards and ethics. It was founded as an Association in 1977 after many years as a Standing Conference. The Association is established:

i to promote and provide education and training for counsellors . . . with a view to raising the standards of counselling for the benefit of counselling and in particular for those who are the recipients of counselling.
ii to advise the education of the public in the part that counselling can play generally and in particular to meet the needs of those members of society where development and participation in society is impaired by mental, physical or social handicap or disability. (BAC, 1991)

From relatively modest beginnings it has grown to an organization of over 9,000 members in 1993, making it one of the largest counselling associations worldwide. Its membership spans an enormous diversity of cultural, professional and personal experience. It is also an association in which, although the counsellor's voice predominates, the views of clients are also present because of the policy of maintaining an association for everyone interested in counselling rather than acting as an exclusive forum for counsellors. Although the organization has many of the characteristics of a professional association, it has always sought to have a wider brief and membership than this. Successive chairpersons have emphasized the significance of the name of the association. It is *'for* Counselling' and not *'of* Counsellors' as it is sometimes misrepresented by the press and some of its own members. This width of membership and aims has sometimes complicated the process of establishing ethical principles and standards of practice. As someone who has been a member of the Standards and Ethics Sub-committee, I have been all too aware of the tensions that can arise in as large and diverse an organization as BAC. However, I believe the costs of diversity have been outweighed by the gains. The debates which have taken place within BAC ensure that the outcomes are more representative of the total membership than of any single group within it, and this adds to the credibility of the Association's policies within, and outside, the world of counselling.

However, the process of achieving this credibility is not always easy or unproblematic. The main focus of effort within the Standards and Ethics Sub-committee has been the production of codes of practice and guidelines. This requires both intellectual and political skill on the part of everyone involved. As this book is substantially based on the latest version of the *Code of Ethics and Practice for Counsellors* (BAC, 1992a), which is reproduced in Appendix 1, it is worth reviewing the process involved in its production. Before I do this, it is useful to consider why the development of codes of practice has been considered important enough to justify the time and resources involved in their production.

The importance of codes of practice

Counselling is not unique in the significance it attributes to establishing codes of practice. Many other roles and professions have developed their own codes as part of a system of self-regulation or statutory accountability. Some of the excitement of being involved in the process of creating codes is the sense of the emerging identity and ideology of a particular role. Although this is important, the main reasons for the production of codes are far more pragmatic. Codes of practice are published in order to:

- provide a framework for counsellors to consult when they are faced with an ethical dilemma or uncertainty about acceptable standards of practice;
- promote standards of practice generally and therefore the quality of service available to clients by giving counsellors guidelines to inform the ways they plan to provide counselling;
- establish a framework within which malpractice can be identified and may become the subject of complaints or disciplinary procedures;
- enhance the image of counselling by demonstrating that, whilst counselling will continue to mature, it has attained sufficient maturity to have established codes;
- focus discussion on ethical issues so that they act as 'stepping stones' towards future improved codes and standards of practice;
- provide a mechanism for the organization that produced the code to act as a self-regulating and self-governing organization.

The development of the Code for Counsellors

The first version of the *Code of Ethics and Practice for Counsellors* was produced in 1984 and was much shorter than the current version. This had a number of advantages. It was better able to catch the spirit of counselling without being too enmeshed in the practical detail. In this sense, it was a code in which the ideological commitments of counselling were to the fore. However, as the experience of the membership of BAC grew, it became apparent that the code was deficient on three major themes of concern to counsellors. Sex, suicide and secrecy acted as the catalysts for the revision of the code.

Sex is an issue which has the potential of evoking strong and deeply held views. The statement in the 1984 code that 'Engaging in sexual activity with a client whilst also engaging in a therapeutic relationship is unethical' remained contentious even after the code had been formally adopted. Those who opposed the view could point to some of the founders of therapies used in counselling, like Carl Jung and Fritz Perls, who are widely believed to have had sex with current or former clients. Some, particularly from within the humanistic traditions, argued against the automatic exclusion of an activity which could be therapeutic in some circumstances. This debate continued and, in the end, resulted in a re-affirmation of the prohibition of sex between the counsellor and client for the duration of the counselling relationship, and the focus of attention has shifted to the prohibition of sex with former clients. The current understanding of sex between counsellor and client as exploitative is considered in more detail in Chapter 8.

The 1984 version gave no explicit guidance over what counsellors should do about confidentiality with regard to suicidal clients. The inference was that the counsellor should always maintain confidentiality even to the exclusion of seeking alternative help for the client. A student counsellor who had relied on this inference found herself cross-examined in the Coroner's Court, after the suicide of one of her clients, about whether the situation really was as simple as that. In particular, the lawyer suggested that such a policy was only sustainable if the counsellor was trained and competent in the assessment and treatment of suicidal clients, otherwise the possibility of seeking additional help for the client, or making a referral, should not be automatically ruled out. The subsequent revision of the code was strongly influenced by this line of argument. One of the consequences of such a change was a re-evaluation of secrecy about counselling, which resulted in bringing the code much closer to the law on confidentiality. This issue is discussed further in Chapter 9.

More detailed accounts of the influence of these issues on the revision of these codes can be found in an article: 'Sex and Suicide in the Development of Counselling' (Bond, 1991a). Important as these debates were, there were also many other activities involved in the production of this code, including:

- the analysis of over 40 other codes of practice of organizations providing counselling, or closely related activities;
- a lengthy process of debate and drafting within the Standards and Ethics Sub-committee at which representatives of most of the main divisions within BAC were present;

- the publication of articles to stimulate discussion and elicit views from the membership of BAC;
- running of workshops to discover what dilemmas most concerned counsellors;
- the presentation of the code in draft form to the Annual General Meeting in 1989 for one year's consultation;
- the revision of the draft into a final version in the light of numerous letters containing detailed comment in response to the consultative version;
- discussion and voting for its adoption at the Annual General Meeting 1990;
- revisions about sex with former clients at the Annual General Meeting 1992.

The outcome of this process resulted in the *Code* which is the basis of this book. Inevitably, no code can be definitive. It has constantly to be revised in the light of experience, therefore I have included in this book an account of issues not directly considered by the *Code* and have given my own personal reflections. I hope that I have written a book which will be useful to all who take on the role of counsellor.

2 What is counselling?

Anyone who has attempted to answer this question will have discovered that it is not as simple to answer as it might seem. Yet the establishment of an agreed meaning is important in delimiting the boundaries of what activities are included within, and what activities are excluded from, the ethics and standards of counselling.

For example, when a pupil approaches a tutor for help with a personal problem, or when a nurse listens to a patient's worries about being away from home, or when a social worker assists parents preparing for the return of their children from residential care, or when a priest helps someone who has been recently bereaved, is counselling taking place? Or is it some other activity, perhaps subject to different standards of practice and ethics?

One of the difficulties in establishing a definition is that the term 'counselling' is used differently according to the context. There are therefore wider and narrower definitions and some which are mutually exclusive.

The meaning of 'counselling' internationally

At the international level there is a definite tendency to make the term 'counselling' all-encompassing, perhaps to accommodate a diversity of cultures and practice. In languages where there is no equivalent to 'counselling', often the terms 'guidance' or 'advice' act as an equivalent. Alternatively, the term 'counselling' is simply imported into the vocabulary of the language. The International Round Table for the Advancement of Counselling (IRTAC), which is recognized by the United Nations as a Non-Governmental Organisation representing counselling, uses an all-encompassing definition. It defines counselling as: 'a method of relating and responding to other people with the aim of providing them with opportunities to explore, to clarify and work towards living in a more satisfactory and resourceful way . . .'. The close relationship between counselling and guidance in many countries is acknowledged: 'Although the counselling process may be primarily non-directive or non-advisory, some situations may call for a more active intervention and counselling may be combined with guidance and the provision of information' (Hoxter, 1991).

In the United States 'counseling', spelt with one 'l' in American

English, is frequently used in its widest sense as a generic word to encompass advising, guidance, psychotherapy and psychoanalysis. As probably the largest counselling organization worldwide, the American Counseling Association (ACA), recently renamed from the American Association of Counseling and Development (AACD), states in its Ethical Standards that it is an organization whose members are 'dedicated to the enhancement of the worth, dignity, potential and uniqueness of each individual and thus the service of society' (AACD, 1988). It would be hard to expand the use of the term 'counselling' any further. However, there are disadvantages to such a wide definition. The code acknowledges the difficulty it poses for establishing standards.

> The Association recognizes that the role definitions and work settings of its members include a wide variety of academic disciplines, levels of academic preparation, and agency services. This diversity reflects the breadth of the Association's interest and influence. It poses challenging complexities in efforts to set standards for the performance of members, desired requisite preparation or practice, and supporting social, legal and ethical controls. (AACD, 1988)

'Counselling' in Britain

Within Britain there is a use of the term 'counselling' in its wider meaning. Stephen Murgatroyd (1985) regards the professionalization of counselling by training and certification as the prerequisite of a select few working in specialist roles. However, in his view, the strategies used in counselling should not be confined to this select few. Therefore, he argues in favour of deprofessionalizing counselling in order to make its methods available to as many different people as possible. Counselling and helping are therefore synonymous. Philip Burnard (1989, 1992) reaches a similar view about the meaning of the term 'counselling', but offers a different explanation for doing so which arises from his experience of working in the health service. As a nurse tutor, he was concerned to discover that nurses are reluctant to use facilitative skills with patients. This is not merely a matter of skills but of an attitude and a belief that the nurse knows best, or at least better than the patient. This is contrary to the growing practice of involving patients in decisions about their own care. Therefore, Burnard is interested in extending the nurses' skills to include more facilitative interventions which involve the patient in making decisions for himself about his treatment. He draws on John Heron's six categories of therapeutic intervention as the underpinning model. Heron (1990) divides the possible interventions into authoritative and facilitative. Authoritative interventions include: prescriptive (offering advice), informative (offering information) and confronting (challenging). Facilitative interventions include: cathartic (enabling expression of pent-up emotions), catalytic (drawing out) and supportive (confirming or encouraging). Burnard concluded that it is desirable for nurses to use the full range of interventions and therefore defines counselling as the effective use of verbal interventions involving 'both client-centred *and* more prescriptive counselling' (his emphasis). He is therefore taking an all-encompassing view of counselling.

In contrast to this wider definition of counselling, there are two narrower definitions in popular use which are mutually exclusive.

The first of these regards counselling as the same as giving advice. This view has had a long tradition which reaches back to at least the seventeenth century. In 1625 Francis Bacon in his essay wrote 'On Counsel', *'The greatest Trust, betweene Man and Man is the Trust of Giving Counsell'*. It is a reasonable inference that he is thinking of advice because as he develops his argument he identifies the 'Inconveniences of Counsell'. These include 'the Danger of being unfaithfully counselled, and more for the good of them that counsell than of him that is counselled'. He also states that only people with expertise are suitable to provide 'counsell'. This use of counsel to mean giving expert advice is the main definition given in the 1982 edition of the *Concise Oxford English Dictionary*. 'Counsel' is defined as 'advise (person to do); to give advice to (person) professionally on social problems etc.; recommend (thing, that)' (Sykes, 1982). This meaning is still actively used in legal and medical circles. Recently, while I was working on a report about HIV counselling, a doctor who was committed to this usage wrote to me to express exasperation at all the fuss being made about counselling which he regarded as merely a 'popular term for giving advice to people' (Bond, 1991b). This narrow definition of counselling is valid, but is incompatible with an increasingly prevalent use of the term 'counselling' which has a history stretching back at least seventy years. The most recent edition of the *Concise Oxford English Dictionary* recognizes that a distinction in meaning has developed between 'counsel' and 'counselling'. It defines 'counselling' as '1 the art or process of giving counsel. 2 the process of assisting and guiding clients, esp. by a trained person on a professional basis, to resolve esp. personal, social, or psychological problems' (Allen, 1990).

This more modern use of the term has emerged from, and is a reaction against, the traditions of psychoanalysis and psychotherapy. It has its origins in the 1920s in the USA. When Carl

Rogers started working as a psychologist in America, he was not permitted to practise psychotherapy, which was restricted to medical practitioners. Therefore he called his work 'counseling' (Thorne, 1984). However, Carl Rogers was not the inventor of the term 'counseling'. It is widely believed in North America that the originator of 'counseling' was a radical social activist. Frank Parsons (1854–1908) was energetic in his condemnation of American capitalism and competition. He advocated the replacement of capitalism with a system of mutualism, a combination of co-operation and concern for humanity. He was a political activist proposing public ownership of utilities and transportation, the vote for women and a managed currency. He has been called 'a one man American Fabian Society' (Gummere, 1988). In 1908 he invented the 'counseling center' when he founded the Vocation Bureau in the North End of Boston, a part of town crowded with immigrants. The centre offered interviews, testing, information and outreach. Parsons placed more emphasis on social action and the importance of the social culture than most modern counsellors. In North America, attention is periodically drawn to the origins of counselling and Frank Parsons especially when it appears that 'counseling' is in danger of becoming 'overly parochial and perhaps irrelevant' (Zytowski, 1985).

In Britain, the association of counselling with political activism has probably been greatest in the women's and gay movements. Elsewhere counselling is less obviously associated with political activism, but many use it as a means of quiet revolution, drawing attention to the need to humanize education, health care and the essential human qualities of relationships in society. Paul Halmos (1978) pointed out that even tough-minded social scientists may think counsellors are wrong in many of their beliefs but on the whole they are assessed as having a good influence on society. Insights from counselling and psychotherapy have changed hospital procedures which separated mothers from young children. Counsellors have had an important role in exposing the long term human suffering caused by the physical, emotional and sexual abuse of children. This quiet revolution is inspired by the counsellor's faith in the need to love and be loved, and one of the characteristics of most models of counselling is the counsellor's emotional warmth towards the client or concern for the client's well-being as the foundation of the counselling relationship.

Although counselling has changed since it was first espoused by Frank Parsons, the emphasis has remained on counselling as the principled use of relationship with the aim of enabling the client to achieve his own improved well-being. Two fundamental ethical principles are closely associated with this way of counselling: respect for the client's capacity for self-determination and the importance of confidentiality. This is the use of the term 'counselling' espoused by the British Association for Counselling. The definition used within the *Code for Counsellors* (BAC, 1992a) makes specific reference to the client's capacity for self-determination:

> The overall aim of counselling is to provide an opportunity for the client to work towards living in a more satisfying and resourceful way. The term 'counselling' includes work with individuals, pairs or groups of people, often, but not always, referred to as 'clients'. The objectives of particular counselling relationships will vary according to the client's needs. Counselling may be concerned with developing issues, addressing and resolving specific problems, making decisions, coping with crisis, developing personal insight and knowledge, working through feelings of inner conflict or improving relationships with others. The counsellor's role is to facilitate the client's work in ways which respect the client's values, personal resources and capacity for self-determination. (3.1)

Sometimes 'self-determination' is also referred to as 'autonomy', 'self-reliance' or 'independence'. The choice of word often depends on personal preferences but the essential meaning is the same. The concept is fundamental to counselling and acts as the cornerstone of its values from which the ethical principles are derived and ultimately standards of practice are set.

Counselling and other roles

Identifying overlaps and distinctions between counselling and other roles is no longer a concern simply of practitioners. It has become a matter of social policy as the government is becoming more interested in encouraging a systematic approach to the delivery of counselling services in the voluntary and statutory sectors. A major project is in progress sponsored by the Department of Employment to organize a progressive sequence of training for workers offering befriending, advice, guidance and counselling or using counselling skills. This is an ambitious programme involving many people. I have been a member of a team concerned with one part of it: role differentiation (Russell et al. 1992). As so often happens, the moment I concentrate on a particular theme, in this case the differences between the roles, the opposite leaps out at me. Despite the well-established arguments which distinguish counselling from advice and the other roles, I became conscious of a different perspective about their common roots.

From an historical perspective, the development of befriending, advice, guidance, counselling skills and counselling is strongly associated with movements to enable citizens to become better able to participate in the democratic process and to take control of their own lives. Advice and guidance services have received state funding in response to a series of government reports going back to the 1920s to help people cope with the complex network of benefits and laws that form part of modern society. Befriending has a history in social welfare which goes back at least as far as 1879 when lay missionaries were appointed by magistrates to advise, befriend and assist offenders, who were often too illiterate to understand court procedures and too poor to afford legal represen- tation in the courts. Befriending has continued to be used to reach out to socially isolated groups of people whose needs are not adequately met within formal social welfare services. Counselling and counselling skills have been adopted not only as methods of problem-solving or therapy, but also to serve other functions. Within education and health services, they are used to help people make informed choices about the options open to them. In this way, the increasing use of counselling and counselling skills in the statutory sector is linked with a shift from viewing the users of services as wholly dependent on the expert providers of services, such as doctors, teachers, social workers, etc., towards enabling the users of those services to participate in decisions about their own future. It seems to me that there is a closer relationship between the roles of advice, guidance, befriending, counselling skills and counselling than I had previously appreciated. In different ways, they are all rooted in a movement towards democratizing society and empowering the individual to exercise control for herself. In this sense, they all share similar origins and can properly be regarded as belonging to a single family or 'genus' of roles. However, there are also important distinctions to be made between each of the roles. Metaphorically, if they were to be included in a biological classification, they are separate species within the same genus. Therefore, it is worth considering what is distinctive about each of these roles.

Counselling and advice

The *Code for Counsellors* states, 'Counsellors do not normally give advice' (B2.2.2). Advice is generally thought of as an opinion given or offered as to future action. It usually entails giving someone information about the choices open to them and then from a posi- tion of greater expertise or authority a recommendation as to the best course of action. Rosalind Brooke (1972), writing about Citizens Advice Bureaux, describes the advisory process as having two aspects, 'The advisor not only may interpret the information in order to sort it to the needs of the enquirer, but may also offer an opinion about the wisdom of obtaining a solution in a particular way.' This description highlights the difficulty 'advice' poses for the counsellor. The aim of counselling is to enable clients to discover their own wisdom rather than have wisdom imparted to them from the counsellor. The counselling process is intended to increase the clients' ability to take control for themselves rather than depend on others. This difference between counselling and advice does not mean that advice is an inappropriate way of offering help. It is a different method and perhaps more suitable for practical problems than making decisions about relationships, or coping with transitions or other psycho-social issues.

In more recent times advice-giving and counselling have grown closer together in their methods. In a recent discussion paper prepared for the National Association of Young People's Counselling and Advisory Services, Arthur Musgrave (1991) observed, 'Most advice work training focuses on content. All too often workers are left to learn what they can of strategies and tactics as they go along.' He rejected this practice and advocated combining training in advice work with counselling skills. Similar views can be found in the recent publications of the National Association of Citizen's Advice Bureaux, 'The adviser should structure the interview to enable clients to explore the problem fully and choose their own course of action. Advisers should not, for the sake of speed or their own satisfaction, encourage clients to become dependent . . .' (NACAB, 1990). When advice is delivered in this way it is much closer to the methods and process of counselling than when it is given authoritatively.

Counselling and guidance

'Guidance' has been used in as many different ways as 'counselling'. During the 1970s, a time when guidance services were expanding rapidly in social welfare and education, the terms 'guidance' and 'counselling' could be used interchangeably. Aryeh Leissner, writing in 1969, defined guidance as:

> being available for an occasional chat to help a troubled person to gain some insight and better perspective with regard to relatively minor problems. It may take the form of more structured short-term counselling aimed at 'working through' some difficulties or changing certain irrational attitudes. Guidance may also entail the process of enabling a client to understand the need for referral to more intensive, specialised treatment services, and to prepare the client for the referral.

The implication of her definition is that longer term work of a more intensive kind would be regarded as 'therapy', which is beyond the scope of guidance or counselling. In her thinking, both guidance and counselling are a longer form of contact than advice.

It appears that some time since the 1970s, the use of guidance has developed in two different directions. One trend has emphasized the kinds of values and methods of working associated with counselling. This trend is characterized by a very strong emphasis on working in ways which enable the recipient of guidance to make his own decisions. In this sense the guide is like a signpost, pointing out different possible routes and helping people to select their own destination and way of getting there. Information-giving and advising may be more prominent in the worker's interventions than would be the case in counselling, but the emphasis on values based on the client's autonomy mean that this form of guidance and counselling are very closely related, and in some instances the same kind of activity. This use of 'guidance' has become well established in educational settings and is encouraged by many writers and commentators on educational advice, guidance and counselling services (Woolfe et al., 1987).

An alternative use of 'guidance' appears to have developed in reaction against the use of 'counselling' to mean 'non-directive interventions'. In this use 'guidance' is deliberately used to fill the gap left by non-directive counselling in order to validate information-giving and advising. The provider of guidance is therefore more than a signpost but actively indicates the best route and may guide someone along it. For example, I have been told that the Department of Health had considered re-naming 'pre-test counselling' for HIV antibodies (the indicators of HIV infections and the potential development of AIDS) as 'pre-test guidance'. This is in order to escape any confusion about pre-test counselling being directive or non-directive. The policy-makers who wish to substitute the term 'guidance' are doing so to indicate that they wish whoever conducts the pre-test sessions to feel free to offer expert opinion and to guide or direct people sensitively towards behaviours which reduce the likelihood of HIV infection. In other words, the realities of HIV infection should be borne in mind by the person conducting the session, who should actively seek to prevent further infection. Her Majesty's Inspectorate of the Department of Education and Science have reached similar conclusions with regard to the realities of situations which are faced by interviewers offering careers guidance.

> Both the concept and practice of guidance concentrates attention on a very real dilemma which lies at the heart of much careers work in schools. On the one hand education of quality encourages independence

of mind; on the other hand local or national economic circumstances and employment opportunities and pupils' ability impose an inevitable limitation on the exercise of choice. The challenge for any teacher involved in guidance is how to respect, support and encourage autonomy, without fostering false hopes. While there can be no easy solution to such a problem the teacher who is well informed, effectively trained and properly supported by coherent and relevant school and LEA policy is in a position to offer the most valuable support to pupils – the sort of impartial, balanced and considered help and guidance most likely to reconcile economic reality and individual pupils' needs, aspirations and abilities. (HMI, 1988)

In both these examples, the realities of the situation are perceived as restricting the options of the person receiving guidance. The distinctive characteristic of this use of 'guidance' rests on the emphasis of the interviewer using her expertise and experience to identify and direct people towards realistic options rather than helping the recipient to discriminate for himself between what he perceives as realistic and unrealistic. This shift in emphasis is important and distinguishes this use of the term 'guidance' from counselling.

Whether a more directive form of intervention is required in the circumstances of the two examples I have given is a matter for debate. However, I am sure that there is a need for a term which validates advising and giving information. In the English vocabulary 'guidance' is the obvious candidate. It would reduce some of the confusion over roles if the term 'guidance' was used for this purpose. This would mean that 'non-directive guidance' would be better known as counselling. For a more directive kind of intervention, I increasingly prefer to use guidance in this sense rather than to use it in ways which are almost indistinguishable from counselling.

As with giving advice, the potential directiveness of guidance is reduced by the use of counselling skills to maximize client choice within the parameters offered by the interviewer. Therefore, the use of counselling skills helps to make even a directive form of guidance quite different from merely telling someone what they should, or should not, do.

Counselling and befriending

The best known of the organizations committed to providing a befriending service is the Samaritans. Chad Varah, their founder, had a strong preference for providing a befriending, rather than counselling, service. He believed that befriending is a role which is more readily understood by callers and one which is more attractive to people who may feel socially isolated and unable to

approach people they already know about their problems. A substitute 'friend' has a more powerful appeal in these circumstances
than a 'counsellor', which term might be perceived as emphasizing
the difference in emotional vulnerability between helper and helped
and thereby increasing the sense of the caller's personal isolation
rather than focusing attention on the usefulness of the human relationship.

The use of befriending to counter the social isolation of specific
groups of people is a goal shared by all providers of this service.
The social isolation may be due to physical circumstances, for
example people who are housebound due to illness or disability, or
public attitudes, for example people who are mentally ill or have
learning difficulties, the dying, and offenders. National FRIEND is
an example of an organization which provides befriending for
people who may feel set apart by their sexuality and who want the
support of people who share similar experiences of being gay,
lesbian or bi-sexual.

As an organization which provides both befriending and counselling services for people affected by HIV or AIDS, the Aled
Richards Trust, Bristol, has had to consider the boundary between
these roles. Meg Price, the Co-ordinator of the Buddying Services,
wrote to me about how they distinguish between counselling and
buddying, the American term for befriending. She observed:

> Counselling occurs within the framework of a specific contract – to
> look at agreed issues, usually one hour sessions on a regular basis, and
> in a specific setting (usually the counselling room or the client's home).
> Whilst Buddies are not trained as counsellors, their role is to listen
> and to be available at times of particular stress and they may well often be
> the only person that the client can really talk to and confide in.
> Buddies, like counsellors, attempt to work in as non-judgmental a way
> as possible but also have the freedom of a higher level of self-disclosure
> than have most counsellors. Boundaries are far wider and more flexible
> in buddying, buddies usually being expected to perform practical tasks
> for the client, to engage in social activities (e.g. have meals together,
> visiting the pub, going to the cinema, etc.) and occasionally the client
> may become involved in the buddy's personal life (e.g. meeting his/her
> own family and friends). None of these things would be seen as
> appropriate for a counsellor to be undertaking. (Bond, 1991b)

Counselling and psychotherapy

The *Code for Counsellors* contains the observation: 'It is not possible to make a generally accepted distinction between counselling
and psychotherapy. There are well founded traditions which use
the terms interchangeably and others which distinguish them' (3.3).
When the terms 'counselling' and 'psychotherapy' are used in their

widest sense they encompass each other. On the other hand these terms are sometimes used to distinguish between these two roles. The criteria for the distinction varies according to the speaker's point of view. The potential distinguishing characteristics identified by Brammer and Shostrum from a search of American literature are identified in Figure 2.1.

Counselling	Psychotherapy
Educational	Reconstructive
Situational	Issues arising from personality
Problem-solving	Analytic
Conscious awareness	Pre-conscious and unconscious
Emphasis on working with people who do not have severe or persistent emotional problems	Emphasis on 'neurotics' or working with persistent and/or severe emotional problems
Focus on present	Focus on past
Shorter length of contract	Longer length of contract

Figure 2.1 *Characteristics of counselling and psychotherapy (adapted from Brammer and Shostrum, 1982)*

There is a need for a systematic study of the differentiation between counselling and psychotherapy in Britain. It seems likely that some of the findings of Brammer and Shostrum about the differences will also be applicable on this side of the Atlantic. They trace a history of counselling as dealing with problems which are primarily pressures from the outside environment rather than deeply embedded difficulties resulting in rigid, neurotic patterns. In this sense, counselling is about helping people who have the capacity to cope in most circumstances but who are experiencing temporary difficulties, or making transitions or adjustments in their life. Issues arising from difficult relationships at home, making decisions, coping with serious illness, bereavement, addiction, etc., may all be within the scope of counselling. If issues are merely symptomatic of something deeper, or the client is experiencing more entrenched problems such as persistent phobias, anxiety states, low self-esteem or difficulty in establishing relationships, then psychotherapy may be more appropriate. This would imply that there is a difference in training and expertise between counsellors and psychotherapists. In my experience, this distinction does not exist in the UK, as neither counselling nor psychotherapy is wholly regulated in the UK and this means that they do not have established national standards followed by all practitioners. Therefore it is not possible to assume that the psychotherapist always has a different area of experience or is better trained than the counsellor. This situation seems certain to persist for many years to come.

In a paper delivered to the 16th Annual Training Conference of the British Association for Counselling, Brian Thorne suggested that the quest for difference between counselling and psychotherapy is illogical and invalid. He argued that implicit in the kinds of distinctions most frequently made between counselling and psychotherapy is the idea that counselling is concerned with cognitive problems and psychotherapy with affective problems. He debunked this line of argument in the following way:

> I would suggest that it takes only a moment's reflection to reveal the uselessness of such distinctions. Clearly cognition and affect are both involved in all behaviours. No choice, for example, can ever be simply logical and rational. What is more, a serious personality problem usually brings with it many situational and environmental dilemmas and a situational problem may well have its source in a personality distur-bance. It would, of course, be highly convenient if problems could be categorised and circumscribed so neatly but to suggest that they can is to fly in the face of the facts. (1992)

In his paper he argued against all the distinctions between counsell-ing and psychotherapy made by Brammer and Shostrum and many others. I have no doubt this debate will continue unresolved for some considerable time. The debate may have more to do with status and money than with substantive differences. I am frequently told that in the private practice the label 'psychotherapy' attracts higher fees from clients than 'counsellor'. However, so far as I can tell, there is a great deal of common ground between counselling and psychotherapy. Clients talk about their experience of being on the receiving end of counselling or psychotherapy in very similar terms. Fee differentials notwithstand-ing, the difference between the two appears to be more important to practitioners than to clients. From an ethical perspective, it is clear to me that counsellors and psychotherapists work within the same ethical framework. It may be that if differences between the two roles can be established, there will be some corresponding differences in standards of practice, but even these may simply be details in comparison with the many standards shared in common.

Counselling and counselling skills

This has arguably been one of the most important distinctions to emerge in recent years. It is also one which has been subject to considerable misunderstanding.

The most obvious misunderstanding is based on the idea that 'counselling skills' is a label for a set of activities unique to counselling. Although the term 'counselling skills' is sometimes used on this basis, it is quickly discredited because any attempt to list specific 'counselling skills', such as active listening, paraphrasing, using open questions, reflective responses, etc., quickly looks indistinguishable from lists labelled social skills, communication skills, interpersonal skills, etc.

In order to understand what is meant by 'counselling skills', it is useful to take the two words separately.

'Counselling' is an indication of the source of the concept historically. It indicates that even though these skills are not unique to counselling, it is the way they have been articulated in counselling that has been useful to other roles. For example, advice-giving has a much longer history than counselling skills, but the tendency has been to concentrate on the content of the advice rather than the way it is delivered. However, the methods advisers use to communicate with clients can be adapted to improve the way advice is given and maximize the 'client's' involvement in the decision-making. 'Counselling' in this context is acknowledging the source of the concept and method of communication. Similarly, nurses, tutors, personnel managers, social workers, and many others have all recognized that there are advantages of adapting the methods of communication used in counselling to aspects of their own role. One way in which an outside observer might detect that counselling skills are being used is the pattern of communication. This is illustrated in Figure 2.2. Imparting expertise involves the expert in communicating her knowledge and expertise to the recipient and therefore takes up most of the time available. This contrasts with conversation, where both participants tend to contribute for equal lengths of time and in a pattern which flows backwards and forwards. The use of counselling skills will usually change the pattern of communication in favour of the recipient, who speaks for most of the available time. Part of the expertise in using counselling skills is learning how to communicate briefly in ways which do not interrupt the flow of the speaker but at the same time help the speaker more effectively to address the issue

Style	Pattern of flow	Time ratio
Imparting expertise	Interactor ⇒ Recipient	80:20
Conversation	Interactor ⇔ Recipient	50:50
Counselling skills	Interactor ⇐ Recipient	20:80

Figure 2.2 *Different patterns of communication*

which is concerning her. When counselling skills are being used, an outside observer might notice that the recipient is encouraged to take greater control of the agenda of the dialogue than in the other styles of communication. In other words, the values implicit in the use of counselling skills are similar to those of counselling which place an emphasis on the client's capacity for self-determination in how help is sought as well as for any decisions or actions that may result.

Other things which might be apparent to an outside observer would be the way the recipient is encouraged or enabled to participate in deciding the agenda for the total transaction. In other words, the values implicit in the interactions are similar to those of counselling with an emphasis on the client's capacity for self-determination.

The term 'skills' in 'counselling skills' is sometimes taken in a very literal sense to mean 'discrete behaviours', but this is not the way the term 'skills' is understood in the social sciences. Skills which are used to enhance relationships can be distinguished from 'physical skills' as in sport or work, and 'mental' and 'intellectual' skills not merely on the basis of observable behaviours. They are inextricably linked to the goal of the person using them. For instance, Michael Argyle (1981) defines socially skilled behaviour as 'behaviour which is effective in realising the goals of the inter-actor'. In the context of counselling skills, those goals are to implement the values of counselling by assisting the self-expression and autonomy of the recipient.

One of the ways in which an independent observer might be able to distinguish between 'counselling skills' and 'counselling' is whether the contracting is explicit between the two people. This is highlighted in one of the alternative definitions for counselling which is still in popular use: 'People become engaged in counselling when a person, occupying regularly or temporarily the role of counsellor, offers or agrees explicitly to offer time, attention or respect to another person or persons temporarily in the role of client' (BAC, 1985). This definition was originally devised to distinguish between spontaneous or *ad hoc* counselling and formal counselling. The overt nature of the latter involving 'offers' and explicit agreements was seen as 'the dividing line between the counselling task and the *ad hoc* counselling and is the major safeguard of the rights of the consumer' (BAC, 1985). The definition also provides a useful basis for distinguishing when someone is using counselling skills in a role other than that of counsellor or when they are counselling.

The *Code of Ethics and Practice for Counselling Skills* contains a useful test for the distinction.

1.2 Ask yourself the following questions:
  a) Are you using counselling skills to enhance your communications with someone but without taking on the role of their counsellor?
  b) Does the recipient perceive you as acting within your professional caring role (which is *not* that of being their counsellor)?
  i If the answer is YES to both these questions, you are using counselling skills in your functional role and should use this document.
  ii If the answer is NO to both, you are counselling and should look to the *Code of Ethics and Practice for Counsellors* for guidance.
  iii If the answer is YES to one and NO to the other, you have a conflict of expectations and should resolve it.
  Only when both the user and the recipient explicitly contract to enter into a counselling relationship does it cease to be 'using counselling skills' and become 'counselling'. (BAC, 1989)

Ideas about counselling skills have continued to evolve since the publication of this code. My discussions with a wide variety of users of counselling skills suggest that there is a growing emphasis on 'counselling skills' sharing the same values as 'counselling'. In particular, counselling skills are most appropriate to situations where their user is intending to empower someone or maximize the capacity for self-determination. Therefore, as a matter of definition, 'counselling skills' are inappropriate to situations in which the user's goals have priority over those of the recipient or 'client'. For example, it is becoming increasingly inappropriate to think of selling, interrogation or persuasion, as involving counselling skills. These are activities which are better thought of in terms of communication skills, a term which is more neutral about values. On the other hand, counselling skills are appropriate to many roles including advising, guidance, befriending and psychotherapy where the user aims to empower someone. One of the consequences of this development is that users of counselling skills and counselling are once again becoming more closely identified with each other. Therefore many of the ethical issues which interest counsellors are also relevant to the users of counselling skills.

There are three frequent misconceptions that I encounter in discussions about counselling skills. These are:

Using counselling skills is always a lower-order activity than counselling. This need not be the case. Perhaps this is just as well, because arguably the user of counselling skills may be working under more demanding circumstances than the counsellor who usually has the benefit of more extended periods of time which have already been agreed in advance. In comparison, the user of counselling skills may be working more opportunistically with much less certainty about the duration of the encounter. Users of counselling skills can be more or less skilled, just like counsellors. However, using counselling skills is not a role in itself but something important to enhance the performance of another role. This means that the capacity to use counselling skills effectively depends not only on being skilled in their use but also on someone's competence in their primary role, such as nurse, tutor, etc. For all these reasons, using counselling skills can be more skilled than counselling. It certainly cannot be assumed that using counselling skills is a lower level of activity.

People in occupational roles other than counsellor cannot counsel. This would mean that doctors, nurses, youth workers, etc., cannot counsel but can only use counselling skills. This is not the case. With appropriate training, counselling supervision, and clear contracting with the client in ways consistent with counselling, it seems to me anyone can change roles to that of 'counsellor'. There are important issues about keeping the boundaries between different roles clear and managing overlapping roles or dual relationships. But not all dual relationships are undesirable provided the boundary between the relationships can be clearly identified and is respected by both the counsellor and client. Usually it is easier, whenever possible, to avoid the potential pitfalls of dual relationships by ensuring that the counsellor is independent of the provision of other services and other relationships, whether personal or professional, with the client.

Anyone with the occupational title 'counsellor' is always counselling. This is not the case. As the concept of counselling has narrowed down into a specifically contracted role, there is a need for 'counsellors' to distinguish between when they are counselling and when they are performing other roles, such as training, supervision, managing, etc. In each of these other roles a counsellor is likely to be using counselling skills. BAC has produced codes of ethics and practice for other roles closely associated with counselling including:

- *Code of Ethics and Practice for Counselling Skills*, which applies to members who would not regard themselves as counsellors, but who use counselling skills to support other roles;

- *Code of Ethics and Practice for the Supervision of Counsellors*, which exists to guide members offering supervision to counsellors and to help counsellors seeking supervision;
- *Code of Ethics and Practice for Trainers*, which exists to guide members offering training to counsellors and to help members of the public seeking counselling training;
- *Complaints Procedure*, which exists to guide members of BAC and their clients resolving complaints about breaches of the Codes of Ethics and Practice.

Copies of these and other guidelines and information sheets relevant to maintaining ethical standards of practice can be obtained from the BAC office, 1 Regent Place, Rugby CV21 2PJ. *Telephone Helplines: Guidelines for Good Practice* is another guideline, intended to establish standards for people working on telephone helplines (sponsored by British Telecom). A new edition was produced in late 1992. Single copies are available from BSS, PO Box 7, London W3 6XJ.

Conclusion

'Counselling' is a word which has several different meanings. One of the most important differences is whether it is being used in a wider or narrower sense.

There are many examples of words carrying wider and narrower definitions. For example, in social policy the term 'social services' has a wider and narrower meaning (Mays et al., 1975). The narrower meaning refers exclusively to local authority social service departments, in contrast to its wider meaning which incorporates education, housing, health services, etc.. Similarly, the term 'counselling' has narrower and wider meanings. The codes of BAC use 'counselling' in its narrowest sense to describe a specific role. There is another use of 'counselling' which is more generic and all-encompassing to incorporate any or all of advice, guidance, befriending, counselling skills, psychotherapy and psychoanalysis. Confusion can be avoided from the outset by clarifying what meaning is intended in any instance.

3 The framework for ethics and standards of practice

Counselling has had only a relatively short life, compared to other professional roles, in which to develop its ethics and standards of practice. The relative brevity of its history means that counselling can learn from some of the longer established roles. The first code for counsellors, produced in 1984, was strongly influenced by social work ethics and the code developed by the British Association for Social Workers. Medicine, with its longer history, also has insights to offer as well as cautionary examples of how ethical endeavours can be counter-productive. In my opinion, one of the challenges for counselling is how to be as systematic in the development of ethics as in the current practice of medicine, but without taking on the worst excesses of professionalization which could create an unbridgeable gap between counsellor and client. I have been impressed by the way some doctors and nurses use their ethical framework to inform difficult decisions in patient care. For example, how do a clinical team decide between the needs of a severely brain-damaged child dependent for life on his incubator, and a recently born child with good prospects provided that the child can be put into the incubator occupied by the other child? In the final resort this is an ethical decision. Good clinical practice provides the information on which the likely outcome of giving the incubator to either child can be predicted, but this still leaves a choice to be made. In comparison with medical staff, counsellors are seldom faced with such highly charged and irreversible ethical dilemmas, but we can learn from the way such decisions are made.

The framework within which medical ethical decision-making is made involves consideration of information from four separate sources. These are:

1 Moral philosophy:	What should we do?
2 Law:	What are we legally prohibited from doing and/or what are we legally required to do? What are we legally entitled to do?
3 Resources:	What is possible?
4 Practitioners:	What do we want to do?

It is useful to consider each of these in turn as they apply to counselling.

Moral philosophy

I have already observed that the history of counselling within Britain is comparatively short compared to that of medicine. The history of the British Association for Counselling is even shorter. The inaugural meeting of BAC took place in London in 1977 in inauspicious circumstances of 'chaos, ghastly food which was allegedly vegetarian, and a public address system which was determined to break the language pattern of every speaker' (Hooper, 1988). Since then, BAC has made enormous progress and has acted as a national forum for establishing standards of practice for counsellors. However, so far as I can tell, there has been no significant interest from moral philosophers in these endeavours.

This may be for a number of reasons.

1   It is only as the role of counsellor becomes more clearly defined that consideration of the issues becomes possible and attractive to philosophers. It is difficult to be as precise and clear as philosophers like to be, when the object being analysed is elusive and lacking clear identity.
2   The rapidity with which counselling has grown has required pragmatic decision-making. Of necessity, this has run ahead of the much slower process of the academic deliberations of moral philosophy.
3   The origins from which counselling has emerged may be less sympathetic to moral argument than scientific justification. Jeremy Holmes and Richard Lindley (1989) have suggested this is the case with psychotherapy. They point out that the founders of major movements within psychotherapy, such as Freud and Jung, explored their theories in scientific terms and attempted to justify them by scientific criteria. It seems that scientific justification was, and probably still is, perceived as having the highest status. Resources tend to flow towards those who can claim a scientific basis for the efficacy of their work. These observations about psychotherapy seem equally applicable to counselling.

For whatever reason, it looks as if it will be some years before counsellors will have available to them books which explore the application of moral philosophy to counselling in ways which assist the counselling practitioner. However, it is possible to extract a number of principles from moral philosophy which have proved useful to other professions. These are:

1 Beneficence: What will achieve the greatest good?
2 Non-maleficence: What will cause least harm?

3 Justice: What will be fairest?
4 Respect for autonomy: What maximizes the opportunities for
                                everyone involved to implement their
                                own choices?

I have expressed each of the principles as a question because this
is how most people apply the principle to actual situations. Behind
each question is a statement that it is better to do good, avoid
harm, be just and respect autonomy. However, these principles do
not always work in harmony. For example, the counsellor's desire
to do good for the client can lead to parentalism, a term which I
am using to include either paternalism or maternalism. Parentalism
overrides the freedom of the clients to make their own choices in
order to achieve what the counsellor believes to be in the client's
best interests.

> Sam reveals that he has financial problems due to a compulsion
> to gamble, which is unknown to his wife and children. He
> believes he could overcome this problem before it reaches
> disastrous proportions if he could enlist the support of his
> family, but can't bring himself to tell them about his problem.
> His counsellor is increasingly concerned because time is slipping
> by and, as the debts mount, the risk of the family losing their
> home is only a few weeks away. Should she warn the family and
> seek to enlist their support for Sam?

In such circumstances, the principles of beneficence and respect for
autonomy are working in opposition to each other. If the
counsellor informs the family about Sam's gambling, she may help
to avert a devastating financial crisis and would therefore be doing
good, but at the cost of sacrificing respect for Sam's autonomy,
literally 'self-rule'. How can the counsellor choose between them?
Perhaps one of the other principles will be decisive. The counsellor
may wish to consider what will cause least harm? The harm which
faces the family lies mostly in Sam's inaction. His inaction means
that they are deprived of taking any action for themselves for as
long as they remain in ignorance of the problem. On the other
hand, if the counsellor informs them, harm will be caused to Sam
who will be perceived as someone unable to act for himself in the
eyes of his family. There may well also be betrayal of the trust Sam
has placed in the counsellor to keep confidences. Any betrayal of
confidentiality may also harm other clients who may lose trust in
this particular counsellor, or even in counselling in general, if such
breaches of confidence come to be viewed as accepted practice. It
is clear that although the potential harms may not be equally

balanced, there is no way of proceeding without some harm occurring.

Will the question of justice be decisive? Questions of justice are not merely matters of law. In determining what is just, it is sometimes necessary to ask more fundamental questions about what is meant by 'fair', and who should be taken into account in deciding what is 'fair'. These are philosophical and sociological questions and the subject of academic study. Much of this academic study is an extrapolation and examination of the different moral frameworks that individuals have internalized from their own culture and personal background. Would the questions of what is 'fair' be different between Anglo-Saxon and other cultures? What are the expectations of the counsellor and client, derived from their culture and their personal experience, including moral training particularly as a child? I doubt that every counsellor would wish to engage in academic debate about the moral basis for determining what is 'fair', but all counsellors ought to spend some time examining their own personal values and the implications of these for how they reach personal decisions about what is fair. My own experience of undertaking this sort of exercise in groups is that people with apparently similar values can come to different conclusions. This is a useful experience for counsellors and helps to develop an important therapeutic attitude of being cautious about judging clients in moral terms. It also points to the difficulty of determining on one's own what is 'fair'. The answer to this kind of question, and indeed all the questions associated with these basic principles, needs to take into account the opinions of others. On questions of justice, the law can often be a useful source of ideas, because, although the law has not always managed to deliver justice, it has over the centuries developed a conceptual framework and series of methods in which many people have committed themselves to obtaining and giving justice. In this particular example, the law would emphasize the importance of confidentiality, and the client's consent to any breach of confidence. A counsellor might also want to consider the collective experience of counsellors as represented in their codes, and would find a similar conclusion.

After considering all four of the fundamental principles, it would seem that the counsellor needs to act within the client's consent. However, care is needed before this becomes generalized into a principle which applies to all cases. This analysis of what is morally desirable is based on the assumption that Sam has approached the counsellor for counselling for himself and the counsellor has agreed that she will counsel on this basis. Would the situation be different if the counselling was provided in a different set of circumstances? What if the counsellor was a social worker working for a child protection agency who was therefore primarily concerned with the well-being of the children and Sam sought counselling from her with knowledge of this? How should she proceed in a morally acceptable way?

Psychologically, counsellors tend to concentrate on the relationship between themselves and their client. This is inevitable. Within the privacy of the counselling room, no-one else is immediately visible. The counsellor's concentration is directed towards the client. The counsellor's training will have been primarily directed towards learning to work with the client's inner world and perceptions and possibly the dynamics of the relationship between the counsellor and client. The values which form the basis of counselling, as will be explained later in this chapter, emphasize respect for individual autonomy. On the whole, I believe these moral principles support this client-centred perspective, but there may be times when counsellors need to take a wider view of their moral responsibilities in their dealing with individual clients. Careful consideration of the application of these principles helps to identify such situations. These principles also point to a moral basis for questioning the counsellor's contribution to society and the impact of society and the ways society is organized on individual autonomy. The questions posed by these moral principles invite us to increase our understanding of counselling in a wider context, as well as to help us to make decisions about working with individual clients.

The law

I think I detect a recent shift in attitude as it is becoming clearer that the law has much to offer both clients and counsellors in terms of protecting their entitlements, for example over confidentiality. These benefits outweigh the problems arising from differences of emphasis within legal and counselling culture. The emphasis in legal matters is inevitably on facts, evidence and the rational application of rules. Such rationality contrasts with much of the counsellor's experience of working with people's subjective experiences, fantasy and feelings. However, recent experience gives grounds for hope that, when counselling is explicitly considered by legislators, it is treated with sensitivity and in ways which are helpful to both clients and counsellors. In Chapter 9, I refer to an instance where a Law Commission on confidentiality considered the duties of a psychologist to maintain confidentiality over personally sensitive information vis-à-vis the client's employer unless a matter of public interest is involved, such as the health and safety of fellow employees. These recommendations would apply to all counsellors, and are of particular interest to employee counsellors.

The Human Fertilisation and Embryology Act 1990 provides another example of counselling and the law moving in the same direction. This Act is the only legislation I am aware of which establishes a new counselling service on a statutory basis and sets out its duties. The approach taken by the Act and the Code of Practice published by the Human Fertilisation and Embryology Authority (HFEA, 1991) demonstrates how a statutory duty to provide counselling need not conflict with the ethics and practice of counselling, and can have the effect of protecting what the client and counsellor are entitled to. The Act is concerned with the regulation of medical intervention to alleviate infertility and reduce the risk of inherited abnormality. It was devised in response to a moral panic in the media about new medical interventions such as the use of donor sperm and gametes, *in vitro* fertilization, etc. The statutory provisions affirm a general duty to give relevant information to ensure that patients are in a position to give an informed consent to any proposed medical intervention. The patient *must* be given 'such relevant information as is proper' (s. 13(6), Schedule 3, para. 3(1)(b)). In addition, patients must be given 'a suitable opportunity to receive proper counselling about the implications of taking the proposed steps' before they consent (Schedule 3, para. 3(1)(a)). No-one is obliged to accept the counselling that is offered. However, the HFEA Code of Practice states that counselling is 'generally recognised as beneficial' (6.3). The provisions about record-keeping and confidentiality are of particular interest to all counsellors and not just those involved in this particular setting. This code requires that: 'A record should be kept of all counselling offered and whether or not counselling is accepted' (6.24). And furthermore, 'All information obtained in counselling should be kept confidential' (6.25) even from the rest of the team working with the patient unless the patient has given consent or if the information 'is of such gravity that confidentiality *cannot* be maintained . . .' (3.24). The provisions recognize that the conditions for effective counselling require it to be set apart from the other work of the clinical team but at the same time recognize that counselling has an important and complementary role within the total service offered to patients. The legislation and HFEA code of practice are a good example of what can be achieved when lawyers and counsellors co-operate. There are many advantages in such an outcome because both counsellor and client have the full weight of the law protecting their respective rights.

However, most counsellors are providing services which are not established on a statutory basis and are therefore covered by the general principles of law which have been developed without explicit consideration of counselling. This means that in some circumstances counsellors and anyone directly affected by the work of counsellors, such as clients and counsellors' employers, are faced with some difficulty in establishing their legal rights and obligations. Part of the difficulty is the enormous volume of law in existence and determining what out of this great mass is applicable to counselling. A further complication is that on some issues, counsellors may be concerned with issues which cross over the boundaries or fall between the traditional ways in which the law is classified. For example, a counsellor faced with a request by an employer to make her records available to an auditor concerned with assessing the quality of the service being provided could potentially be concerned with contract law regarding her relationship with the client, employment law about the relationship between the counsellor and employer, common law about confidentiality and privacy and administrative law about any statutory powers involved. Even once the relevant areas of law have been identified, there may be a degree of uncertainty about how they will be applied. Counsellors are so seldom involved in court cases that there is a dearth of court decisions to provide precedence upon which the outcome of cases can be predicted. This is clearly a much less satisfactory position than where the role of the counsellor has been given careful consideration and been enacted in law, as in the instance of human fertilization and embryology.

As most counsellors work in situations where an understanding of the legal basis of their work is still at an exploratory stage, a word of warning is required about the law contained in this book.

A cautionary note about the law contained in this book

Statements about the law contained in this book should not be regarded as definitive. They are preliminary explorations of issues. Because of the difficulties already mentioned in determining the application of the law to counselling, any explanation of the legal position could hardly be more than this. It is also probable that during the lifetime of this book the law will change on significant points. It is therefore important that anyone with specific concerns about legal issues should obtain up-to-date professional advice. Legal advice may be obtained by consulting:

- a solicitor
- law centres
- legal advice lines, which are one of the services made available in some schemes of professional indemnity insurance
- associations for counselling.

Throughout the counselling relationship both the counsellor and the client remain citizens and are subject to the law. Despite the difficulties in determining what this means in practice, the *Code for Counsellors* (BAC, 1992a) reminds everyone of some basic legal principles.

> B.2.6.1 Counsellors should work within the law.
> B.2.6.2 Counsellors should take all reasonable steps to be aware of current legislation affecting the work of the counsellor. A counsellor's ignorance of the law is no defence against legal liability or penalty . . . (BAC, 1992a)

Whenever it seems relevant in the chapters which follow, I have included reference to the law. However, one of the problems is that Britain has two separate legal systems. The Scottish system is based on a different tradition from the rest of Britain and therefore produces different law. There are also significant legal provisions which relate only to Northern Ireland. Therefore most of the law mentioned within the book relates to England and Wales. Where possible I have indicated if it has a wider application. As a separate country, Southern Ireland or Eire has its own legal system which has not been considered in the preparation of this book.

A further source of potential confusion exists within the law because the terms 'counsel' and 'counselling' do not necessarily carry the same meaning as counselling in the context of psychological and social care. Reference to 'counsel' in a court is likely to be to a barrister. 'Counselling' in this context often means giving advice about the law. In criminal law, 'counselling' has a specific meaning relating to accomplices to a crime. A counsellor is someone who conspires with others to commit a crime, or encourage, or knowingly gives assistance to the participants in a crime before the crime is committed (Smith and Hogan, 1992: 126).

Resources

Resources are an important factor to be taken into consideration in any ethical decision-making. They often determine what is feasible and there are occasions when counsellors need to campaign for adequate resources to maintain an acceptable standard of practice.

The principal resource required for counselling is time. If the counsellor is working voluntarily then she bears this cost. In private practice, the client pays for the counsellor's time. If counselling is provided as part of someone's paid employment, there is a significant cost to the employer in wages. In employee counselling, the employer may be paying for both the client's and the counsellor's time. This means that there is always a need to address issues such as:

- Do the counsellor and client have the time available?
- Will the likely outcome justify the time spent?
- What will be the consequence of not investing the time?

In addition to the use of time for the provision of counselling, there are additional resource implications for an established counsellor; the largest of these is obtaining regular counselling supervision. For trainee counsellors, there is usually a substantial use of resources in the time and cost involved in obtaining both training and counselling-supervision.

Some resources may be required in order to provide a suitable environment for the counselling to take place. Most counselling takes place in a room which needs to be private and reasonably free from extraneous noise. There are two problems with extraneous noise: it can be disturbing; and, because sound travels both ways, a client may reasonably conclude that what is said inside the counselling room can be heard as well outside the room as sounds from outside are heard coming into the room. However, it is worth noting that although the usual requirement is for an appropriately furnished room free from extraneous interruptions, this is not a universal requirement. Counsellors report that some clients find such an environment intimidating and off-putting. In particular, counsellors working with drug users or young people state that some of their clients associate a private room with being in trouble and that their clients prefer to obtain privacy in other ways, perhaps by seeing the counsellor in a busy public space where the meeting may pass unnoticed. The anonymity of such a meeting creates an alternative method of obtaining privacy. This contrasts sharply with the unsatisfactory situation in which the counsellor is forced to see clients in a corridor or some other public space due to an absence of suitable facilities.

The requirements of good practice may also include adequate resources for insurance, as well as a telephone or panic button system if the counsellor's or client's safety requires this (see next chapter), and a secure place in which to keep any records or notes about the counselling (see Chapter 12).

Practitioners

Practitioner counsellors have an important contribution to make to the development of an ethical understanding of their role and to the setting of standards of practice. It was the accumulated experience of the members of the British Association for Counselling as reflected in the correspondence between some of the membership and the Standards and Ethics Sub-committee which initiated and influenced the revision of the 1984 version of the *Code of Ethics and Practice for Counsellors* into the 1990 and 1992 versions, and will lead to future revisions. One of the inevitable consequences of including statements about an ever increasing number of issues which have caused counsellors concern is that the code steadily lengthens. The 1990 version of the code is over twice as long and much more detailed than its 1984 progenitor. It has also moved from making general statements of principle to becoming much more specific. In order to make the contents of the code accessible to readers it was structured and cross-referenced.

The *Code* starts with an introduction which includes a definition of counselling (see previous chapter) before the Code of Ethics elaborates the values, and then the ethical principles derived from these values. The Code of Practice which follows sets out the standards of practice required to fulfil the ethical principles. It is useful to consider the values, ethical principles and code of practice more fully.

Values of counselling

Values act as the foundation upon which ethical principles and standards of practice are built. The worth of counselling depends upon them. The values identified in the *Code for Counsellors* are defined in Figure 3.1. These values are not unique to 'counselling' in its narrow sense. They are also the values explicitly mentioned in the *Code of Conduct* of the British Psychological Society (1991) which states: 'In all their work psychologists shall value integrity, impartiality, and respect for persons and evidence. . .'. These are values shared by most of the caring professions in democracies.

Value	Definition
Integrity	wholeness, soundness, uprightness, honesty
Impartiality	fairness, absence of prejudice
Respect	esteem felt and shown towards another person

Figure 3.1 *The values of counselling*

The challenge for counsellors, as for all other roles which have adopted these inspirational values, is to convert them into concrete practice. The intermediate step in this process is to re-express the very non-specific values into general statements of ethical principle.

Ethical principles

The *Code for Counsellors* identifies a number of ethical principles derived from the values to inform practice.

Avoidance of harm   This is a commitment to avoid harm to the client by exploitation: 'Counselling is a non-exploitative activity' (A.1), to work ethically; 'Counsellors should take the same degree of care to work ethically whether the counselling is paid or voluntary' (A.1); and to ensure client safety; 'All reasonable steps should be taken to ensure the client's safety during counselling' (A.2). This last statement carries with it the implication that, even if a client cannot be helped, he should not be left in a worse condition than when he arrived. This applies equally to physical and psychological states. It sets a baseline beyond which standards ought not to fall. However, merely attaining this standard would be insufficient grounds for the worth of counselling. People seek counselling not to avoid harm but in the hope of some benefit. This requires a degree of competence on the part of the counsellor.

Competence   The *Code* states: 'Counsellors shall take all reasonable steps to monitor and develop their own competence and to work within the limits of that competence' (A.4). In the worst case, would someone who is incompetent necessarily be aware of their inadequacy? How can someone know what they lack the competence to know? It is possible for someone to continue in a state of what Francesca Inskipp (1986) has identified as 'unconscious incompetence'. Therefore it is important to involve others in any evaluation of competence. The *Code* specifies that taking all reasonable steps to monitor and develop competence 'includes having appropriate and on-going counselling supervision/consultative support' (A.4). When someone moves from a state of 'unconscious incompetence' to 'conscious incompetence' this is an important step in the learning process but is often associated with uncomfortable feelings of anxiety, a sense of being de-skilled, although some may become excited at the prospect of new learning. Once the new learning has taken place and can be implemented, a state of 'conscious competence' follows. This is the third stage and can feel artificial. As the learning and practice are integrated into the counsellor's personal style and usual ways of working, a loss of self-consciousness occurs and a state of 'unconscious competence' is reached. This is the objective of monitoring and developing levels of competence and the learning cycle is completed until a new competence is required.

The ethical requirement of on-going counselling-supervision is not merely a safety net against incompetence but is also intended to serve the positive function of enhancing the quality of counselling by competent counsellors. Further consideration of the ethical basis of counselling-supervision can be found in Chapter 11.

Clear contracts The pre-eminence of respect for a client's capacity for self-determination which forms part of BAC's definition of counselling carries with it certain consequences. On ethical grounds alone, it makes it impossible to impose any absolute ethical principle, for example that counselling be totally confidential, because this could be a violation of the client's own wishes and capacity for self-determination. For example, what if the client wants the counsellor to inform someone that the client has been receiving counselling? A respect for someone's capacity for self-determination requires that his wishes about how the counselling is provided and on what terms should be taken into account by the counsellor. The process of negotiating a clear contract between the counsellor and client is therefore an important part of the recognition of the client's capacity for self-determination and preferable to a list of conditions determined by the counsellor in advance.

Not all clients will have strong views about the terms on which they wish to be offered counselling. In these circumstances it is important that, 'The terms on which counselling is being offered should be made clear to clients before counselling commences. Subsequent revisions of these terms should be agreed in advance of any change' (A.3). It is as a direct consequence of the fundamental principle of respect for the client's capacity for self-determination that clear contracting has become so prominent in counselling. In Chapter 5 I suggest that clear contracting shows a higher level of respect for the client's autonomy than merely seeking informed consent.

Confidentiality The omission of a statement about confidentiality as an ethical principle at the time of the 1990 version of the *Code for Counsellors* was deliberate. It was intended as a signal that confidentiality ought not to be regarded as an absolute principle. With hindsight, I believe this was an over-reaction by me and other co-authors of the *Code*. It is a decision which was understandable in its context. The earlier version of the code contained the statement 'The counselling relationship is by its nature confidential.' It continued to contradict so absolute a statement by permitting counsellors who 'believe that a client could cause danger to others . . . may break confidentiality' and by the requirement that, 'Counsellors monitor their counselling work through regular supervision . . .' (BAC, 1984). In contrast, confidentiality is given an extended consideration within the 1990 version of the *Code of Practice* and some of the logical inconsistencies of 1984 are avoided. Now, some years on, I find it strange that confidentiality should not also be regarded as an ethical principle. Were I to rewrite the *Code of Ethics* substantially, I should include two closely related statements about confidentiality: 'Confidentiality is important in order to protect personal information about clients and ought to be treated most seriously in the practice of counselling. Each client should be informed by the counsellor where he or she stands with regard to confidentiality.'

The importance of confidentiality as an ethical principle is a corollary of the respect for the client's self-determination. Disclosure of personal information without the client's consent clearly erodes a client's ability to keep control of his own situation. For example, a client may be feeling resentful towards someone but uncertain how to deal with the situation. From the moment the existence of these feelings is communicated by someone other than the client, it is most likely that the client will have lost the time or space to formulate his own plan of action and may be overtaken by events. Confidentiality is also important practically. Without it, few clients would feel able to trust their counsellor with personally sensitive information. This important topic is given further consideration as an aspect of practice in Chapter 9.

Ethics and standards of practice

Most of this book and three-quarters of the *Code for Counsellors* are concerned with standards of practice because counselling is ultimately a practical endeavour. However, before we move on to these considerations, it is useful to explore the relationship between ethical principle and standards of practice.

First, the ethical principle establishes the spirit in which the counsellor ought to act. The *Code of Practice* is based on the experience of many counsellors and sets out how they have applied those principles to their practice. However, if a specific provision in the *Code of Practice* appears likely to undermine an ethical principle then the latter is more important. A code of practice cannot envisage all possible circumstances for all counsellors and clients. Nonetheless, it is anticipated that the circumstances in which the *Code of Practice* could conflict with an ethical principle will be rare. It is intended that the *Code of Practice* should set out achievable methods of implementing the ethical principles.

Second, the standards of practice set by the *Code* are the basic standards for acceptable practice. Failure to achieve these standards constitutes grounds for complaint against a BAC member which can be pursued under the Association's *Complaints Procedure* (BAC, 1992b). On the other hand, it is possible to achieve higher levels of practice. There are many examples mentioned throughout the book, especially with reference to record-keeping and monitoring counselling, where there are significant differences between what is considered the minimum standard of practice and an ideal standard of good practice. Generally speaking, the accreditation schemes for counsellors, supervisors and training courses run by BAC have tended to set criteria above the minimum standards of acceptable practice.

Conclusion

In this chapter I have considered four of the major elements which contribute towards what is considered ethical and of an adequate standard of practice in counselling. These are moral philosophy, law, resources and the views of practitioners. To date, the last has been the most influential. However, as more attention is given to the law and moral philosophy, it seems likely that these will become more important resources available to counsellors who wish to enhance their practice. I think it is important that all these elements are given sufficient attention by researchers and writers in order to make them accessible to practitioners. Each element acts as an important check and balance in the total system of ethics and standards of practice, and thus helps to ensure that standards set by the practitioners themselves are not merely self-serving. I believe that the involvement of practitioners in setting out their own code of practice has so far been in the spirit of enhancing the service to clients. I hope this is how it will always be. However, this cannot be guaranteed and it is salutary to reflect that some other longer established codes than those produced by counsellors have come to be seen as protecting the interests of practitioners rather more than the users of their services.

4 Client safety, legal liability and insurance

Responsibilities to the client are the foremost concern of the counsellor. The justification of counselling rests on this work being undertaken in a counsellor–client relationship. However, before a principled relationship, which is the basis of counselling, can be established a number of issues require careful consideration. Thorough preparation not only makes it easier to avoid harming the client, but also increases the possibility of the client benefiting from the counselling.

Client safety

The *Code for Counsellors* (BAC, 1992a) states: 'Counsellors should take all reasonable steps to ensure that the client suffers neither physical nor psychological harm during counselling' (B.2.2.1). This is the minimum requirement of the ethical principle of non-maleficence. Some fictitious examples provide illustrations of the kind of harm that could befall clients.

Liability for physical injury

Bill was so nervous when he entered the counselling room that he did not notice a shelf at head level. He bumped his head so badly that he required medical treatment.

The risk of physical injury to a client during counselling is usually fairly unlikely, provided that the counsellor has anticipated any sources of danger and removed them. Nonetheless, there is always the potential for a client tripping, falling off a chair, or bumping into something. In these circumstances, the client may seek compensation for any injury, particularly if it appears that the counsellor has been negligent. Normally this claim would be against the 'occupier', which is defined in law as a person who has sufficient control over premises to put him under a duty of care towards those who come lawfully upon those premises (Rogers, 1989). In many circumstances this could be the counsellor. Normally the claim would be covered by existing public liability insurance if the counselling is taking place on business or public premises. If the insurance cover is inadequate, however, the claim would have to be met by the counsellor personally. This has important implications for both counsellor and client. If Bill's injuries were serious or resulted in disability any award for damages could be substantial. A recent record award of damages for bodily and psychological injury in the UK is £1,700,000 in a road accident case, which indicates that substantial amounts of money may be involved. Bartlett Insurance Brokers, who provide the insurance schemes for BAC and the British Psychological Society (BPS), have observed, 'The chances of a counsellor's causing an injury of this severity must be extremely remote but counsellors, when selecting an insurance limit, should always look to the worst possible scenario because the premium is set at a low level reflecting the very low probability' (Bartlett, 1992).

Many counsellors work from home and may be relying on their household insurance for protection. However, most household insurance policies exclude cover from premises, or parts of premises, used for business purposes. In these circumstances, the counsellor could be personally liable to pay damages. It is therefore important that the counsellor seeks advice from a competent insurance broker about whether she requires 'public liability insurance'. This insurance is included within the insurance schemes provided in association with BAC and BPS.

Counsellors who use physical activity with clients, such as beating cushions, pushing against the counsellor, etc., will also be interested in obtaining insurance to cover themselves in case the client is accidentally injured.

Liability for psychological harm

An example will illustrate the sort of situation in which a claim for compensation for psychological harm could arise and the difficulties any client may encounter in obtaining damages.

> Peter approached a counsellor for assistance with a bereavement. Despite the counselling he felt progressively worse and became more withdrawn. Eventually he was treated by a psychiatrist for depression. On his recovery, he considered suing his counsellor.

If the counsellor has created a contract with the client promising improvements or the absence of deterioration, the client could sue for breach of contract. However, Kenneth Cohen observed that:

> counsellors and psychotherapists wisely therefore, tend to be very cautious about predicting outcomes, and the very wisest of them promise nothing at all! Some who do choose to make extravagant claims for their brand of counselling or therapy offer no quibble money back guarantees to disappointed clients: this is a sensible precaution against claims for misrepresentation and breach of contract. (1992)

In the absence of any contractual terms relevant to the claim, the client's case would be based on the alleged negligence of the counsellor. In order to establish this case the client would need to show the existence of:

- a duty of care
- breach of that duty
- damage that resulted.

The duty owed by counsellors is the same as that owed by any other professional. They are required only to exercise reasonable care and skill in rendering their services to clients. The duty of care does not require that there should be no deterioration or even actual improvement. Reasonable care will be assessed by a court by examination of the standards of the profession, particularly its guides to ethics and conduct, its leading textbooks and the testimony of its leading practitioners. If, as is the case in counselling, there are differences of view about what constitutes acceptable professional behaviour, such as variations between theories and methods of counselling, this poses a problem for the court. In these circumstances the court does not get involved in assessing which treatment is more effective and, as a consequence, label less effective treatments as negligent. An assessment of effectiveness would be fraught with problems and would leave no room for differences of opinion between conscientious and generally competent practitioners. Courts have therefore adopted a different approach which judges that a professional is not negligent if she follows the practice accepted at the time as proper by a reasonable body of professional opinion skilled in the particular form of treatment (Rogers, 1989). The test used to decide whether this is the case was formulated in *Bolam* v. *Friern Hospital Management Committee* (1957) about medical negligence but now has much wider application. Kenneth Cohen has indicated the kind of question that a judge might ask himself: 'Even though there is a body of competent professional opinion which might adopt a different technique, did the practitioner act in accordance with a practice accepted as proper by a responsible body of professional opinion skilled in the particular form of treatment?' (1992).

If the counsellor can show that he acted in accordance with a reasonable body of competent professional opinion then there is likely to be a complete defence, but there are uncertainties about how a counsellor would establish this defence. Courts already attach great weight to medical opinions within psychiatry but the status of non-medical opinions is unknown. It seems probable that the official views of an established organization will carry more weight than an individual's, but again, there is uncertainty about this.

In order to succeed the client must also establish that the breach of the duty was the cause of the harm suffered. 'Cause' is defined strictly to mean 'materially contributing' rather than 'determining'. This means that conjectural and speculative explanations of the cause of the harm are inadequate. The question may be put as 'Would the loss or harm have happened but for this duty?' The existence of more than one possible explanation, particularly explanations not involving the counsellor, could discredit or reduce the claim. In Kenneth Cohen's opinion there may also be an inherent anti-litigation bias within counselling arising from the difficulty the client has in establishing the counsellor's responsibility for the harm suffered in a relationship where the client retains a high level of responsibility for the outcomes of the counselling. 'Many would say that in the long run, a good counsellor or therapist seeks to empower and encourage his client to locate causality operating in her life more and more within herself, rather than others, including in particular the counsellor' (Cohen, 1992). On the other hand, an empowered client might become more active in pursuing grievances against the counsellor if she has been negligent in the way she has worked.

There are other legal rules which may adversely affect a client's ability to sue for negligence in these circumstances. However, even if the client could satisfy all these, there are further complications arising from the provisions for compensating psychological injuries. No compensation is available for hurt feelings alone in this kind of case unless they are of sufficient duration and severity to amount to mental illness. The circumstances causing the mental illness are also defined so restrictively that they are unlikely to occur within counselling.

It is a general legal principle that no damages can be recovered for negligence resulting in emotional suffering short of psychological illness unless there was also physical injury. This principle was re-affirmed in the recent case of *Nichols* v. *Rushton* in which someone suffered 'severe shock and shaking up' in a car accident but could not be awarded damages because this did not amount to psychological illness and was not accompanied by physical injury (*Times Law Reports*, 1992). The same principles would apply for claims arising from negligence in the counselling room.

It is evident that a client is likely to experience considerable difficulties in bringing an action against a counsellor for negligence resulting in psychological harm. Nonetheless, a counsellor could incur considerable legal expenses in defending such an action and therefore professional indemnity insurance to cover such costs may be advisable.

The difficulties clients encounter in using the courts to seek remedies against counsellors is one of the reasons why it is so important that counselling organizations have effective complaints procedures. This is a matter of both justice to clients and also ensuring that allegations of practice are adequately investigated to protect the reputation of counselling as a whole.

In England, there is only one case of negligent psychotherapy recorded in the law reports. In the case of *Landau* v. *Werner* (1961) it was held that the defendant, a psychoanalytically orientated psychiatrist, was liable for negligently causing a deterioration in his client's condition by engaging in social contacts with her in a misguided attempt to resolve her transference. Her deterioration had been such that she attempted suicide. This judgment in the High Court was upheld by the Court of Appeal. Both courts came to this view whilst rejecting allegations that the defendant had had sex with his client.

The lack of British cases against counsellors based on negligence is in sharp contrast to the USA, where the rules for establishing liability are much more favourable to the client and therefore litigation is a much more frequent occurrence.

Avoidance of advice-giving

At first sight it may seem strange that the *Code for Counsellors* includes the statement 'Counsellors do not normally give advice' (B.2.2.2) as a matter of client safety. It could equally well be viewed as a matter of autonomy. The reason why this statement is included here is that advice-giving carries with it additional legal responsibilities. This is recognized in law by making it much easier for a client to bring an action for negligent advice. Unlike in the action for negligence (see previous section) the client would only have to show he acted in reliance on the advice, rather than proving a causal connection between the duty of care and the harm. Unlike in negligence, the client would also be able to claim for purely economic losses, such as loss of earnings suffered as a result of bad advice, even though there has been no damage to person or property and no legally recognized contractual relationship between counsellor and client.

There is a general principle in medical negligence law that failure to advise of risks of treatment can be as negligent as giving bad advice (*Sidaway* v. *Bethlem Royal Hospital*, 1985). However, in Kenneth Cohen's opinion, it is unlikely that a failure by a counsellor to advise risks would be actionable because there is no professional body opinion that such risks ought to be disclosed. 'It is evident that there is no consensus at the moment in the world of therapy and counselling as to whether the risks are great enough to impose a duty of care' (Cohen, 1992).

On the other hand, situations sometimes arise when a counsellor may feel a moral or ethical duty to advise someone to seek specialist help other than counselling. For example, if a client seeks counselling for stress-related problems and complains of constant headaches which could be stress-related or have physical origins, such as a brain tumour, a conscientious counsellor would recommend a medical examination in order that both he and the client have more information about the nature of the symptoms and to decide what kind of treatment is most appropriate. Unlike doctors, who hold themselves up as medically qualified, and could be expected to be held liable for treating someone for depression when they have a diagnosable brain tumour, the counsellor does not claim medical expertise. This lack of medical expertise reduces the possibility of legal liability for failing to advise clients to seek appropriate medical diagnosis, but paradoxically increases the moral grounds for doing so. It is because the counsellor lacks the expertise to interpret physical symptoms until organic origins have been eliminated that the client should be encouraged to seek a medical examination.

Counsellors who advise homework for clients (as opposed to facilitating the client setting his own homework between counselling sessions) may incur liability. Kenneth Cohen gives two speculative examples:

> Suppose . . . a client says in effect: 'I confronted my boss as we agreed I would. But now he's fired me and I wouldn't have lost my job but for your bad advice'. Or suppose a client is arrested by the police for engaging in sexual activities which his counsellor had negotiated with him as homework without realising they are illegal. (1992)

These examples not only illustrate the risks of advice-giving but also demonstrate the need for counsellors to be clear in their agreements with clients about who takes responsibility for the outcome of the counselling.

Libel and slander

Counsellors are often much more concerned about the possibility of legal actions for negligence being taken against them than they are about libel and slander. However, this may be a misplaced concern. Some insurers and lawyers believe that in actual practice actions for libel and slander could generate more law suits against counsellors than claims for negligence. Like all citizens, counsellors have a responsibility to avoid making defamatory statements. However, the nature of our work means that counsellors need to take particular care over this responsibility.

Both libel, which is in writing, and slander, which is oral, are forms of defamation. Defamation is defined in law as the publication of a statement which adversely reflects on a person's reputation by lowering him in the estimation of right-thinking members of society generally, causing him to be shunned or avoided (Rogers, 1989). In ordinary language it is the communication of something to at least one person, other than the person defamed, which damages that person's reputation. The damage to reputation might result in hatred, contempt or ridicule.

There is clearly potential for counsellors to defame each other's reputations by statements against each other about malpractice or incompetence. Although generally counsellors are fairly tolerant of each other, sometimes in heated debate or as a result of clashes of personality things are written or said which are defamatory.

Another potential source of liability arises from what clients say about others. Many of the things said about people in counselling are defamatory. However, so long as what is said remains confidential between the counsellor and client, no actual damage is caused to the reputation of the persons defamed, nor will they learn of what has been said, therefore no legal action is likely to occur. This has implications for couple, family and group counselling because the defamation is communicated to a larger number of people and is therefore less likely to remain confidential.

The risk of legal action for defamation is one of several reasons why counsellors need to be extremely careful over their practice of confidentiality. Avoiding the use of names or personally identifiable information during supervision or if cases are discussed in training makes it much less likely that the counsellor would take on liability for any defamation of others by clients. This is important because every repetition of defamatory words creates the possibility of a separate case and therefore, in repeating what a client has said, the counsellor may also become personally liable.

If a defamatory statement is made, there are a number of legal defences. The first of these is that the statement is true, and this defence is known as justification. Minor inaccuracies in the defamatory statement would not prevent this defence. However, this is a defence which would present a problem for a counsellor who was being sued for the subsequent communication of something told to her by a client in confidence. She would almost certainly require the co-operation of the client in establishing the truth, a client who could have legal grounds for a separate action against the counsellor for breach of confidence.

A second legal defence is known as 'fair comment'. This means that it must be in the public interest, which is defined quite widely, and covers both matters in which the public is legitimately interested as well as matters in which it is legitimately concerned. This defence is usually used by people sued because of the publication of stories in newspapers about the conduct of someone in public life, but it is not exclusive to this situation and could be used to defend criticisms made at a public event such as a conference or on a training course. For the defence to apply, there must have been an expression of opinion rather than fact, and it must be 'fair' in the sense of based on true facts.

The defence which is likely to be of most interest to counsellors with regard to clients could apply to the situation where the counsellor is passing personally identifiable information on to someone to prevent serious physical harm being caused to the client or others. For example, a client may have alleged that serious sexual physical assaults are being conducted by her father against members of her family. Clearly it is impossible to pass on this information without being defamatory against the client's father. The counsellor would be protected by a form of qualified privilege; in circumstances where there is a reasonable occasion requiring communication and the statement was honestly made, then such communications are protected for the common convenience and welfare of society. This defence will operate only in so far as the range of people informed is restricted to people with a legitimate interest; in these circumstances this would include people directly affected or people able to take action to prevent the assaults, such as the police, social services, etc. Again, careful observation of the BAC *Code of Practice* with regard to confidentiality increases the likelihood of this defence being available to a counsellor.

Breach of confidentiality

Breach of confidentiality is actionable in law. This is a complex subject, but because it is so central to the work of counsellors, I have considered the ethical and legal issues together in Chapter 9. In many ways I think the keeping of confidences is the most demanding of responsibilities placed on counsellors. It is also the responsibility which is most easily broken accidentally or even in the belief that the communication is in a client's best interests but without his consent.

Conclusion

The recommendation contained in the *Code for Counsellors* that all counsellors should review their need for insurance periodically is clearly a matter of prudent self-protection. The complexity of the law and the existence of many different potential sources of liability mean that it is unrealistic to expect counsellors to be able to anticipate every way in which they might incur liability. The examples given are by no means exhaustive. Even though a claim may be unsuccessful, a counsellor may incur expenses in seeking legal advice and defending the action.

However, there is probably a more important reason than self-interest why counsellors should give serious consideration to adequate insurance. For a client to have a successful claim against a counsellor, there must have been a corresponding harm. Ethically it is desirable that the client be compensated in such a way as to put him in as good a position as if that harm had not occurred. As most counsellors lack the financial resources to meet claims for compensation, insurance is a prudent alternative method of rectifying any harm to a client.

Counsellors committed to good practice would wish to offer this protection to clients. Any insurance package ought to include:

- professional indemnity (malpractice, errors and omissions)
- public liability
- libel and slander insurance
- product liability.

The need for the first three has already been mentioned. Product liability insurance would be particularly relevant to counsellors who supply such items as relaxation tapes.

Bartlett Insurance Brokers report, on the basis of running the BAC insurance scheme for over one year and the BPS scheme for five years, that they have had around a dozen cases reported as potential claims and none of these has involved actual claim payments by insurers. In several situations the counsellor benefited from free legal advice or representation. This may indicate that it is the most prudent counsellors who are seeking insurance, and therefore by definition are least likely to have claims launched against them. On the other hand, the cost of defending even unsuccessful or malicious actions against counsellors can be substantial when this occurs. I am aware of uninsured counsellors who have had to spend substantial sums of money on legal advice. Certainly, it is important that counsellors review their need for insurance and balance the relatively low cost of cover against the ethical desirability of being insured as a protection to clients and themselves.

5 Client autonomy

Autonomy means the right of 'self-rule' or 'self-government'. In moral philosophy, Raanan Gillon has defined the essential meaning of autonomy as 'the capacity to think, decide and act on the basis of such thought and decisions, freely and independently and without, as it says in the passport, "let or hindrance"' (1985). Autonomy is not unfettered licence to do anything regardless of the consequences to others. In most ethical systems, the right to have one's autonomy respected extends to the point where one person's autonomy is consistent with the respect for the autonomy of others. John Stuart Mill, a founding father of utilitarianism and ethical theorist, argued strongly for the importance of respecting another's autonomy. However, he imposed two restrictions. First, respect for another's autonomy should not lead to the harm of another's autonomy. Second, the person whose autonomy is respected should possess a fairly basic level of maturity and therefore be capable of taking responsibility for his or her own autonomous actions. As a philosopher, he was primarily concerned with the rationality of people and this is reflected in his test for an adequate level of maturity, which he defined as 'a capability of being improved by free and equal discussion'. This test may not transfer easily into counselling because of the inherent inequality of power between counsellor and client, but the concept of individuals having the capability of taking responsibility for their own autonomous actions is important. For example, it is absurd to offer respect for someone's autonomy if for some reason that person is incapable of taking responsibility for her own actions, perhaps due to neurological damage. A different set of criteria about acting in that person's best interests is required. We shall return to exceptions to the principle of autonomy later in this chapter and the next. Before doing so, it is important to explore some of the implications of autonomy in counselling.

Respect for someone's autonomy is so fundamental that it influences many different aspects of the counselling relationship. The *Code of Ethics and Practice for Counsellors* (BAC, 1992a) establishes the basic principle:

> B.2.2.3 Counsellors are responsible for working in ways which promote the client's control over his/her own life, and respect the client's ability to make decisions and change in the light of his/her own beliefs and values.

This section applies to all clients whether or not they are assessed as being in an autonomous state. It requires counsellors working with clients who temporarily lose their autonomous state due to severe psychological or physical illness, severe emotional distress, or drugs, to work in ways which will help these clients back to a state of taking control of their own lives. In practice, this might mean trying to avoid irreversible decisions about the client's lifestyle, such as disposing of a home, or, when there is a choice of interventions, choosing the one which is most likely to enhance the client's control over her own life. Anyone who has worked with people who are diagnosed as severely mentally ill will recognize the potential conflict between choosing interventions which make the patient's condition more manageable for staff and relatives, perhaps by sedation, and using interventions which take account of the patient's own wishes. During periods of severe mental disturbance or physical illness, counselling is unlikely to be an appropriate intervention but in some circumstances the counsellor may have a role in acting as an advocate for the person's wishes expressed when the client was still in control of her life. For example, someone may indicate what they wished to be communicated to relatives in the event of a mental illness, perhaps about how household pets should be taken care of. It is reasonable to assume that the knowledge that these declared wishes have been followed will assist a client to regain a sense of control over her own life as the crisis passes. These are the kinds of exceptional circumstances in which a counsellor might act on a client's behalf.

However, most clients possess at least a basic level of autonomy. The counsellor's role is to enhance this capacity for personal autonomy. Subjectively, people experience their own sense of autonomy differently. For example, some people may be so hurt by previous experience that they feel trapped by their past. Others may feel enmeshed in a difficult relationship or overwhelmed by a current crisis. Objectively, people take different levels of control of situations which are potentially within their control. Sometimes this is due to a lack of relevant knowledge or personal and social skills. The role of the counsellor is to enhance the client's subjective and objective autonomy.

Counsellors can assist or frustrate their client's growth towards autonomy in many ways. This is not only a therapeutic issue but also a matter of ethics. Most of this chapter will be concerned with ways counsellors can work to enhance their client's autonomy but it is worth spending a few moments reflecting on how counsellors can work against the development of the client's autonomy. A danger sign is the conviction that the counsellor knows what is better for a client than does the client herself. This is particularly the case if such a belief is reinforced by a determination that the client's experience should conform to the counsellor's own personal experience or to a particular theory. For example:

> Sue's partner has recently died. Her counsellor frustrates Sue by appearing to expect that Sue will be helped by the same things that had helped the counsellor in a similar situation. Sue also finds that the way she is expected to follow a series of stages in her grieving, which do not fit her experience, is unhelpful. This situation could resolve itself in several ways. Sue could lose confidence in her own experience and start to conform to her counsellor's personal and theoretical expectations. This is clearly a move away from autonomy towards dependency. Sue could abandon the counselling as unhelpful. An opportunity lost. Sue could challenge the way in which the counsellor is working, a risky thing to do and she may not have the emotional energy for this course of action when she is feeling so vulnerable. The best outcome is that the counsellor is sensitive to Sue's reactions and invites her feedback, and perhaps with the help of counselling-supervision modifies her approach, thus demonstrating respect for Sue's personal experience and her autonomy.

This example reveals the power held by counsellors over vulnerable clients, and how, through too great an enthusiasm for a particular theory or approach, autonomy can be eroded and a client's dependency inadvertently encouraged. The example I have given assumes that the client has sufficiently developed insight to be able to recognize what is happening and the capacity to take the initiative. Other clients may be so used to having their experiences invalidated that they fail to recognize what is happening to them. In these circumstances the counsellor is in a very powerful position and is dangerous unless he is aware of the possibilities of using this power to undermine the development of a client's autonomy. Alice Miller (1990) characterizes such situations as potentially 'poisonous'. She is particularly concerned with the way orthodox psychoanalysis, until recently, dismissed clients' accounts of childhood sexual abuse as fantasy. Psychoanalytic theories had the effect of automatically, and unconsciously, acting as blinkers which exclude from view the real experience from the client's childhood. Almost all counsellors would now accept the possibility that clients may be recalling actual events when they describe childhood sexual abuse. The widespread acceptance of this point of view has taken place as recently as the 1980s. However, it is salutary to wonder whether there are other theoretical 'truths' in the counsellor's repertoire which blinker counsellors against the client's experience and therefore exclude something from view which needs to be taken as true if a client's right to act autonomously is to be respected rather than poisoned by a counsellor's disbelief or interpretation. This is not an ethical argument against theory or making interpretations of what is communicated by the client. It is an argument for avoiding investing theories with too much certainty and attempting to impose a point of view on a client, especially if it contradicts the client's reported experience. Both clients and counsellors need a degree of emotional health in order to recognize these situations. In Miller's words, 'Only a feeling person can grasp the way an empty theory may function as a means of power, for he or she will not be intimidated by incomprehensibility' (1990).

It is to avoid abusing their power over emotionally vulnerable clients, and to avoid fostering dependence, that counsellors generally avoid giving advice. Appropriate advice can be enabling and empowering if the client is seeking help with a practical problem but it is much less appropriate to working with feelings, where it can be experienced as a denial of the validity of the client's own emotional experience. As most issues raised in counselling have an emotional basis, advice should be used, if at all, only infrequently. The *Code of Practice* states: 'Counsellors do not normally give advice' (B.2.2.2). This self-denying ordinance is out of respect for the client's own autonomy. Even good advice encourages reliance on the counsellor's judgement rather than helping the client to develop her own capacity to make personal judgements.

One of the ways in which counsellors have attempted to ensure the client's autonomy within the counselling relationship is to emphasize the importance of boundaries of responsibility within the counselling relationship and to avoid acting in ways which intrude upon what is properly the client's area of responsibility. Some of the ways this ethical principle have been elaborated are considered next.

Autonomy as a division of responsibility between method and outcome

John Rowan has described the boundary of responsibility within counselling as a division of responsibility between method and outcome. The counsellor is responsible for the methods she uses but responsibility for the outcome is the client's. This point is most readily grasped in terms of its implications for how counsellors think and talk about their role. Rowan observes that it is tempting to describe achievements in counselling in terms like:

- Produce a breakthrough in client;
- Cure client;
- Enlighten client;
- Get client to go from adjustment to ecstasy;
- Ability to facilitate client change of self-direction;
- Ability to get client catharsis/insight/body change/pivotal attitude change.

> But these are all, ultimately, things the client does, rather than things the therapist or counsellor does. What I think works on a list like this is to stick to things which the therapist [or counsellor] does. (Rowan, 1983)

This issue is sometimes approached metaphorically in the search for similes and images to describe the role of the counsellor. In *Therapists' Dilemmas* (1985), Windy Dryden interviewed 14 well known therapists or counsellors about issues of uncertainty which have arisen during their work. Frequently, when the interviewees touch on boundaries of responsibility between the counsellor and client, they use metaphorical images or react against images chosen by others.

Albert Ellis, the founder of rational–emotive therapy, advocates the role of therapist as 'scientific healer' with characteristic personal vigour. When interviewed by Windy Dryden he commented on the situation where the RET practitioner knows the solution to the client's problem,

> . . . why should you waste therapeutic time collaborating 50–50 with the clients when you can effectively help them zero in on what their philosophic problems are? . . . Indeed, if you do try to maintain a fully collaborative stance, I think you are adopting a hypocritical pretense. . . . My hypothesis is that many therapists, who are scared shitless of making mistakes in therapy, like 'full collaboration' because they can cop out of taking risks and of doing a great deal of the therapeutic work themselves. . . . They are in a word afraid of being directive. (Dryden, 1985)

Ellis believes that it is unavoidable that the therapists will try to fit clients into their system as opposed to modifying their system to fit the client. He also asserts that it is legitimate to try to talk clients into something that he believes on theoretical and practical grounds is therapeutic. The degree of autonomy he leaves the client is to refuse to be persuaded or to choose someone else as their therapist. This is an extremely robust view of the counsellor taking responsibility for the methods used. There is a fine line between such an authoritative view of the counsellor's role and the counsellor being perceived as taking responsibility for the outcome of the counselling.

Few counsellors are comfortable with the authoritative healer approach of Ellis which, in his rhetoric and practice, can seem to some quite authoritarian. Even counsellors who do think of themselves as 'healers' recognize that the transition from the counsellor making a diagnosis of what is wrong with the client to obtaining the client's co-operation in the 'treatment' needs to be handled more sensitively than Ellis acknowledges. Failure to do this runs the risk of creating dependence on the therapist. Care taken over ensuring the client consents to the interventions and maximizing the client's involvement in negotiating the terms of her participation minimizes the risks of dependence. However, the imagery of 'counsellor' as healer can never totally fit into a clear distinction between responsibility for method and outcome.

John Bancroft, a psychiatrist, author of *Human Sexuality and its Problems* and contributor to a course on sexual counselling, experiences the dilemma between being a 'healer' and being an 'educator' quite acutely. He acknowledges the attractions of being a healer and how it can be effective, particularly in the short term, but it cannot get away from being the 'expert' and the implication, 'this is what you should do'. He argues that the disadvantage of the healer role arises at the end of the therapy. He comments about his work with couples that,

> If they leave a course of counselling thinking that they have been 'treated' then they are not going to see themselves as equipped with new resources to deal with problems that may arise in the future. So, it is a very important part of my 'educator' role to get the couple, by the time they have left me, to have a clear understanding of what has happened, why it has been helpful, so they can apply these principles themselves. (Dryden, 1985)

Bancroft has observed that the association of 'healing' with 'expert' and 'higher dependence' also contributes to a higher rate of relapse following counselling. In contrast, the educator who acts in the role of 'guide' fosters a greater sense of self-reliance and the end result is less relapse.

However, in the British culture, the role of teacher and educator is not always associated with being less authoritarian and collaborative. When Emmy van Deuzen Smith (1988) likened her approach to existential counselling to a 'tutorial relationship', she encountered considerable misunderstanding of what she meant. Instead of the 'self-directed tutorial' she envisaged, some counsellors took her to mean a pedagogic relationship in which the teacher disseminated expertise and knowledge rather than working collaboratively. The value of the metaphor of counsellor as 'educator' depends on it being used in ways consistent with its literal meaning of 'drawing out' something which the client already possesses.

Other metaphors have been used to describe the counsellor's role, with the purpose of maintaining an emphasis on the client's responsibility for his contributions in counselling and for its outcome. Sometimes the counsellor is presented as a 'resource person', with the emphasis on the client choosing how to use those resources. Alternatively, the counsellor may be presented as the 'facilitator', where the focus is on the counsellor's expertise in helping the client achieve something the client has chosen.

The metaphorical descriptions of the roles of the counsellor as 'educator', 'resource person' and 'facilitator' all fit more easily into a division of the boundaries of responsibility between method and outcome than those of 'healer'. However, sometimes the boundary of responsibility has been presented as a choice between polarized opposites: being either directive or non-directive. I think this way of approaching the issue of respect for the client's autonomy is more deceptive than illuminating. Counselling is not a neutral activity in the way 'non-directive' seems to imply. The values of counselling, namely respect, integrity and impartiality (see Chapter 3) mean that there is an implicit tendency to direct clients towards taking personal responsibility for their own lives and there are times when this may even be explicit. Counsellors are in the business of influencing people towards relating to each other as autonomous individuals on an adult/adult basis. There is another reason why presenting the choice of being directive or non-directive as though it is a choice between absolutes is deceptively polarized. In practice, there are intermediate stages of being less or more directive. A counsellor who simply tells a client what to do regardless of the client's consent to engaging in this process is both being directive and also clearly acting outside the boundaries of responsibility considered acceptable in counselling, because she is invading the client's zone of responsibility. This kind of intervention is more directive than that of the counsellor who has negotiated with the client an agreement or consent which permits her as a counsellor to give authoritative interventions towards a goal selected by the client. This in turn is more directive than that of the counsellor who abstains from giving clear personal opinions but seeks to elicit a personal view from the client. A range of responses, between being directive and being non-directive, is possible. An authoritarian way of working is clearly outside the ethical boundaries of counselling. Equally, there is the danger of the counsellor taking too little responsibility and leaving the client with excessive responsibility for method and outcome. The counsellor has to find a way between these two extremes.

The interviews reported in *Therapists' Dilemmas* (Dryden, 1985) would suggest that counsellors are most acutely confronted with what is the appropriate boundary of responsibility either when they believe that they can see a solution to the client's problems which has not yet occurred to the client, or when the client asks the counsellor to express a personal opinion like 'Do you think my marriage is dead?' or 'Do you think I am capable of overcoming this problem?' These are dilemmas which are intrinsic to counselling and have to be evaluated in the light of the specific circumstances. Part of this involves asking:

- 'Am I as counsellor taking on responsibilities which are more properly the client's?'
- 'Is there a way I could respond which maximizes the client's autonomy and minimizes his dependence on me?'

Counsellors who systematically ask themselves these questions are much more likely to stay within boundaries which give clients their appropriate responsibility for the outcome of the counselling.

One of the consequences of the division of boundaries in counselling is the emphasis on the counsellor's responsibility for the methods used with his clients. This is not merely a matter of the kinds of interventions used by the counsellor but the basis on which the counselling relationship is founded.

Counselling as a voluntary activity

It is a basic principle that counselling is a voluntary activity for the client. In most circumstances this is clearly the case. The client has sought out a counsellor as a matter of personal choice rather than feeling obliged to receive counselling or having been sent for counselling as an alternative to something worse, perhaps disciplinary action.

However, counsellors working in organizational settings report that there are situations where a client may be seeking counselling because she is compelled to do so by someone else. For example, employee counsellors may have someone sent to them as an alternative to disciplinary procedures or as part of a disciplinary procedure. Counsellors in education also experience having clients sent to them, usually to resolve troublesome behaviour, but sometimes because a member of staff has recognized that a pupil is deeply distressed and needs help. Usually the person sending the client is doing so out of a commitment to help and is wanting to act constructively. However, this person's action poses a number of difficulties for the counsellor. First, it challenges the client's ability to exercise choice about whether to participate in counselling. Second, there may be pre-determined expectations about what the outcome of the counselling will be, which are not necessarily those of the client. This may not be too much of a problem if the aim is to reduce distress, as the client is likely to share this aim. However, expectations about changes in the client's behaviour are likely to be much more problematic. For example:

> Carl is sent to see a school counsellor to stop what his teacher sees as disruptive behaviour. During the counselling it emerges that Carl feels misunderstood and picked on by his teacher. He wants to find ways of expressing his views more effectively rather than become more compliant.

Any attempt by the counsellor to impose the teacher's views on Carl in these circumstances would clearly be in breach of the spirit of the voluntary nature of counselling and indicate a lack of respect for the client's autonomy.

A parallel situation also occurs with adults. Sometimes adults are sent to counsellors by employers as an alternative to disciplinary procedures. Again, this is usually done out of compassion for the client. For example,

> Joan is sent to an employee counsellor to help her reduce her lateness at starting work and her unexplained absences. The personnel officer who sent her suspects that she has relationship problems at home and has chosen this course of action rather than dismissing her as she is unlikely to be employed by anyone else.

There is considerable potential for confusion over the client's autonomy and the counsellor's role in these circumstances. What if Joan, unknown to the personnel manager, has been preparing to establish her own small business and this is why she is absent and is reluctant to offer an explanation? What if the personnel officer is right about the relationship problems causing the absence but Joan is happy to use them as an excuse and wants to go to counselling as a means of postponing the day of reckoning? In both these situations the counsellor may feel caught between the client's wishes and those of the personnel officer. Certainly, the counselling is unlikely to be effective because the client is not committed to the process, rather she is using mere attendance as a shield against a less liked alternative. This situation can be avoided by better management systems which establish a clearer differentiation between disciplinary and counselling procedures. Joan would be in a better position to decide whether or not to attend for counselling had the personnel officer said, 'Unless your attendance record reaches a specified level by a particular date then disciplinary or dismissal procedures will be started. I realize there may be problems which are contributing to your poor attendance record and I would like to help. You may find it useful to talk to the counsellor who may be able to help you solve these problems. In the end I must act to ensure acceptable attendance levels.' If the choice of whether or not to attend counselling is put in these terms, it becomes much clearer that the outcome of the disciplinary procedure does not depend on whether Joan attends for counselling, but on whether her attendance record reaches satisfactory levels. If she seeks counselling it will be because she wants it for herself and therefore she is more likely to engage actively in the process.

It sometimes happens that a counsellor is not in a position to influence others in ways which prevent a client being 'sent'. For instance, a client may attend in compliance with a partner's wishes or under threat of someone else doing something which the client wants to prevent. The classic example would be someone accepting a detoxification from alcohol or drugs which includes counselling as an alternative to a custodial sentence. Can there be such a thing as a voluntary client under threat of imprisonment? This is one of many situations in which the counsellor cannot assume that it is the client's wish, rather than someone else's, that he receive counselling. In such circumstances it is good practice for the counsellor to help the client establish his options including not proceeding with the counselling. This may be a very quick process or may involve several sessions of 'pre-counselling' before the client is clear about whether he wants to proceed.

Choice of counsellor

The growth in popularity of counselling and psychotherapy has meant that both activities have been subject to scrutiny by consumer watchdogs. Counsellors will be interested in the recommendations that have been made to potential clients. In order to avoid the risks of incompetence and sexual exploitation, people are encouraged to 'shop around'. The Consumers' Association has recommended four steps to help people choose a counsellor or therapist who is most likely to meet their needs. Steps 1–4 are intended to apply to all counselling. Steps 2 and 3 apply mostly to private counselling.

1 Decide what you want
   ● What do you want to get out of therapy – why are you seeking it, and what result would mean it had been successful?
   ● Do you want long-term support or help with a short-term problem? How much can you afford?
   ● What type of therapy would suit you?

2 Find possible therapists
   ● A recommendation by a friend or GP is a good way to find a therapist.
   ● Contact the British Association for Counselling . . . They can send a list of therapists in your area. Some are accredited by the BAC, with a minimum 450 hours' training and 450 hours' experience. However, most are not.
   ● Contact therapy organisations to ask whether any of their members practise in your area. You can get lists of organisations from BAC, from the UK Standing Conference for Psychotherapy, and from MIND.

3 Choose a therapist
   Contact a few therapists and discuss the following points:
   ● What qualifications do they have, and what was the training that led to the qualifications?
   ● How many years have they been practising, and how many hours of experience have they acquired?
   ● Are they members of any professional organisations?

4 Don't be pressured
   ● Don't be afraid to rely on your gut feeling: if you don't like the therapist, or feel they aren't helping you, then stop. Therapy is for your benefit – you have no obligation to the therapist.
   ● If at any stage you think the therapist is behaving improperly, discuss it with them, stop seeing the therapist, or report them to their professional organisation.
                 (Consumers' Association, 1991, *Which? way to Health*)

These recommendations are very much in accord with the counsellor's ethic of respect for the client's autonomy. As this advice becomes more widely adopted by potential clients it is increasingly likely that counsellors will be asked to provide pre-counselling meetings and pre-counselling information.

Pre-counselling information

The Consumers' Association guidelines for potential clients set out the sort of information needed by clients which could be given in a brief booklet. Such booklets are being produced in increasing numbers, written and presented in a language and style appropriate to their potential clients and presented in bright colourful covers.

The leaflet produced by the Red Admiral Project, London, is clearly titled 'HIV/AIDS – Free Confidential Counselling Service for People Affected'. What makes this leaflet stand out is that after a brief introduction to the range of services available and the background of the counsellor, including his training, the rest of the leaflet (75 per cent, six pages of A6) is made up of personal statements made by six named people who have been differently affected by HIV/AIDS. These accounts cumulatively give a clear picture of what a potential client could expect of counselling and what is expected of them.

A somewhat different but equally effective approach has been taken by York and Scarborough College of Midwifery and Nursing Counselling Network. Again in an attractively designed cover, the leaflet contains a mission statement, operational policy, methods of access to the service, a helper's charter (which contains the entitlements of service procedures), a client's charter, complaints procedure and an evaluation form for users of the service. Of most interest from the viewpoint of giving pre-counselling information is the client's charter. With the author's consent, I am quoting it in full because I know that many counselling services are considering the production of similar statements as part of their pre-counselling information and I believe this version of a client's charter provides a useful prototype.

The client has the right to:
Ask for help from the service, and choose a helper from a list of helpers.
Withdraw at any time from the service.
Clear boundaries of confidentiality.
Skilled helpers who will be non-exploitative.
Feedback any issues and concerns about the service to the administrative secretary.
Have your queries and concerns answered by either the helper or their supervisor.
Control the level and extent of any disclosure.
Complain about the conduct of the service in any respect.

The client can expect:
A non-judgmental approach. A respectful, open and genuine helper.
To be given no advice, direction or solution to their problem or issue.

The opportunity to develop personal insight into their problem, strengths, and resources.

The helper to explain the approach they are taking and clarify any actions or techniques that are used when these are unfamiliar.

To be helped within the following definition:

The term 'Counselling' includes work with individuals, pairs or groups of people, often but not always referred to as 'clients'. The objective of particular counselling relationships will vary according to the client's needs. Counselling may be concerned with developmental issues, addressing and resolving specific problems, making decisions, coping with crisis, developing personal insight and knowledge, working through feelings of inner conflict or improving relationships with others. The counsellor's role is to facilitate the client's work in ways which respect the client's values, personal resources and capacity for self determination. (BAC, 1992)

The client's responsibility:

To use the time made available by the helper for significant issues and to work profitably.

To respect the contracts made between yourself and the helper.

To express any doubts and seek clarification should any of the helping process be unclear.

To act in accordance with own values, and to speak out if these boundaries are not respected.

(Dexter, 1991)

One of the issues confronting anyone writing a leaflet about a counselling service is what to say about confidentiality. It is advisable to avoid statements like 'Counselling is *totally* confidential' because this arguably misrepresents the ethics of counselling and certainly the law (see Chapter 9). If there are known circumstances in which confidentiality cannot be offered this should be mentioned, or alternatively, if the circumstances have only a remote possibility of arising in actual practice, potential clients could be encouraged to raise any issues about confidentiality with their counsellor. This might involve making a statement like: 'The counsellors understand that confidentiality can be very important to anyone seeking the counselling. If you would like further information about the level of confidentiality we offer or any other matter, please ask the counsellor about it at the beginning of the session.' The basic principle is that all clients should know the terms on which they are being offered confidentiality. In particular, they should know all the reasonably foreseeable conditions in which confidentiality is *not* being offered. Michael Megranahan has made a clear recommendation about the standard of practice for employee counselling which, in my opinion, ought to be transferred to all settings where counselling is offered:

The person seeking help may either directly ask the questions: 'How do I know what I say will be confidential?', 'What guarantees do I have?', or assume that the conversation is confidential. It is essential . . . that the limits (if there are to be any) governing confidentiality are unambiguous, pre-defined and agreed with at the beginning of any counselling organisation as well as communicated at the beginning of any counselling interview to every person seeking help. The extent of the confidentiality should be public knowledge for every person who has access to the counselling facility and be in writing, e.g. in an employee handbook. (1989)

I have often been asked whether counsellors should routinely give clients copies of the BAC *Code of Ethics and Practice for Counsellors* as part of the pre-counselling information. On the whole, I do not think this is appropriate. The *Code* is not sufficiently specific to the particular circumstances of the counsellor-client relationship. I think it is much better that clients are informed of its existence and a copy is readily available to clients when it is requested. It is much better to produce information which is specific to the counselling being provided and in a style appropriate to the client group. Sometimes this will require providing information in languages other than English. It may also require imaginative use of drawings for clients who are unable to read or the opportunity for preliminary pre-counselling discussions with a receptionist or counsellor about the suitability of counselling.

Contracting

Counselling is not unique in attaching considerable importance to the client's autonomy. There has also been an increasing emphasis on autonomy in professions which have sometimes been considered paternalistic in their concern to do good for someone. Reiter-Theil et al. observed: 'Derived from the principle of *respect for autonomy*, informed consent has become one of the predominant rules discussed in medical ethics since the 1970s' (1991).

Informed consent is someone's agreement to treatment after having:

- understood the procedures or methods to be used,
- understood any risks and benefits,
- been informed of relevant alternatives.

It must be guaranteed that the client consented without coercion or manipulation and that the client is able to make a rational decision based on the information provided.

However, consent is the absolute minimum standard of practice in counselling. It is more appropriate to situations where the person has something done to them, rather than as in counselling where the client is an active participant in the process. The codes of practice require a higher standard of actively engaging the client in the contracting process. The *Code for Counsellors* states:

> 2.2.10   Clear contracting enhances and shows respect for the client's autonomy.
>
> 2.2.11   Counsellors are responsible for communicating the terms on which counselling is being offered, including availability, the degree of confidentiality offered, and their expectations of clients regarding fees, cancelled appointments and any other significant matters. The communication of terms and any negotiations over these should be concluded before the client incurs any financial liability.

The question of whether key terms in the contract should be communicated orally or supplemented with written records is currently being debated. In situations where the client is paying for the counselling, it is important to both client and counsellor that they know where they stand financially and with regard to other matters. In these circumstances, it seems highly appropriate routinely to send a letter stating the terms of the agreement to all new clients after the first session, or whenever key terms of the contract have been agreed. The letter can be written in user-friendly everyday language. On the other hand, if the counselling is being provided free of charge, counsellors are currently less likely to send out a letter which records the nature of the agreement between themselves and clients. Both counsellors and clients are more likely to rely upon written pre-counselling information as the basis of their agreement and the counsellor's own record of what was agreed. This probably is satisfactory in most cases, although I think ideally all clients should have a written record of the agreement between themselves and their counsellor. However, the cost of doing this compared to the gains has to be taken into account when the service is provided free of charge. One way of reducing costs is to have a standard letter or contract which can be amended to record any variations to the standard terms. The provision of a written record of the terms of the agreement is a formal acknowledgement of the importance of the client's autonomy and respect for his or her part in any negotiations about the contract.

There is a need for periodic review and renegotiation in the light of experience. The *Code of Practice* states: 'Reasonable steps should be taken in the course of the counselling relationship to ensure that the client is given an opportunity to review the terms on which counselling is being offered and the methods of counselling being used' (2.2.12). This permits progressive clarification of terms as they become relevant. The alternative of trying to anticipate all possible eventualities in the initial contracting would be counter-productive. Usually when clients seek counselling, they have a sense of urgency and wish to start the process as quickly as possible. This means that the initial contract may be relatively simple and may require elaboration as the relationship proceeds. The crucial point is that the client ought not to incur liabilities retrospectively. Agreements stand from the time at which they are made. This applies particularly to financial matters and as far as possible to issues relating to confidentiality and privacy.

During the contracting it is considered desirable that clients should be informed about any records that are kept about the counselling.

> 2.2.14 If records of counselling sessions are kept, clients should be made aware of this. At the client's request information should be given about access to these records, their availability to other people, and the degree of security with which they are kept.

Further consideration of record keeping can be found in Chapter 12.

Contracting is important ethically because it enhances the client's sense of her own autonomy. Many of the issues addressed in the contract will be the kinds of ethical and practical issues already mentioned. The client's sense of personal autonomy can be further enhanced by using contracting about the therapeutic aims of the counselling. It increases the alliance between counsellor and client when the client is actively engaged in planning the goals of the counselling and making choices between alternative methods of working. These therapeutic contracts require periodic review in the same way as contracts about the other issues considered in this section.

Relationship between counsellor's and client's autonomy

The optimum standard in counselling is that both counsellor and client are working together as a deliberate and autonomous choice. This is most likely to happen when both counsellor and client share important personal values in common. However, this is not always essential. Counselling may take place where there are differences in values provided the counsellor's own personal values are consistent with respect for a client's own values, beliefs and choices and working within these. In reality, I suspect this is what most frequently happens. Counsellors and clients work together satisfactorily where their personal values are compatible rather than identical. The onus is on the counsellor to provide the client with sufficient space to work within her own value system with the counsellor's own value system validating this relationship and avoiding the imposition of the counsellor's own personal values. Without the counsellor's own autonomous commitment to respecting the client's values and capacity for self-determination the relationship lacks integrity. Integrity requires that both counsellor and client are acting autonomously.

However, establishing relationships in which both counsellor and client are acting autonomously is a high standard to maintain and it is not always easy to do so. What should a counsellor do when he finds himself working with a client whose personal values are so antagonistic to his own that both the integrity of the counselling relationship and the counsellor's own personal integrity are threatened?

For example:

> Mark is a committed pacifist for religious and personal reasons. He has counselled soldiers recovering from post-traumatic stress disorder who are returning to civilian life. Does respect for a client's values, beliefs and capacity for self-determination mean that he should also be willing to counsel soldiers wishing to return to active military service?

Mark's dilemma is encountered in many forms. To what extent does respect for the client's autonomy require that counsellors work with clients who choose to act in ways which conflict with the counsellor's deeply held views?

When this issue was put to the Standards and Ethics Sub-committee, a baseline for practice was identified. This is the counsellor's willingness to support the client in finding a source of counselling which would offer more support in their chosen course of action when the counsellor has a conscientious objection to the client's proposed actions. Over the years, a number of examples of the application of this principle have been considered. Two have arisen several times.

Pro-life counselling

Some counsellors hold strong personal views against abortion and treat this as a matter of conscience. Such a counsellor may be working in settings where she sees clients about a wide range of issues so that the question of abortion may be raised only infrequently, or she may be working in one of the pro-life organizations as a counsellor with the explicit aim of providing alternatives to abortion. What should a counsellor do if a client decides she wants an abortion? It is incompatible with even a minimal level of respect for the client's autonomy merely to say 'I disagree with your choice and can do no more. Come and see me again if you change your mind.'

The minimum level of respect is to give the client sufficient information to enable her to implement her choice. Ideally, the counsellor would actively enable a referral to someone who could be more supportive of the client's autonomous choices.

Christian counselling

There is a type of counselling known as 'Christian counselling' which raises serious ethical issues. Usually this is a label adopted to describe a form of counselling which is associated with fundamentalist Christianity. The question arises about whether it can be considered 'counselling' in the sense defined by BAC. The answer is complicated by the existence of several different movements using the label 'Christian counselling'. It is quite clear that if a counselling service is no more than a concealed way of obtaining converts to a particular religious point of view, then it is incompatible with 'counselling' as the term is used by BAC. Indeed, it is hard to see how such a service can have much integrity even in its own terms if duplicity is involved. The advertising of such services to the general public without revealing their religious affiliation in order to attract vulnerable people by the offer of help is morally questionable, particularly if clients are then subjected to techniques more appropriate to the pulpit than the counselling room to persuade them to join religious movements. From time to time concern has been expressed about counselling programmes which are not open about their religious affiliations and are exclusively committed to changing people from homosexuality to heterosexuality. Such programmes are incompatible with 'counselling' as it is defined by BAC because of a lack of respect for the client's autonomy over choice of lifestyle.

Even if a Christian counselling service is open and straightforward with clients about its religious affiliations, it may still be offering counselling in ways which are not compatible with BAC's requirements. The fundamental question is how much respect is shown for a client's autonomy. In my view, it is inappropriate for a counsellor to require the client's autonomy to be exercised according to Biblical principles, or within a framework of

Christian commitment, insight and values. Respect for a client's autonomy requires that the counsellor is open to the possibility of the client choosing a faith other than Christianity or no religious belief. It is sometimes suggested that counselling, as defined by BAC, is fundamentally based on humanist values and is therefore exclusively secular in character. This is also a misunderstanding if it is being implied that counselling seeks to promote a humanist view of life. It is more accurate to think of counselling as a humanitarian activity in the sense of promoting general well-being, regardless of the recipient's belief system. Therefore, I have some unease when proselytizers of any kind organize themselves into counselling organizations because my experience suggests that the missionary nature of their belief system frequently leads to an undermining of a client's autonomy.

The type of Christian counselling just described should not be confused with counselling which is provided by someone who has Christian beliefs but respects the client's right to hold different religious beliefs or no beliefs at all. There is a long established tradition of pastoral counselling which is based on respect for the client's autonomy over religious beliefs (Hiltner, 1949; Wise, 1951; Foskett and Lyall, 1988). The Association for Pastoral Care and Counselling was one of the founding organizations of BAC and is still one of its largest divisions.

Racist or sexist clients

It is ethically consistent with the core values of counselling of respect, integrity and impartiality that counsellors should strive to provide counselling services on the basis of equality of opportunity for users of the service. A deliberately racist or sexist counsellor could not subscribe to counselling values with personal integrity. This raises the question of how a counsellor should respond to a client who does not share these values. From time to time I have been approached for guidance by counsellors who have been deeply troubled by the racism and sexism of some clients. For example:

> Rachel is conscientious in attempting to establish relationships with her clients which have the qualities of integrity, impartiality and respect. Tom, the client, is deeply committed to views which are intolerant and often exploitative of people with different ethnic origins from his own, and these are the basis of his chosen courses of action. How should Rachel respond?

Most of the counsellors with whom I have discussed this issue accept that there can be no automatic duty placed on the counsellor to challenge her client's views. Counselling needs to be provided in ways which permit clients to express views which differ considerably from those of the counsellor. The client's right to express anti-social views and negative feelings towards others has always been an important part of respect for the client's capacity for self-determination. It is also part of the therapeutic process, in which such feelings sometimes change. Therefore, the counselling relationship is not appropriate for campaigning for greater social tolerance but on occasion it may have this effect by resolving areas of personal pain which fuel intolerance. However, this analysis does not resolve Rachel's dilemma. She is faced with a client whose personal values are so different from her own that she no longer feels able to offer respect for his capacity for self-determination without sacrificing her personal integrity. In her view, the situation is not resolved by maintaining clear boundaries between her own value system and those of her clients. In these circumstances it seems appropriate to consider discussing the conflict of personal values with the client directly. It is only once the issue has been discussed openly between the counsellor and client that each of them will be in a position to decide whether it is desirable to continue counselling together. How to raise the subject and the timing of the discussion may need to be considered in counselling-supervision. However, to continue without raising the subject is open to objections from both counsellor's and client's viewpoints. It is not possible to help someone conscientiously towards living their lives according to their own values when you strongly disapprove of those values. Equally, the client may have valid moral grounds for objecting to being counselled by someone who has kept disapproval of his values secret from him. It could be viewed as covertly undermining his autonomy. The integrity of the relationship requires finding a basis on which both the counsellor and client can proceed respecting each other's autonomy. Alternatively, it may be better to discontinue counselling and for the counsellor to assist the client in finding an alternative source of help if this is requested.

Issues of this degree of difficulty are best discussed in counselling-supervision or with another experienced counsellor before deciding how to respond to the client. The example given is about racism but could equally have been about prejudices based on gender, disability, sexuality, class, religion or age. Ethically, it is important that the counsellor responds to this dilemma in a way which is both consistent with the counselling model being used and respectful of the client's choice of outcome for herself. To act otherwise is to move outside the ethical boundaries of relationships in counselling. For example, persuasion and manipulation to seek to change someone's point of view, even for what are widely held as socially desirable ends, are an intrusion into an area of responsibility which is properly the client's. At times, some counsellors may feel frustration about the need to respect a client's responsibility for the outcome of the counselling. One way some counsellors have found of resolving this ethically is to accept the constraints on their range of personal responses when in a counselling role with particular clients, but, independently of counselling, to offer workshops, lectures, write or campaign to try to change attitudes. There is a tradition within counselling which goes back to Frank Parsons, probable originator of the term 'counselling', and his campaigns on behalf of the urban poor people in Boston during the early 1900s which combines counselling with social and political action. In Britain, this tradition has continued in some areas of the country and within movements to empower disadvantaged people, particularly women and gay or lesbian people. Equally there has been a tradition which is less activist and is politically quietist. It seems to me that both traditions are valid. They present potential clients with a range of choice between a variety of counsellors with different values and personal views about how best to implement those values.

Conclusion

The management of the counselling relationship in ways which respect both the autonomy of the client and the counsellor is a complex task which involves many different aspects of this relationship. The setting of boundaries of responsibility in the relationship and establishing a language and imagery consistent with these is only part of what is required. Ensuring that the client is entering counselling on a voluntary basis, adequately informed about his rights and responsibilities, active contracting, when it is appropriate, and being willing to raise and face differences in personal values in a counsellor may not only contribute to respect for the client's autonomy but also help to ensure that the relationship itself has integrity because it is based on the autonomous actions of both counsellor and client.

Throughout this chapter, I have taken it for granted that the client is capable of exercising his own autonomy. There are times when clients appear so ill or disturbed that the counsellor considers them to be incapable of autonomous actions. This situation may involve temporarily stepping out of a counselling role into one which takes greater responsibility for the client's actions. As this often involves questions of confidentiality, this situation is considered further in Chapter 9. Situations where the client is suicidal can be particularly anxiety-provoking, and these are considered separately in the next chapter.

6 The suicidal client

Working with suicidal clients is a situation which not only challenges the skill of the counsellor but also raises an important ethical issue. Is this a situation in which the counsellor's traditional ethic of respect for the client's autonomy is adequate? The counsellor is faced with a choice between maintaining a policy of respect for the client's autonomy and right to choose, and acting to prevent self-destruction in the interests of preserving the client's life.

This choice between ethical principles can be resolved in a number of ways. There are those who take the position that one or other of the ethical principles ought to take precedence in all circumstances.

One view is based on the primacy of life as an ethical cornerstone. This is founded on the belief that life is the most valuable thing we possess: life is so obviously good that it requires no theoretical argument to justify its position as a primary value. It is asserted that the sanctity of life is self-evident, especially in the case of one's own life. The act of questioning its value is therefore in itself symptomatic of crisis, illness or abnormality. From this moral perspective it is easy to justify acting to prevent someone taking their own life. The force of this justification would even override a client's own autonomous wishes in order to compel that client to accept treatment or confinement without the opportunity to kill herself. The experience of many mental health professionals appears to match this particular analysis. They report that suicidal feelings are often short-lived and transitory. If someone can be protected from acting on these feelings, then the will to live often returns and the problems which have caused the individual to become suicidal can be tackled.

There is an alternative point of view that the persistent occurrence of suicide challenges claims to the self-evident sanctity of life. Occasions arise when the desire to preserve life may be overridden by a preference for death. From this perspective, suicide is the ultimate expression of someone's choice of how to live or die. Therefore, it follows that counsellors ought to respect a client's right of choice over his suicide in the same way as they would over other matters. R.D. Laing (1967) has argued that suicide is an ultimate right of any individual. Thomas Szasz (1986) has argued that any attempt at coercive methods to prevent suicide contradicts the concept of individuals as moral agents who are ultimately responsible for their own actions. Some counsellors take this view and apply it consistently to all situations involving suicide. This stance is particularly attractive if, like Laing and Szasz, the counsellor disagrees with medicalization of mental illness and does not accept that behaviour which others have defined as mental illness erodes an individual's moral responsibility for his own actions. It is also a point of view which appeals to therapists working with the large number of people who go through the motions of attempting suicide but who appear to have no real intention of killing themselves. This form of parasuicide is primarily a cry for help disguised as attempted suicide. Part of the counsellor's role is to encourage the client to communicate what is wanted more directly and therefore to act with a greater sense of control over her autonomy. To rush into a course of action designed to prevent suicide would be counter-therapeutic. It may reinforce any manipulative or 'blackmailing' component in the parasuicide rather than reinforce the client's ability to act more straightforwardly in his quest to resolve his problems.

The proponents of each of these views can argue that their opinions are founded on both an ethical analysis and a constructive framework which enhances therapeutic work with significant numbers of the suicidal. How should a counsellor choose between them? My own opinion is that it is not necessary to choose one viewpoint to the exclusion of the other. I suspect that counsellors who cling exclusively to one opinion or the other do so out of an attempt to control their own anxiety in a potentially extremely anxiety-provoking situation. Suicidal intentions occur in such a variety of different circumstances, that I have come to the view that it is a matter for assessment as to which of the two ethical principles ought to prevail. Some examples may help to illustrate what I mean.

Suicide as self-administered euthanasia

Sally has terminal cancer and has been told by doctors that her illness is well advanced with an increasing number of secondaries. She has announced to her family and her doctor that she does not wish to battle futilely against her imminent death. She would prefer to die at home at a time of her own choosing. Her family and doctor attempt to dissuade her or suggest alternative ways of providing good-quality terminal care but Sally remains committed to her planned suicide and has discussed her plans with her counsellor over several months.

This is the kind of situation where there can be little doubt that the client is making a decision which is authentic, deliberate and clear-headed. She has sustained her point of view over a period of time and is acting under her own volition, not under the influence of others. It may be that the counsellor will want to check that the client is aware of the alternative ways of receiving care during a terminal illness and that her aims would not be better met by home nursing or the use of a living will, in which the client sets out how she wishes to be cared for medically, or going into a hospice. Even if the client was unaware of any of these, or feels that they are inadequate to enable her to take control of her dying, I doubt whether there are grounds for the counsellor to intervene to attempt to prevent the suicide. David Heyd and Sidney Bloch (1991) express the view that although doctors will find it psychologically and legally difficult to co-operate actively in such a suicide, no psychiatrist would consider the forced hospitalization of such a person. This means that even if a counsellor wanted to intervene there would be very little that could be done as any attempt to prevent the suicide would almost certainly require the co-operation of doctors.

The counsellor may experience further dilemmas. What if the family seek the counsellor's support in trying to persuade Sally out of self-administered euthanasia? This is a situation where the counsellor needs to consider the nature of the contract with the client and, assuming that this contract is with Sally, the counsellor may have to explain tactfully that her primary responsibility is to Sally who retains control of the outcome of the counselling. If the family feel unable to communicate their feelings about Sally's proposed actions directly to her, then they may wish to find the assistance of another counsellor to facilitate such a discussion. For Sally's counsellor to undertake an additional role on behalf of the family could raise all the problems of conflicting loyalties, particularly as there is a substantial difference of view between them.

An alternative possibility is that the counsellor feels strongly supportive of Sally's decision to take control of her own dying. How far should she go in offering emotional encouragement or active support? Legally there are definite limits in how far a counsellor can go without risking prosecution. Unlike in Dutch law, there is no provision for doctors or anyone else to assist someone to end his own life. The legalization of euthanasia is discussed periodically, but it seems unlikely that it will be legalized in the foreseeable future. Until there is a change in the law, it is an offence to assist someone to kill himself or herself. Although the Suicide Act 1961 stopped attempted suicide and suicide from being a criminal offence, it also created a new offence. Section 2 states: 'A person who aids, abets, counsels or procures the suicide of another or an attempt by another to commit suicide, shall be liable on conviction on indictment to imprisonment for a term not exceeding fourteen years.' To 'counsel' in this legal context means to conspire, advise or knowingly give assistance, which are not activities usually encompassed within counselling.

A recent judgment in the Court of Appeal reported in *The Independent* Law Report (1992) has some relevance to this situation because one of the points under consideration was the right of adult patients to refuse treatment even if this could result in their death. The case concerned a member of the Jehovah's Witnesses who expressly refused to receive a blood transfusion which might save her life. Lord Donaldson, Master of the Rolls, stated that the appeal is not about 'the right to die' but about the 'right to choose how to live' even if the choice might make an early death more likely. An adult patient who suffered from no mental incapacity had an absolute right to consent to medical treatment, to refuse it or to choose one rather than another of the treatments offered. The right of choice existed notwithstanding that the reasons for making the choice were rational, irrational, unknown or even non-existent. That was so in spite of the very strong public interest in preserving the life and health of all citizens. He suggested a threefold test that doctors should use to determine whether they were bound by a patient's refusal of treatment: (1) whether the patient's capacity to make the decision has been affected by the effects of shock, pain or drugs; (2) whether the patient's capacity had been overborne by outside influence; and (3) whether the patient's decision had been intended to apply to the circumstances which had arisen (*Re T*, 1992).

I have given the judgment in some detail because it contains a clear assertion of an individual's right to refuse treatment. Such a refusal of treatment might well form part of a planned suicide. The tests the judge suggests to decide whether such a refusal is valid are primarily about whether the individual has the capacity to make such a decision autonomously or the autonomy is eroded by circumstances or the influence of others. This judgment relates only to adults.

The right of someone under eighteen years old to consent to or refuse treatment was also considered by the Court of Appeal at about the same time as *Re T*, 1992. At an earlier case the House of Lords had already established that a child of sufficient intelligence and understanding, could consent to medical treatment even if the parents did not consent or had expressly forbidden the treatment (*R.* v. *West Norfolk and Wisbech Area Health Authority, ex parte Gillick*, 1985). The implications of this case with regard to confidentiality are discussed in Chapter 9. The question which faced the Court of Appeal was whether the court had the power to order medical treatment which a 'Gillick competent child' (see Chapter 9) had refused. In *Re J (a minor) (Medical Treatment)* (1992), J was suffering from anorexia nervosa of such severity that there was a serious risk of irreversible damage to her brain and reproductive organs and her life was in danger. The Court of Appeal granted an emergency order enabling J to be treated despite her lack of consent. Although J maintained her refusal to consent she accepted that the court order would have to be complied with. The Court of Appeal explained the decision in the following terms:

> No minor of whatever age has the power by refusing consent to treatment to override a consent to treatment by someone who has parental responsibility for the minor. Nevertheless such a refusal was a very important consideration in making clinical judgements and for parents and the court in deciding whether themselves to give consent. Its importance increased with the age and maturity of the minor. (*The Guardian* Law Reports, 1992)

This judgment creates uncertainty about the powers of someone under eighteen to refuse medical treatment when faced with terminal illness. The judgment recognizes the right of the young person's choices to be taken into account but these can be overruled. Nonetheless, the general trend in recent decisions has been to increase the weight given to the young person's views. A counsellor working with a terminally ill young person who wishes to refuse treatment to shorten her life or in preparation for suicide would be well advised to seek legal advice.

Suicide as an escape from problems and emotional pain

Another example describes a kind of situation which most counsellors encounter more frequently,

> Brian is overburdened by financial problems and social isolation following the ending of a longstanding relationship. He is becoming increasingly depressed and is talking about suicide as a way out of his problems and to escape the emotional pain he is experiencing.

In this example Brian's suicide is not an alternative to an imminent and inevitable death but represents a substantial foreshortening of his lifespan. There is also an element of doubt about whether his choice is authentic, deliberate, clear-headed and rational or he is acting irrationally, impulsively and based on judgements distorted by extreme personal distress or loss of a sense of reality. It is in circumstances like these that a counsellor most acutely experiences the choice between respect for the client's autonomy and acting to prevent self-destruction. The counsellor is in a situation in which whatever she does will be at a cost. The balance of cost between non-intervention and intervention is represented in Figure 6.1.

Non-intervention	Intervention
The client's decision is taken as authentic, deliberate, clear-headed and rational.	The client's decision is taken as irrational, impulsive, distorted by distress or loss of a sense of reality.
The client's decision is treated as irreversible with the result that the irreversible act of suicide becomes inevitable because no steps are taken to prevent it.	The client's decision is assumed to be reversible and therefore steps which are also reversible are taken in order to prolong life until the client changes his mind.
The client's autonomy is respected and the liberty to kill himself is treated in the same way as any other decision.	The counsellor sets the importance of serving life as a priority and acts to make this outcome more likely. Other people's wishes may have priority over the client's.
The counsellor may appear indifferent to the client's distress.	The counsellor shows her care by intervening to rescue the client from self-destruction.
The counsellor takes the client's side rather than that of partners, friends, family who may wish the counsellor to intervene. The client's interests take priority over others.	The counsellor may not be acting in a way which corresponds to the client's wishes.
The price: missed opportunities, the infinite loss involved in death, possibility of the most 'tragic mistake'.	The price: acting to undermine the client's choice which, if it is effective, may prolong mental and physical misery, serious disrepect of autonomy.
Underlying assumption: 'nothing in life is as much under the direct jurisdiction of each individual as are his own person and life' (Schopenhauer).	Underlying assumption: the instinctive drive to save other people's lives and the public interest in saving life. While there is life there is hope.

Figure 6.1   *The balance of cost in a suicidal case (adapted from Heyd and Bloch, 1991)*

A subsidiary issue arises because the counsellor will not usually have the power to intervene directly. In order to act to prevent self-destruction, the counsellor is likely to have to communicate confidential information about her client to either a doctor or a social worker with the statutory powers to give compulsory treatment under the Mental Health Act 1983. *The Code of Ethics and Practice for Counsellors* (BAC, 1992a) gives some guidance on this issue but does not give a comprehensive procedure for how counsellors ought to respond to suicidal clients in situations like this example. I shall therefore give my own personal reflections based on over twenty years of working with suicidal clients in a wide variety of circumstances.

Assessment procedure

The starting point ought to be an assumption that the counsellor will respect the client's choice and autonomy. This assumption will only be overruled when (1) there is evidence that the client lacks the capacity to make his own decisions, (2) there is a substantial risk of suicide, and (3) the counsellor can do something which has a reasonable chance of averting the suicide or involve someone who has the power to prevent the suicide. Merely being suicidal is insufficient evidence of a lack of capacity to act autonomously. The client would need to be exhibiting loss of sense of reality due to extreme distress, mental or physical illness; or seeming very confused; or being substantially influenced by others.

Methods for conducting the assessment may vary between counsellors according to their background. Counsellors who prefer to avoid conventional psychiatric classifications may prefer the assessment process described by John Eldrid (1988) which is derived from his experience as a director of the Central London Branch of the Samaritans. Counsellors with a psychiatric training may prefer the assessment procedures advocated by Keith Hawton and Jose Catalan (1987). Although the procedures are described in different terminology they address the same tasks. These can be summarized as an assessment of:

(a) Suicidal intentions: strength of feelings about going on or ending it all; degree of planning and preparations already accomplished; exploration of client's intentions in any recent attempt at suicide.
(b) Clarification of current difficulties: exploration of nature of problems and duration, e.g. loss of close relationship, job, finance, status, sexual or addiction difficulties, etc.

(c) Psychological state: comparison between usual psychological state and present with particular regard to hopelessness, anxiety, guilt, obsessions, anger, dependency, inner isolation.

(d) Psychiatric history: previous history of mental illness and attempted suicide; and any evidence of current mental illness including depression.

(e) Resources for coping: the availability of support from social network of partner, friends, family, etc. and religious faith; previous coping strategies for problems.

The assessment procedure often involves difficult decisions. It is in both client's and counsellor's interests that the counsellor holds appropriate discussions with a counselling-supervisor or experienced counsellor and if necessary seeks the opinions of professionals with relevant experience. The purpose of these consultations is to provide support for the counsellor and to clarify issues which require consideration, and to provide any additional information not already known by the counsellor or the client, especially about the kinds of help available from non-counselling services. Information about these services and the ways counselling can help clients who are feeling suicidal helps to ensure the client is in a position to make informed choices.

Any consultations by the counsellor with people outside the counselling relationship which are undertaken as part of the assessment stage should either be with the client's consent or be undertaken in such a way that the client's personal identity is not disclosed. The assumption of respect for the client's autonomy carries with it the high standards of practice and confidentiality associated with counselling until such time as it becomes clear that the client needs someone temporarily to take responsibility for his care. These consultations are not an alternative to the client's making these enquiries for himself which is the usual practice in counselling. It is highly desirable that whenever possible the client makes his own enquiries as a means of taking control of his own destiny.

At the end of the assessment process there are usually three possible conclusions.

First, the client is competent to take decisions for himself including whether to consent to counselling or other treatments and to take control of his living or dying. Counselling would continue by agreement with the client. In order to emphasize the client's responsibility some counsellors obtain written agreements from their clients that if they feel suicidal they will contact their own general practitioner and if this is not possible the Samaritans. An alternative method is to obtain agreements from clients that they will not attempt suicide while the counselling is continuing. None of these agreements are enforceable against a suicidal client but they emphasize the client's responsibility for his own well-being and show that the counsellor has taken his suicidal intentions seriously. A contemporaneous record of such agreements signed by the client may assist towards establishing that the counsellor has acted with reasonable skill and care in any subsequent legal hearings, although there is some doubt about their legal standing.

Second, the mental state of the client may be such that there is real doubt that the client has the capacity to take responsibility for himself and there is a substantial risk of suicide. Ethically, this situation is most easily resolved if the client will agree to seek a second opinion from a doctor, psychiatric nurse or approved social worker. If the client is unwilling to do this, then the counsellor may need to break confidentiality in order to obtain help. The *Code of Ethics and Practice for Counsellors* (BAC, 1992a) contains the following guidance:

> B.4.4   Exceptional circumstances may arise which give the counsellor good grounds for believing that the client will cause serious physical harm to others or themselves, or have harm caused to him/her. In such circumstances the client's consent to a change in the agreement about confidentiality should be sought whenever possible unless there are good grounds for believing the client is no longer able to take responsibility for his/her own actions. Whenever possible, the decision to break confidentiality agreed between a counsellor and client should be made only after consultation with a counselling supervisor or an experienced counsellor.
>
> B.4.5   Any breaking of confidentiality should be minimised both by restricting the information conveyed to that which is pertinent to the immediate situation and to those persons who can provide the help required by the client. The ethical considerations involve balancing between acting in the best interests of the client in ways which enable clients to resume taking responsibility for their actions, a very high priority for counsellors, and the counsellor's responsibilities to the wider community.

The decision about whether or not to break confidentiality in these circumstances is often very difficult. It is worth noting that the *Code* does not require the counsellor to break confidentiality but it is a matter for the counsellor's judgement. If the counsellor breaks confidentiality too readily, particularly if the client's reputation or interests are harmed by it becoming known the client is suicidal, the counsellor may be sued for breach of confidence – see Chapter 9. The counsellor has to balance the expressed wishes of the client against the counsellor's assessment of the client's capacity for taking responsibility for himself. The potential for the client being significantly helped by such a breach of confidence would also need to be taken into account. For instance, there is no point in breaking a confidence if no additional service will be made available.

The third possible conclusion is that the client either lacks the maturity to understand the consequences of his actions or is so distressed or mentally disturbed that he lacks the capacity to take responsibility for his own actions; there is a high risk of suicide; and, there is a reasonable likelihood of compulsory treatment under the Mental Health legislation. In these circumstances the counsellor should try to find a way of proceeding with the client's consent. These are probably the circumstances in which the client does need someone to take responsibility on his behalf on a temporary basis. The counsellor can only do this by seeking the assistance of a doctor or approved social worker. In the case of adults any compulsory treatment would usually be provided under the terms of the Mental Health Act 1983. The view of most professional mental health workers is that merely being suicidal would be insufficient grounds on its own for compulsory treatment. Serious mental illness would need to be established, of which being suicidal might be one of the symptoms. In the case of people under the age of sixteen, although the Mental Health Act 1983 could be used, it is more usual to use Place of Safety Orders or Care Orders available for the protection of children rather than mental health legislation and this was the practice in *Re J* (1992) which concerned a young person over the age of sixteen but below eighteen years old. Advice about the applicability of both these procedures can be obtained from a local Social Services Department or MIND.

It will be clear from my argument so far that, in my opinion, it is only in the most exceptional circumstances that a counsellor ought to act in a way in which the protection of the client from self-destruction overrides respect for the client's autonomy, and then only after careful assessment, unless the client is a young person lacking the maturity and intelligence to have the capacity to make her own decisions and falls within the scope of child protection legislation, or the client is an adult who lacks the capacity to make independent decisions for herself. In these exceptional circumstances it may be ethically more desirable to take responsibility for the well-being of the client temporarily, if there is no way of proceeding with her consent.

The process of assessing suicidal clients is often therapeutic to clients who actively participate in the assessment procedure. Often what seems an overwhelming and ill-defined sense of hopelessness does change into a differentiated series of separate problems which can seem more manageable. Perhaps most important, the counsellor is giving the client permission to explore his suicidal feelings and to discover what they really mean for him, with the possibility of finding alternative outcomes. Used this way the assessment process is therapeutic in its own right. It is often a time when clients have a sense of getting started at dealing with the issues which really concern them. This sense of a new start is often accompanied by a willingness to put suicidal intentions to one side for the time being in the hope of making changes to make life more rewarding.

For the counsellor, a systematic assessment procedure provides a means of resolving an ethical dilemma in a considered and conscientious way. Although it is not always possible to be infallible in one's assessments, at least the counsellor knows that she has done all that can reasonably be expected of her and has also maximized the likelihood of the client making an authentic and considered choice.

Many counsellors working with suicidal clients would also assert the importance of not taking significant decisions without consultation with at least one other person. If a client does commit suicide, the counsellor may experience regret and concern that, perhaps, something more could have been done to prevent it. It is at times like this that it is useful to know that the decision was not taken on one's own. Consultations with a counselling-supervisor, doctor, or social worker are a simple way of helping to minimize some of the inevitable distress following some suicides.

Attempted suicide in the presence of the counsellor

Fortunately this is a very rare occurrence. However, it is worth planning how you would respond because if it happens there may be little time for careful consideration. Three different potential scenarios are considered separately.

> Sarah has said she is feeling suicidal. She has enough tablets for a lethal dose with her and is threatening to take them in the counsellor's presence or use some other method which is only likely to harm herself.

Ethically, it is appropriate to try and talk the client out of her proposed action. Even Thomas Szasz, who is a leading advocate of respecting the individual's right to choose to commit suicide, concedes that the professional ought 'perhaps to persuade him or her to accept help' (Szasz, 1986).

Legally, the act of challenging the client's threatened suicide protects the counsellor from committing the offence of being an accomplice to suicide, which is an offence under section 2 of the Suicide Act 1961. It is possible that if a counsellor did nothing then this could be construed as encouraging an attempted suicide. However, it does not appear appropriate to go further than verbal challenges by using physical restraint because attempting suicide is no longer an offence. Therefore the right (not duty) to use such force as is reasonable in the circumstances in the prevention of crime under section 3 of the Criminal Law Act 1977 does not apply. The use of force in these circumstances could constitute an assault in both civil and criminal law. If a client is sufficiently mentally disturbed to have been placed under a compulsory treatment order authorized by the Mental Health Act 1983, then minimal force to prevent the taking of the tablets or some other form of suicide is legally permissible. Counsellors are unlikely to be working with patients under compulsory treatment orders unless they are working in psychiatry or social services.

> Penny takes a potentially lethal dose of tablets in the presence of her counsellor or does something else, such as cutting her wrists, which could be dangerous to herself but is unlikely to harm others.

There are different views about how a counsellor ought to act ethically. Some would insist on calling for medical assistance straight away regardless of the client's wishes or agreements about confidentiality. Others would try to obtain the client's consent to calling for medical assistance and would respect the client's wishes until she loses consciousness and then would call for medical assistance. It is agreed that this shows greater respect for the client's autonomy. It is unclear to me whether one course of action is preferable over the other from a legal viewpoint. Certainly, to do nothing could amount to being an accomplice to suicide which is a criminal offence. It is therefore important that the counsellor seeks medical assistance at some point and probably it is legally safest to do so at the earliest opportunity.

> Tom is suicidal and is threatening to commit suicide by jumping out of a window into a public thoroughfare or some other method which is reckless as to potential injuries or death caused to others.

Ethically, this is a situation where merely attempting to talk someone out of their proposed course of action could be inadequate. The risk of serious injury or death to others, in my opinion, would justify the counsellor in calling for outside assistance even if this meant breaking confidentiality. It would also be legal to use such force as is reasonable in the circumstances in order to prevent the client's proposed course of action. The amount of force used would not be based on the prevention of the suicide, as suicide is no longer illegal (Suicide Act 1961). The level of force should be 'reasonable in the circumstances' to prevent the risk of serious bodily harm or death to someone by the suicidal person, perhaps as in the example, by landing on top of a pedestrian or driver. The standard of reasonable force would take into account circumstances in which the force was considered necessary. Even a reasonable person cannot be expected to assess the minimum level of force to a nicety (Smith and Hogan, 1992).

It is less clear what a counsellor ought to do if, for example, the client leaves the room stating he intends to kill himself by driving recklessly until he has an accident which could result in serious injury or death to others. In these circumstances, the counsellor has to choose whether to seek the assistance of the police to frustrate the client's intentions. On balance, I think this would be an appropriate course of action if the counsellor had reasonable grounds for believing there was a substantial risk of serious injury to others.

Other ethical dilemmas

During the writing of this chapter I have been consulted by counsellors about two situations which caused them difficulty in deciding how to proceed. You might like to consider how you would respond if you encountered them by using the guidelines suggested in this chapter.

Peter has a long history of psychiatric treatment but has chosen to see a counsellor privately rather than be re-admitted into hospital. After a period when he seemed to be recovering, he suddenly appeared to deteriorate. He would drive to remote places and phone his counsellor at any time of the day or night sounding very confused, quite suicidal and would plead for his instant help, particularly that the counsellor should drive out to collect him. The counsellor noted that, despite his apparent confusion, he always remembered the counsellor's telephone number and could give directions to where he was. How would you respond as Peter's counsellor?

Felicity has had a long sequence of different treatments, both psychiatric and counselling for what she believes to be 'manic depression'. She feels she can no longer cope with the mood swings which occur without medication or the extreme discomfort of 'dry-eyes' which are a side effect of the medication. She is seriously suicidal and both she and her counsellor believe that at the current state of knowledge she is unlikely to find any better form of treatment. What should the counsellor do if Felicity tells him that her plans to commit suicide are well advanced? What should the counsellor do if later on he finds Felicity unconscious after an overdose?

After a suicide

A counsellor may be called to give evidence at the Coroner's Court. The main purpose of this court is to establish the identity of the deceased and to determine the cause of death. However, the Coroner, who is usually a local solicitor or doctor, has considerable personal discretion in how he conducts hearings. This means that it is difficult to give counsellors detailed guidance on what to expect.

If a counsellor is summoned to appear, it will usually be in order to establish the cause of death. This means that the counsellor will need to decide how much she is willing to say in open court. The central issue will be the agreement about confidentiality made with the client. It is accepted practice by counsellors that agreements about confidentiality continue beyond the client's death. This is a requirement of B.4.10 of the *Code of Ethics and Practice for Counsellors*. If the counsellor expects to be asked questions about confidential matters I would recommend seeking legal advice in advance of the hearing and if necessary arranging to be legally represented in court. The Coroner has the legal powers to require answers to questions and, if someone refuses to answer without lawful excuse, may impose a fine of up to £400 under s. 10 of the Coroner's Court Act 1988 or use the contempt of court procedure to compel an answer. If the counsellor has not obtained legal representation, I would carefully explain to the Court the nature of the agreement with the client about confidentiality and request the Coroner's guidance. The Coroner may use his discretion to waive his powers to require answers or may restrict questioning to matters which are of central importance to the function of the court. The counsellor would not incur legal liability for breach of confidence if she answers questions at the direction of the Coroner. However, in some circumstances, the counsellor may feel that there is an ethical dilemma which is not wholly satisfied by a strictly legal analysis. For example, a counsellor might feel willing to answer questions in general terms about a client being depressed because of relationship difficulties but may know there are some things which the client had stressed as being confidential such as specific feelings about a named sexual partner or a relative. Again, I would recommend that the dilemma is explained to the Coroner and he is requested to use his discretion. If the Coroner takes the view that an answer is still required and the counsellor maintains the view that she is unable to answer then it is probably appropriate to ask for an adjournment to seek legal advice. If the counsellor has already anticipated that this situation might arise then she would be well advised to attend the Court with a solicitor or barrister from the outset.

After a suicide it is not unusual for relatives to want to discover whether everything had been done which could be done by those caring for the person who committed suicide. If they were unaware of the mental and emotional state of the person who died, they may also want as much information as possible. Out of their anger and grief they may wish to show that the counsellor was either incompetent or uncaring. This can lead to some challenging questions, either in court or elsewhere. It goes without saying that a counsellor who has been clear from the outset with a client about her qualifications, experience and policy over respect and autonomy or intervention to prevent suicide, is in as strong a position as it is possible to be in these circumstances, particularly if she has also conducted an appropriate assessment in consultation with others and then acted on it. Evidence of clear agreements that the client would abstain from suicidal attempts for the duration of counselling or that the client would contact specified people or organizations should he become suicidal all help to add to the credibility of the counsellor and to an understanding of the counsellor's position with regard to client autonomy. Members of the general public, and particularly distressed relatives, may assume that a counsellor has a clear duty to intervene in all circumstances to prevent suicide and may also have unrealistic expectations of what can be done even if the counsellor has attempted to intervene.

The issue of keeping written records is highly relevant to any situation which might result in a court appearance. This is discussed in Chapter 12.

Conclusion

Suicidal clients provide the counsellor with both an ethical and a therapeutic challenge. It is recommended that most clients will be counselled within a framework of respect for their autonomy. Exceptionally a counsellor may, after appropriate assessment and consultations with a counselling supervisor, act in ways which temporarily assume responsibility for the client by taking steps to prevent the client's self-destruction. In this chapter I have argued that the counsellor's decision between these two outcomes depends on systematic assessment. Ideally, because suicidal feelings are common, I believe that it is desirable that all counsellors should be trained in assessment but, in the short term, this is not a realistic expectation. What should a counsellor do if she feels lacking in sufficient competence, even after consultations with her counselling-supervisor and others, to make an assessment? I have argued elsewhere that counsellors should monitor their own competence and act within it (see the next chapter). So what does this mean in the context of suicidal clients?

One response which may be widely used seems to me to be inappropriate. I have been contacted by clients who have been distressed by the counsellor adopting a policy of insisting that either the client tells her general practitioner of her suicidal feelings or the counsellor will do so. This is a violation of respect for the client's autonomy. In my view, medical assistance should not be imposed on a client unless the client is so mentally disturbed as to satisfy the criteria outlined earlier in this chapter. For most counsellors, these criteria would be quite exceptional, and the decision to place the client in the double bind of 'either you inform a doctor or I will' should be used only on the basis of a competent assessment and after trying to obtain a client's agreement to medical or alternative assistance has failed. A counsellor's lack of competence to conduct an assessment of a suicidal client is an inadequate reason for disregarding the client's consent or opinions. A client may have good reasons for her doctor not knowing about her suicidal feelings, either because she suspects that the GP will be unsympathetic or she does not want it put on her medical records, perhaps because she is employed in the kind of work where medical references are required. Whatever the reasons, it is important that they are respected. There are also legal dangers to a counsellor passing on information about suicidal clients routinely. A counsellor could be sued for breach of confidentiality – see Chapter 9. Instead of having an automatic policy of informing the GP or making referrals, it seems to me that it is better if the counsellor tells the client why she feels unable to provide an adequate service for the client. Once the client understands the situation, she is in a better position to decide whether she is willing to continue working with the counsellor, with or without her GP's knowledge, or to be referred. The counsellor may also wish to make a personal choice about whether to continue counselling the client.

British counsellors are, on the whole, more fortunate than their American counterparts. In the USA counsellors and therapists are vulnerable to legal action if they fail to take action to prevent a suicide or if they overreact and breach clients' rights. Although British counsellors walk this tightrope ethically, so far as I know no legal action or formal complaint to a counselling association has resulted.

7 Counsellor competence

It goes without saying that it is desirable that a counsellor should be competent at providing counselling. This general ethical principle is widely agreed. What is much more difficult is to describe in precise terms what constitutes a basic standard of competence in a way which is acceptable to most counsellors. If it is difficult to achieve this to the satisfaction of most counsellors, who are presumably familiar with their subject, then how can a client, who may not know very much about counselling, assess whether a particular counsellor is sufficiently competent to meet that client's needs? These issues are fundamental to the credibility of counselling. Before I look at the strategies counsellors have adopted to ensure their competence, I will explore some of the difficulties inherent in the task. Counsellors are not alone in facing this issue. Other occupations have differences of view amongst themselves about what is competent practice. It is therefore useful to discover what are the legal obligations of practitioners and how the courts have approached the problem of deciding what is competent.

Difficulties in determining what is competent counselling

There is no globally accepted understanding of counselling. The nature of the subject means that it is unlikely that there ever could be a single model of counselling universally recognized as the 'truth'. Counselling is closely linked to human experience, which is so diverse and varied that there will always be different models of counselling, each partially representing an aspect of the 'truth'. This has implications for a client who asks the seemingly simple question, 'Was my counsellor competent?' Whether or not a particular intervention is likely to be judged competent will depend on the context and the theoretical orientation in which it is used. For example:

> Sue is distressed by her counsellor telling her that he feels antagonistic towards her when she does or says certain things. She asks, is it appropriate for a counsellor to disclose that he feels angry and frustrated or is he being incompetent?

I am told there are more than 50 different models of counselling.

To illustrate the way the answer to Sue's question depends on the theoretical orientation of the counsellor, I will restrict myself to four models chosen at random from the Counselling in Action series.

From a psychodynamic perspective, such an intervention would be assessed as counter-productive. In order to help a client gain insight into her transferences, 'the counsellor deliberately keeps him or herself, as a human being, in the background'. Michael Jacobs states that one of the ways transference can be resolved occurs because

> the counselling setting provides a chance for strong feelings to be expressed [by the client] for as long as is necessary, until they cease to exert so much pressure on the client. . . . It is frequently the fear that love or hate drives others away that leads people to push down their strongest emotions. As they realise in counselling that the counsellor is not shocked, is not hurt, is not put off, does not misuse the client's feeling, or does not respond in any other inappropriate or damaging way – in other words, does not repeat the reaction which the client has experienced in the past – the very strength of the feelings can diminish. (1988)

The counsellor's interaction is therefore an act of incompetence in psychodynamic counselling.

However, this is not the view of a person-centred counsellor, whose objectives and methods are rather different. The person-centred counsellor focuses attention on the quality of the relationship between counsellor and client. Congruence is an essential quality in this relationship. Brian Thorne and David Mearns (1988) observe that, 'The counsellor is "congruent" when she is openly being what she *is* in response to her client . . . when her response is what she feels and is not a pretence or a defence.' Therefore the intervention could be highly appropriate and competent provided the counsellor's feelings are genuine and spontaneous, and communicated appropriately.

In rational–emotive counselling this kind of disclosure would be more likely to be viewed as irrelevant. The type of self-disclosure recommended by Windy Dryden is directed towards encouraging clients to internalize a new rational philosophy. The counsellor 'is to disclose not only how you as a counsellor have experienced a similar problem in the past, but also how you overcame it. Thus, for example, . . . I sometimes tell my clients how I overcame my anxiety about having a stammer and therefore stammered less . . .' (1990). The kind of counsellor self-disclosure questioned by Sue is not of this kind and is therefore irrelevant in rational–emotive counselling. To the extent that it disrupted the rapport between her and her counsellor it might be judged more severely as counter-productive.

Not all counsellors are purists in the sense of adhering to a single model. Some, like Sue Culley (1991) seek to integrate skills drawn from a variety of models in a systematic way. From her viewpoint, provided the counsellor was acting within her specific guidelines for when to use immediacy, the counsellor would be acting competently. If, on the other hand, the counsellor was randomly eclectic, there might well be no criteria for determining whether the intervention was competently executed.

The theoretical orientation of the counsellor is only one of the contextual variations which might be relevant to assessing the competence of a particular intervention or method of working. The cultural setting, the needs of particular client groups, whether the counselling is one to one, with couples, or in groups, may also be relevant. What is competent in one context may be incompetent in another. This makes it difficult to generalize and to be specific and precise at the same time. Guidelines intended to have a wide application are of necessity written in general terms. For example, a general guideline 'Counsellors should only disclose their immediate feelings about their clients when it is appropriate' might alert counsellors to a potential issue but, because it is written in terms which are intended for universal application, it gives little actual guidance. It is easier to become much more specific once the context, particularly the theoretical orientation of the counsellor, is established.

Counselling is still at a relatively youthful stage in its development in Britain. It is at a stage of rapid expansion, innovation, and therefore a time of creativity and, with that, change. Within large counselling organizations like BAC, RELATE, the Westminster Pastoral Foundation and many training agencies, there are attempts taking place to encourage counsellors to standardize some aspects of their work. This is important and will help to establish realistic expectations of counselling, for both counsellors and their clients. However, even without the differences between schools of thought within counselling, there is a limit to how far this process can go. There will always need to be sufficient flexibility to allow for new ideas and new responses to client needs and research findings. There also needs to be room for honest disagreement about methods between counsellors. Any method of determining what is competent will have to accommodate the inevitable tensions between standardization and innovation.

Strategies for promoting the competence of counselling

Faced with the impossibility of producing a definitive description of what constitutes competent practice, counsellors use several strategies to enhance their own competence. There are five main strategies which have been widely adopted:

First, the responsibility for monitoring competence is placed on the counsellor him or herself. 'Counsellors should monitor actively the limitations of their own competence . . . Counsellors should work within their known limits' (BAC, 1992a: B.2.2.17). Taking on this responsibility can be a more difficult task than it sounds. If someone already knows how to do something to a high standard, they can identify when their standard falls. What if someone does not know what a competent level of practice is? This is sometimes expressed as the conundrum 'How can I know I am incompetent if I do not already know what is competent?' The next strategy responds to this dilemma.

The second method chosen by counsellors is to use someone who can act as a counsellor-supervisor who facilitates the counsellor in the task of monitoring herself. This role is explored more fully in Chapter 11. For the moment it is sufficient to note that members of BAC regard the role of the counselling-supervisor as so important that it is considered unethical to counsel without supervision. It is a method of obtaining informed feedback.

Thirdly, counselling-supervisors are not the only potential source of honest feedback about the counsellor's competence and quality of work. The *Code for Counsellors* also requires counsellors to monitor the limitations of their competence by '. . . seeking the views of their clients and other counsellors' (B2.2.17). The idea of seeking the views of other counsellors, particularly those working in similar ways, is uncontroversial. However, the concept of seeking feedback from clients is more controversial. Two objections to this practice have been argued with some vigour.

Some have objected that seeking feedback from clients can be disruptive to the counselling relationship. In particular, some psychodynamic counsellors have worried about whether seeking feedback from clients could create confusion and disrupt a client's progress in unravelling transferential relationships. Clearly, timing is important but for anyone who has doubts about its value I recommend Patrick Casement's *On Learning from the Patient* (1985).

It has also been argued that clients may be unable to give honest feedback because of a sense of dependence on the counsellor.

Alternatively, clients may be uncritical of the counsellor, by, for example, confusing 'feeling better' with 'getting better'. I think these arguments do not discredit feedback but client's feedback, like all feedback, requires evaluation by the recipient. Feedback is inevitably revealing of the person who gives it, and if it reveals excessive dependence on a counsellor, this highlights something important about the nature of the counselling relationship which needs addressing.

Fourthly, at a national level in BAC and within many counselling organizations a great deal of work is being undertaken to identify the basic levels of training required for counsellors to perform specific tasks. Individual counsellors are expected to 'have received adequate basic training before commencing counselling and should maintain on-going personal development' (B.2.3.2).

Fifthly, the accreditation scheme for counsellors sets a high standard for counsellors based on the recommendations of Professor Brian Foss (1986). In his report he recommended that in order to be accredited a counsellor should have received at least 450 hours' training and 450 hours' supervised practice over a three-year period. Although this standard is higher than most voluntary organizations can achieve, it is becoming the basic standard for the counsellors of students in higher education. Accredited status is also a statutory minimum for counsellors working in Human Embryology and Fertilisation Clinics unless they are qualified social workers or chartered psychologists. The Code of Practice required by the Human Fertilisation and Embryology Act 1990 requires that either the counsellor must be at one of these levels of qualification or 'a person with such a qualification is available as an advisor to counselling staff and as a counsellor to clients as required'.

Counsellors with impaired functioning

One situation has arisen from time to time and is therefore worth considering specifically. Like anyone else, counsellors are vulnerable to all the frailties of the human condition which may affect their competence. Therefore the *Code of Practice* requires that: 'Counsellors should not counsel when their function is impaired due to personal or emotional difficulties, illness, disability, alcohol, drugs or for any other reason' (B.2.2.18). It is reasonable to assume that most counsellors know whether they have been drinking alcohol or taking drugs, medicinal or otherwise, which impair their functioning. Occasionally counsellors are unaware of the effect of this consumption, particularly if they are becoming addicted.

There is another situation in which a counsellor's functioning may become impaired due to an insidious erosion of ability due to illness or disability:

> Trevor has a progressive illness which affects his conceptual abilities and he appears unaware that his interventions are increasingly confusing for clients. What is the responsibility of his counselling-supervisor?

In these circumstances it is widely accepted that the counselling-supervisor has a responsibility to raise the concern with Trevor and perhaps advise him to withdraw from counselling. Fortunately this is a rare occurrence but there is a much more frequent variation of this situation which is less clear cut:

> Margaret has recently been bereaved by the death of her last surviving parent. She knows she is preoccupied with her loss. Should she withdraw from offering counselling?

This is the sort of situation which ought to be discussed in counselling-supervision. Usually it is raised by the counsellor but sometimes the discussion is initiated by the counselling-supervisor. There are four possible assessments of the situation:

1 The counsellor is able to use her current experience of bereavement as a resource for her clients, particularly those also experiencing bereavement;
2 The counsellor finds it too emotionally painful to function with recently bereaved clients but is able to continue working with other clients on non-bereavement issues;
3 The counsellor needs to withdraw temporarily from all counselling;
4 The counsellor needs to withdraw from providing counselling indefinitely or permanently.

Sometimes counsellors in the situations of either Trevor or Margaret are more optimistic about their ability to function than their counselling-supervisor. In situations where there is substantial difference of opinion and the counselling-supervisor believes it is necessary to take positive action in the interests of protecting clients, the following procedure has proved useful:

1 The counsellor is told by his counselling-supervisor of any reservations about competence to practice, in writing if necessary.

2 If the counsellor and counselling-supervisor cannot agree about the counsellor's competence, the opinion of a mutually acceptable third person is sought to make an assessment.
3 If the situation remains unresolved, the counselling-supervisor may withdraw from that role giving reasons, which would usually be in writing.
4 The counselling-supervisor may raise the issue with the counsellor's professional association or in the last resort implement the complaints or disciplinary procedure.

There is no intention that someone should withdraw from counselling merely because of disability, illness or other reason. The test is whether the counsellor's circumstances impair his functioning as a counsellor. There are many effective counsellors who have restricted mobility, or are visually handicapped. Some counsellors with hearing difficulties are able to overcome this by the use of hearing aids, lip reading or counselling using sign language. Some counsellors have managed to turn what might at first sight seem to be a hindrance to their functioning as a counsellor into an advantage.

The law and competence

'Competence' is not a term that is much used in law. Lawyers have approached the issue of identifying adequate standards of practice from a different point of view. It is defined in terms of the service provider, including counsellors, having a duty to exercise 'reasonable skill and care'. It has been important in deciding claims for negligence to determine whether 'reasonable skill and care' has been used. Many of the leading cases relate to medical negligence where the courts have been faced with differences of view about what constitutes reasonable care and skill. Counsellors are not unique in having several established, but conflicting, views about how best to work.

What is *reasonable* skill and care? The same standards are not expected of a passer-by who renders emergency first aid after an accident and a qualified surgeon. Someone who is acting in a voluntary capacity may not be expected to show the same level of skill as someone who is working for reward. If someone practises a profession or holds himself out as having a professional skill, the law expects him to show the amount of competence associated with the proper discharge of that profession, trade or calling. If he falls short of that standard and injures someone as a consequence, he is not behaving reasonably (Rogers, 1989).

How does a court assess what is a reasonable standard? First the court will look to see if the counsellor explicitly promised a result as a term of the contract with the client. This is one of the reasons why counsellors are wise not to make promises, say, to alleviate depression, anorexia, etc., within a fixed time limit. In the absence of such a promise within the contract, the court will assess what constitutes a reasonable standard by using one of two procedures which vary according to whether the court is dealing with professional or industrial procedures. It seems most likely that it is the professional procedure which would be used.

If, as in counselling, there is no agreement about a universal standard of what is proper, then the court will not get involved in choosing between different professional opinions. The test is, did the counsellor act in accordance with a practice accepted at the time as proper by a responsible body of professional opinion skilled in the particular form of treatment? It does not have to be a majority opinion in order to be valid. The practices adopted by a substantial minority of practitioners have been considered reasonable. One problem does arise for counsellors from the way these procedures have developed in medical negligence. It is unclear whether courts will accept the opinions of non-medical practitioners about what constitutes acceptable practice. It is possible that counsellors will either have to rely on the views of medical practitioners or accept the possibility of the court using its own judgement about what is reasonable, which is the more usual practice in industrial cases.

Two other legal points may be particularly relevant to counselling.

First, the standard of reasonable skill and care requires striking a balance between the magnitude of the risk and the burden placed on the counsellor to avoid the risk. This may mean that a higher standard of care is required where the counsellor is working with issues about suicide, HIV infection, or abortion, compared to assertiveness or bereavement.

Second, there is a legal preference for establishing a standard of care and skill with particular posts rather than the individuals who occupy them. In other words, courts expect the same minimum standard of a newly qualified counsellor compared to an experienced practitioner in the same post. Similarly no allowance is made for domestic circumstances or financial worries, or other factors which might contribute to error. This means that organizations are well advised to set the same standards for similar posts throughout the organization. For counselling in general it is becoming increasingly important to establish a series of nationally recognized standards appropriate to different kinds of counselling posts.

Another important factor in deciding what is a reasonable standard is that what ought to be done (or not done) should be commensurate with the risk. This is one of the reasons why counsellors may need to set themselves a higher standard of practice with regard to suicidal clients (see previous chapter) compared to counselling in situations where the risk of harm to clients is less.

Conclusion

This brief review of the law indicates the advantages to counsellors and clients alike if counsellors can agree national standards for specific voluntary and professional posts. This is an enormous task but some groups of counsellors have attempted to identify good practice. The study of HIV counselling sponsored by the Department of Health and BAC was intended primarily to promote standards of good practice but it also has the effect of establishing what falls below acceptable practice (Bond, 1991b). The enormous amount of work being undertaken by the Lead Body on Advice Guidance and Counselling in order to establish a progressive system of National Vocational Qualifications for the Department of Employment seems likely to be an important step forward but it is going to be some time before these standards are determined.

In the meantime individual counsellors need to continue to monitor their own level of competence and to be willing to be accountable to clients and other counsellors for their practice on a day-by-day basis. What can a counsellor do in these circumstances? Probably the minimum standard every counsellor should aspire to is:

(a) Know why you are doing or saying something to your client;
(b) Be sure you are saying or doing what you intend;
(c) Know what its effect is likely to be;
(d) Adjust your interventions according to the client's actual response;
(e) Review your counselling practice regularly in counselling supervision;
(f) Assess whether your level of skill is the same or better than other counsellors offering counselling on similar terms or holding similar posts.

Simple as these principles are, they can act as the foundation of competent practice.

8 Avoiding the exploitation of clients

It is clearly contrary to the values and ethics of counselling to exploit clients. The mere use of the term 'exploit' makes this self-evident because of its negative moral overtones. The difficult and more challenging task is to describe what constitutes exploitation and what amounts to good practice in order to avoid it.

The current wording of the *Code of Practice for Counsellors* (BAC, 1992a) specifies some forms of exploitation.

> B.2.2.6. Counsellors must not exploit their clients financially, sexually, emotionally, or in any other way. Engaging in sexual activity with [a client] is unethical.

This list is not exhaustive but attempts to elaborate the ethical principle stated earlier in the *Code* 'counselling is a non-exploitative activity' (A.1). Each of the listed forms of exploitation is considered in turn.

Financial exploitation

The potential for financial exploitation in counselling occurs in a number of ways.

The most common source of complaint arises from lack of clarity about the financial costs incurred by clients. For example:

Stephanie seeks counselling and agrees to monthly payments of fifty pounds. After the first two months she and her counsellor agree to meet more frequently and change from fortnightly sessions to weekly. The discussion about the new arrangements is hurried and at the end of a session. Stephanie is perplexed and shocked to receive a bill for £120 at the end of the next month. She had wondered what the cost would be, but had calculated that the maximum charge would be for four weekly meetings at £25, a total of £100. When she raises the issue, her counsellor explains that his charges had gone up at a point during the first two months of seeing her and, as this was a new arrangement, he felt obliged to charge at the higher rate.

This is a classic example of where lack of clarity about fees, prior to the client incurring costs, can lead to misunderstanding and can even destroy trust in the counselling relationship. It would have been better if the original arrangement had been an agreed fee for a fixed amount of counselling expressed in hours or sessions. This would have removed uncertainty about the implications of any changes in arrangements. In my opinion, any increase in charges without notice and charged retrospectively is exploitative. It is also unenforceable in law. One of the basic requirements of a legally valid contract is prior agreement about its terms.

Clients are entitled to feel cheated if, after reaching an agreement about the payment, the counsellor is bad at time keeping, particularly if this results in the client paying a full fee for a session when he has only received part of one. Habitual bad time keeping is almost certainly an indication of low standards of practice by a counsellor. However, like anyone else, a counsellor can be unexpectedly delayed by an accident or for some other reason. What should a counsellor do in these circumstances? The obvious course of action is to reduce the fee in proportion to the time missed. If however the purpose of the session has been frustrated by the shortage of time then it may be more appropriate to make no charge. If the client has incurred costs or been inconvenienced to attend a session which has been adversely affected by the time keeping of the counsellor or even the total absence of the counsellor then it may be more appropriate to reimburse those costs and sometimes to pay compensation. One way of minimizing any inconvenience to a client is to have a prior agreement about how long the client should wait for the counsellor before assuming the session is abandoned. Such an agreement would only apply when something unexpected has intervened. It is much better to avoid such situations and if a session needs to be re-scheduled to have reached an agreement about the new arrangements as far as possible in advance.

Counsellors who charge fees for their services are vulnerable to the suspicion that they keep fee-paying clients on longer than is strictly necessary. There are two opposing views about who is responsible in this situation. Some take the view that it is the clients' responsibility to monitor whether or not they want to continue counselling and whether they are getting value for money. This seems appropriate to situations where the counselling is clearly provided on this basis, and the counsellor does not express an opinion about the desirable duration of the counselling relationship. It is arguably another way of respecting the client's autonomy. However, in practice, matters are not always as clear cut as this. For example:

Polly values her counselling sessions, which started when she was having difficulties due to a bereavement. She asks her counsellor how long she is likely to benefit from counselling. He replies that in his experience of comparable situations six months would be the appropriate length. In the event Polly makes more rapid progress and after two months has begun to use the sessions to consider other aspects of her life. She is fee-paying and always pays willingly, which is a relief to her counsellor who is experiencing financial difficulties.

In these circumstances it is more appropriate for the counsellor to draw attention to the change in the purpose of the sessions and to reach a new agreement. The temptation is to allow the counselling relationship to extend itself by the counsellor's inaction to the end of six months or indefinitely. The tendency to extend contracts with wealthy clients is not always deliberate. One way counsellors can check whether this is actually happening is by watching whether they give wealthy clients longer contracts than their poorer clients and by periodically reviewing this issue in counselling supervision. Building in periodic reviews with clients about their counselling contracts also acts as a safeguard. It is a test of the counsellor's integrity whether he can set aside his financial needs in order to negotiate the duration of the counselling relationship so as to take into account the client's best interests.

Sometimes clients want to give their counsellor a gift. This raises issues which involve the integrity both of the counselling relationship and of the counsellor. For example:

Elsie is alienated from her relatives and wishes to leave her counsellor a substantial sum of money in her will.

This situation could threaten the integrity of the counselling relationship if the client's conscious or unconscious intention is to buy the counsellor's loyalty or manipulate the relationship in some way. On the other hand it could be a straightforward way of acknowledging the personal value the client places on the counselling which will only take effect once the relationship is over. The risk to the counsellor's integrity is the suspicion that she may have used her influence to obtain the gift. For all these reasons counsellors are wise to be cautious about accepting gifts and to refuse to do so if the gift would compromise the counselling relationship. If there are no obvious reasons for declining the gift, it is a sensible precaution to protect the counsellor's reputation by discussing it in counselling-supervision and, in the case of substantial gifts, the counselling association. Often it is more appropriate to encourage the client to make a gift to charity rather than tc the counsellor personally.

Sometimes financial exploitation may arise from dual relationships operating concurrently between the counsellor and client. For example:

> Douglas, a car dealer, knows that his counsellor is wanting to buy a car. After some negotiation, the counsellor agrees to purchase a car from Douglas. In the event, the car turns out to be faulty and they are unable to agree how to resolve it. The counsellor sues Douglas.

This case reveals that there are as many dangers in dual financial relationships. At the very least the counsellor has left herself vulnerable to the suspicion that she has used her role in relationship to Douglas to obtain a more favourable deal from Douglas than she could obtain elsewhere. Even if this were not the case, the potential for the business transaction undermining the counselling relationship is a high one if grievances arise in the commercial relationship. It is very unlikely that the dual relationships, counselling and financial, could be kept separate. In the example, it is the client's part of the deal which is faulty but the effect would be much the same if the counsellor had difficulty making payments or if any of many other possibilities arose.

Sometimes counsellors enter into dual relationships out of the best intentions. For example:

> Jon is a fee-paying client in the middle of his counselling when he is made redundant. His counsellor agrees to Jon's offer of doing odd jobs for him instead of paying fees.

There are dangers in this situation for both the counsellor and client. What if the counsellor is dissatisfied with Jon's work? On the other hand, what is a reasonable rate of pay from Jon's point of view? The potential difficulties are such that both these situations need to be considered in advance of entering into such an arrangement. Some counsellors prefer to avoid the risk of such complications by using a sliding scale of fees which could be adjusted according to Jon's circumstances or continuing counselling without any charge.

Bartering goods is sometimes considered as an alternative arrangement in circumstances similar to Jon's. What if Jon agrees to give the counsellor an ornament or some other possession as an alternative method of payment? Again the problems are similar to bartering services. The counsellor needs to consider in advance, what if the object exchanged turns out to be damaged or faulty? Jon needs to be confident he is getting value in the exchange. Probably an independent valuation is required as the starting point for any agreement. So far as I know, there are no British guidelines for these situations where fees are paid by barter. Because of the current economic climate, these kinds of situations are more likely to be considered as possibilities by clients and counsellors. In the United States there is also no widespread standard of practice. However, in a recent publication, Barbara Herlihy reported that the American Psychological Association Ethics Committee was recommending the following standard of practice:

> Psychologists ordinarily refrain from accepting goods, services, or other non-cash remuneration from patients or clients in return for psychological services because such arrangements create inherent potential for conflicts, exploitation, and distortion of the relationship. A psychologist may participate in bartering if (1) the patient or client requests this method of payment, (2) unusual circumstances make it the only feasible option, (3) it is not clinically contra-indicated, and (4) the relationship is not exploitative. When the client or patient is providing services as barter the time required of them must be equitable. (APA Draft, 1991) (Herlihy and Corey, 1992)

Sexual exploitation

Social awareness of sexual exploitation and harassment by people with power over others has increased dramatically over the last decade. It is widely accepted that there is a significant amount of sexual abuse of children by adults and often by members of their own family. There is also an increasing realization that members of the caring professions including psychiatrists, psychologists, social workers and counsellors have also engaged in sexually inappropriate behaviour with their clients (Rutter, 1989; Russell, 1993). Because these studies are recent and probably not as widely known as they deserve to be, I believe there is a need for a thorough review of what is appropriate and inappropriate sexual behaviour by counsellors, followed by a process of counselling education for all counsellors.

There are no means of knowing accurately how frequently clients suffer sexually inappropriate behaviour but there are indications that it is sufficiently frequent to be a real cause for concern. In the USA it is estimated that sexual contact occurs between male therapists and clients in about 11 per cent of cases and between female therapists and clients in 2–3 per cent of cases (Pope and

Bouhoutsos, 1986). Recently there has been a downturn in self-reported cases by therapists, which may indicate that increased awareness of the issue has been successful in reducing sexually inappropriate behaviour. On the other hand, it may be the result of less candid self-reporting (Pope and Vasquez, 1991). In Britain the incidence rate is less certain. It appears that the number of incidents is under-reported but nonetheless allegations of sexual misconduct are one of the most frequent kinds of complaints to the BAC Complaints Procedure. From clients who have approached me about their distress about sexual relationships with counsellors who turn out not to be members of BAC or any other reputable counselling body, it is my impression that sexual misconduct may be even more common outside the membership of BAC. I think that even if the incidence of sexual misconduct by counsellors turned out to be lower than in the USA, and there is no evidence to suggest that this is the case, we need to do everything we can to reduce it further. The effect on clients is so devastating that their reactions have been linked to those of the victims of rape, battering, incest, child abuse and post-traumatic stress syndrome. Kenneth Pope (1988) has described the therapist–patient sex syndrome as involving many of the features of these other traumas:

- Ambivalence: a state of fearing separation or alienation from the counsellor, yet longing to escape the counsellor's power and influence. For as long as the ambivalence persists the client may not report the counsellor out of a sense of loyalty and fear of destroying her professional reputation.
- Guilt: this arises because the client may feel responsible for not having stopped the sexual activity or for having initiated it. However, it is the counsellor's responsibility to monitor the boundaries, even if the client does act seductively, and it is the counsellor who is responsible for maintaining the appropriate level of personal/professional distance, not the client. The client's sense of guilt is often similar to the feelings associated with child abuse, with a similar sense of responsibility for what happened.
- Emotional liability: a long term consequence of counsellor–client sexual involvement can be a sense of being emotionally overwhelmed during the relationship and afterwards. Sometimes these feelings recur with appropriate sexual partners.

Other responses identified by Pope include: identity/boundary/role confusion; sexual confusion; impaired ability to trust; suppressed rage; cognitive dysfunction; and increased suicidal risk. In the course of my work on the Standards and Ethics Sub-committee for BAC I have spoken to several clients who have experienced deep emotional distress and turmoil, sometimes for several years, following sexual relationships with their counsellor, before they have felt able to discuss their experience confidentially with someone else. Sometimes it takes years before someone feels able to make a formal complaint. I am sure many complaints are not brought forward because of the fear of having to relive the painful experience of the original relationship.

The risk of serious emotional distress to the client is only one of the reasons why counsellors in BAC from very early on have adopted a prohibition on sex with clients. There are other reasons why sex between counsellors and clients is considered dangerous. Clients are vulnerable to exploitation because of the inequality of power which is inherent in a counselling relationship. The helper will inevitably hold more power than the person being helped. It is the difference between the provider and the needy. Psychodynamic counsellors have also pointed out the likelihood of a powerful transference growing between the client and counsellor arising from the client's childhood. When this occurs the client is relating emotionally to the counsellor like a child to an adult or a parent. If the counsellor enters into a sexual relationship, it is experienced as sexual abuse or incest. This may explain the level of distress experienced by some clients.

It is sometimes suggested to me that there are situations where it is appropriate for an adult client to take some responsibility and feel guilty for what happens if he engages in sex with a counsellor. I think this must be so if the client is acting as an adult out of an adult psychological state. However, the client does not have the counsellor's additional responsibility of monitoring and maintaining safe boundaries within the counselling. So, even if the client is an adult in an adult psychological state and therefore carries some responsibility, the greater responsibility rests on the counsellor. If the client is regressed to an earlier childhood state or the methods used evoke child-like behaviour or feelings, then there is an even greater responsibility on the counsellor to avoid sexual relationships with clients.

The risks inherent in sex with clients are not confined to the client. The public reputation of counselling in general is at stake. It is important that the public have confidence that they can approach counsellors and discuss personal issues in a safe environment. As part of the counselling process people often become emotionally vulnerable and expose themselves psychologically to their counsellor. Therefore, it is important that the counsellor maintains an appropriate boundary in the relationship to provide the client with safety. The 'no sex' rule for counsellors is out of respect for the clients' psychological vulnerability in the same way as doctors need to respect their patients' physical vulnerability. The prohibition on sex with clients is therefore to protect both current clients and the reputation of counselling in the public mind so that future clients feel able to take the risk of approaching a counsellor.

What is sexual activity?

The prohibition of sexual activity with current clients was adopted in the first *Code of Ethics and Practice for Counsellors* in 1984 and repeated in 1990. This has raised the question of what is sexual activity? The phrase implies that it extends beyond sexual intercourse involving penetration to include other behaviours such as masturbation, 'heavy petting', etc. But where is the boundary in hugging and kissing which are activities which may or may not have an obvious sexual component? The sexual ambiguity of these activities means that it is impossible to produce a definitive list of what constitutes sexual activity. With some activities, it will depend on the intention of the people involved and, just as importantly, the interpretation of the person on the receiving end. Counsellors are wise to be cautious in situations where their actions could be misunderstood.

'Sexual activity' covers many different categories of activity. Three are of particular concern when they arise in a counselling relationship. Sexual assault implies a deliberate attempt to force a client into sexual activity against their will. It is a criminal offence. Sexual abuse may involve force but is more likely to be manipulation into sexual activity under the pretence that it will be therapeutic. It is characteristic of abuse that it involves an abuse of power. Sexual harassment is deliberate or repeated comments, gestures or physical contacts which are unwanted by the recipient or expressed in a relationship where the recipient is in a less powerful position than the person making them. In terms of helping counsellors to think through the issues around sex with clients it is useful to separate these different activities and to realize that any sexual activity with a client is likely to fall into one of these categories because of the inherent power imbalance between the counsellor and client.

'Sexual activity' also has positive connotations. It is associated with intimacy, physicality and relationship, and outside the counselling relationship can be extremely positive and life-enhancing. The prohibition on sex between clients and counsellors is not out of a latter-day puritanism, but it is in the hope that both counsellor and client will find sexual fulfilment independently of each other. My experience of counsellors who have entered into sexual relationships with clients is that they fall into several distinct categories. I think there are a few who deliberately use counselling as a means of obtaining sexual contacts and who appear relatively indifferent to what happens to the client afterwards. Their motivation and behaviour is pathological. More often I encounter counsellors who cross the boundary because of a lack of satisfactory emotional and sexual relationships in their own lives. Such a person may well use clients (and trainees) as a source of social company and hence the possibility of sexual relationships is increased. Counsellors behaving in this way often have considerable confusion over issues to do with personal boundaries which may permeate much of their life and their work with clients. The best way counsellors can avoid this situation is explore their own sexual needs and to ensure that the forum for meeting these is outside the counselling relationship. A counsellor who has done this is in a much better position to deal with sexual attraction which will inevitably arise from time to time.

Sexual attraction

Sometimes it is the client who feels the sexual attraction most strongly and who clearly takes the initiative in attempting to seduce the counsellor. In these circumstances counsellors need to be clear about their role. Rather than comply with the client's overtures it is better to acknowledge openly what appears to be happening and to explore what the client wants from a sexual relationship with the counsellor. If this situation is handled well, it often marks the movement into a new phase in counselling where both the client and counsellor feel able to discuss their feelings about each other more directly. It is often a time when clients are willing and able to disclose more frankly personal needs which are not being met elsewhere in their lives.

For the counsellor, it is important that this kind of situation is discussed in counselling-supervision so that she feels clear and supported in maintaining an appropriate professional boundary. Any alternative approach is usually less satisfactory. To pretend to ignore the client's advances is avoidance of where the greatest energy in the relationship may be currently operating and with it the greatest motivation to work on real needs and issues. To comply with the advances and become involved in sexual activity not only defuses and misdirects potential therapeutic energy but carries with it personal risks for both counsellor and client. For the counsellor, in the event of a complaint there is also the possibility of expulsion from counselling associations.

Counsellors sometimes experience a powerful sense of sexual attraction towards a client. If you have not yet experienced such feelings you can imagine the feelings you might experience if you encounter a client who is your sexual prototype who also has personal qualities you admire. Sometimes in longer counselling relationships of an intimate nature extremely strong sexual attractions develop. The desire to move into a sexual relationship may be enormous. It is not unethical to feel attraction to a client. The ethical response is to acknowledge the feeling to yourself, and to consult a counselling-supervisor and colleagues about the situation as quickly as possible. The decision about whether to tell the client about your feelings of attraction will be a matter of judgement depending on the circumstances and the model of counselling being used. Sometimes seeking your own counselling is useful. So far as I know, very few counselling training programmes include formal training in how to recognize and respond to sexual attraction in counselling. This is a serious omission.

Sex with former clients

It is only very recently that the issue of sexual relationships with former clients has started to be given serious consideration by counsellors on both sides of the Atlantic. Within BAC the first step in the process was taken at the 1992 Annual General Meeting at the University of Warwick which passed the following amendment to the *Code for Counsellors*.

> B.2.2.6 Counsellors must not exploit clients financially, sexually, emotionally or in any other way. Engaging in sexual activity with current clients or within 12 weeks of the end of the counselling relationship is unethical.
>
> If the counselling relationship has been over an extended period of time or been working in-depth, a much longer 'cooling-off' period is required and a lifetime prohibition on future sexual relationships with the client may be more appropriate.

This should be regarded as no more than an interim policy statement at the start of an important discussion about sex with former clients. The proposal of a minimum of twelve weeks' prohibition of sexual activity with former clients is a pragmatic solution to a problem which has arisen in the complaints procedure. Before this amendment, a counsellor could terminate a counselling relationship and one minute later could start a sexual relationship, because the previous code only prohibited sex with current clients. So far as I know, this has not happened but there have been a few instances of counsellors starting sexual relationships within a few hours or days later. Experience of these situations in Britain and the United States suggests that sex with former clients most frequently arises within three months of the end of the counselling relationship, hence a twelve-week prohibition. Even after twelve weeks the counsellor will need to consider what is the appropriate time, if ever, to enter into a sexual relationship. If there is a subsequent complaint the counsellor would have to be able to show that she had acted ethically. The objective of this interim policy is to make the minimum change required to protect clients and to provide a focus for debate about what is a reasonable ethical standard which would apply to all counsellors who are members of BAC.

One of the challenges in reaching an agreed policy is that this is an issue which divides counsellors according to the nature of the work they do with clients and the counsellor's theoretical orientation. Some examples may illustrate these different widely held opinions.

Leslie seeks counselling to help her to manage better a conflict between her and a colleague at work. A combination of problem-solving and assertiveness techniques is successful. After two counselling sessions she has resolved her problem and the counselling stops. Six months later she bumps into her counsellor socially at a party and after a pleasant evening together they decide to meet socially. Neither person is in a relationship with someone else and some time later they start a sexual relationship.

In this example, the counselling work is unlikely to have involved much intimacy or intensity as the theoretical orientation has a strong behavioural component and the focus of the work is outside the immediate counsellor–client relationship. The meeting which precedes the sexual relationship occurs in a setting unconnected with the counselling and on equal terms. It seems inappropriate to prohibit two adults from continuing to develop their relationship in the way that they want in these circumstances. It has been argued that to be too protective of clients in these circumstances is to infantilize them and erode their autonomy. Counsellors who believe this situation is typical argue against any restraint on sex with former clients, or for minimal restraints.

David uses counselling to explore his difficulty in having close relationships which last longer than a few months. During the counselling, which was weekly over five months, attention is paid to his feelings towards his counsellor, Sarah, who points this out when she feels David is trying to distance himself from her. As a result, David becomes aware of how he pushes people away and how this re-enacts a painful period during his childhood. Six months after the end of the counselling David meets Sarah at a charity event and suggests they meet again for a meal. Both of them realize that there is a mutual sexual attraction. What should Sarah do?

In this example the counselling was more intense, intimate and longer lasting. This is the kind of situation where powerful transferences and counter-transferences are likely to arise, whether or not the counsellor is using a psychodynamic model. This is the kind of situation where considerably more caution is required before a sexual relationship is started, if ever. For example, members of the British Association of Sexual and Marital Therapists have adopted a lifetime ban on sexual relationship with former clients. They believe this is essential to protect the integrity of counselling on these sorts of issues. There is anecdotal evidence that some clients are deterred from seeking counselling about marital and sexual issues because they are not confident that counsellors will not engage in sex with them. Many practitioners with a psychodynamic orientation also doubt whether it would ever be possible to enter into a relationship which is truly free of the transferences and power dynamics of the original counselling. This is the focus of one of the debates that is currently taking place. Should the prohibition on sex with former clients be absolute and forever? Alternatively, is it possible that in some situations transferences are resolved and therefore it becomes a matter of judgement about whether sex with a former client is permissible? Even if you take this latter point of view, I think six months would be too soon to consider sex with a former client in the circumstances of this particular case. It requires longer to mark a clear boundary between the counselling and any new sexual relationship. This is more a matter of protecting the integrity of the counselling relationship than whether or not the transference is resolved. It is a characteristic of transferences that they persist over long periods of time, often from early childhood into adult life. Therefore it is improbable that transferences are resolved merely by the passage of time. They are resolved by insight and emotional work. It will be a matter for assessment by both the client and counsellor whether the transference has been resolved. During the debate of this issue, the importance of involving the counselling-supervisor as a relatively independent assessor has been raised several times. It has even been suggested that this might be an exceptional circumstance where the former client and the counselling-supervisor might meet face to face.

It is too soon to anticipate what the final outcome of debate currently taking place within BAC will be. Nonetheless, it is clear that any counsellor entering into a sexual relationship with a former client is taking professional and personal risks. Even if more than three months has elapsed between the end of the counselling and the proposed sexual relationship, I would strongly recommend that the counsellor considers:

- Has sufficient time elapsed to mark a clear boundary between the counselling and the new relationship?
- Have the dynamics involved in the counselling, particularly with special attention to power and transference, been given careful consideration by the counsellor, and are there good reasons for believing these are not influential in the proposed relationship?
- Have the risks to the client been explored with the client?
- Has the support of the counsellor-supervisor for the relationship been obtained?

If the counsellor decides to go ahead with starting a sexual relationship after satisfying these requirements, she needs to be aware of the possibility of the former client experiencing many of the symptoms of the therapist–patient syndrome described earlier. Because of this, most prudent counsellors would prefer to avoid sex with former clients unless the counselling relationship had been extremely brief, lacking in emotional intensity and therefore not involving the dynamics of transference and power which might persist or recur in a subsequent non-counselling relationship. Using these criteria, it would be personally and professionally prudent of Sarah to avoid entering into a sexual relationship with David.

Counselling in an appropriate environment
John Rowan has drawn attention to the way the furnishings of a counselling room communicate to a client what is expected of her. He suggests, for example, that 'Cushions on the floor give much more flexibility and a suggestion that it is all right to be childlike or even childish. A couch or mattress lends itself to fantasy, dreams, deep regression and loss of conscious rational control' (1988). In contrast, it is argued that chairs suggest rationality and the straighter the chair, the greater the emphasis on rationality. Similarly, the presence of a box of tissues may be perceived as

indicating that others have used the room for crying and that the counselling room is a safe place to cry in.

Without wishing to press these observations too far, I think most counsellors would recognize a degree of reality in them and acknowledge the conscious and unconscious influence of the physical environment in which counselling takes place. One of the obvious questions which follows is, why do some counsellors see clients in either the counsellor's or the client's bedroom? This must send mixed messages about the counsellor's intentions. Therefore I think it is better to avoid counselling in bedrooms altogether. If this is not possible, it is better to use a room which is not being used regularly by the counsellor or client, such as a spare room. An obvious exception to this is counselling someone who is bedbound because of illness.

Emotional needs

Much of what has already been said about sexual exploitation is directly transferable to emotional needs. If the boundary in sexual activity is sometimes hard to identify, this is even more so with emotional needs. I cannot imagine that anyone continues with providing counselling unless it is meeting an emotional need of some kind. This is not problematic if the need is complementary to the client's use of counselling and is sufficiently within the counsellor's control to avoid distorting the counselling relationship. A counsellor's emotional needs are not always counter-productive. Sometimes a counsellor's neediness or vulnerability can be used as a resource in order to enhance a client's understanding of her own situation or to break down a sense that the client is unique in having a particular vulnerability. This often represents a high standard of practice and is within the tradition of the 'wounded healer'. The problem arises when the counsellor's neediness is such that the client's needs are eclipsed, or under the pretence of working to meet the client's needs the counsellor is really seeking satisfaction of her own. This can occur in a vast variety of ways. The most obvious are when counsellors cannot end relationships with clients because they are a source of regular companionship and a substitute for developing friendships with people who are not their clients. Perhaps a little less obvious is the counsellor who has such a sense of personal unworthiness that she chooses to work with the most socially stigmatized and disadvantaged clients available to her on the basis that at least they will be grateful for help. Often they are not grateful or appreciative, and the counsellor's disappointment and sense of rejection can become the dominant emotional force in the relationship rather than the client's feelings of vulnerability.

Good practice with regard to emotional exploitation requires that counsellors periodically review what their emotional satisfactions and needs are. It is important that the counsellor has alternative sources of emotional satisfaction outside of counselling for most of their deep needs. Good quality counselling-supervision is invaluable in helping counsellors address this issue.

Responding to exploitation by counsellors

Exploitation involves meeting the counsellor's needs or someone else's at the expense of the client's. Exploitation may be deliberate or unintentional but it is always unethical. What should a counsellor do when she suspects another counsellor of exploiting clients? The course of action must depend on the circumstances in which the suspicions arise if the client is not to be subjected to further harm.

For example:

> Marjorie seeks counselling because she feels troubled by her experience with her previous counsellor. She had been having a sexual relationship with her counsellor which had started while she was receiving counselling. She is aware that this is a breach of the counsellors' code of ethics but does not wish to make a complaint.

In these circumstances the counsellor ought to be bound by his agreement with Marjorie about confidentiality and can only act with Marjorie's consent. He may actively seek this consent or encourage Marjorie to pursue her own complaint but to do more than this must inevitably compromise his own relationship with his client by a failure to work within an agreement about confidentiality and to respect her autonomy. Even though the counsellor may feel uncomfortable with his knowledge, there is little else he can do, otherwise the client's vulnerability is increased by compounding the original harm by a further breach of confidence. The client's needs ought to have priority.

What if the client reveals in confidence a situation where a counsellor is repeatedly exploiting many clients? In these circumstances it will be a matter of judgement whether it would be better to respect an agreement with an individual client about confidentiality or whether it would be better to report the situation in order to prevent further harm to other clients. The significance of considerations of acting to promote the 'public good' with regard to confidentiality is considered in Chapter 9. This is an extremely difficult situation because there can be no hard and fast guidelines. Each person has to assess the situation according to the known circumstances.

An alternative situation could be:

Sandy, a counsellor and colleague, tells you confidentially that he has started a sexual relationship with a current client.

In these circumstances, there is a crucial difference. The counsellor, not the client, has approached you directly. In these circumstances, notwithstanding the agreement about confidentiality, it is probably better either to encourage the counsellor to report the circumstances to his professional association and seek their guidance or, if this does not happen, to take the initiative yourself. A counsellor who actively seeks assistance for himself is likely to be viewed more favourably than someone who waits to be reported. However, even in these circumstances, because the counsellor has approached you in confidence, there should be no automatic breach of confidence. Again, it is a matter of weighing up whether the 'public good' is more likely to be promoted by breaking confidence or by keeping confidence. This constraint does not operate if you are told of the sexual relationship without any pre-conditions over confidentiality.

Sometimes allegations of exploitation occur as rumour. For example:

You are at a party and you hear allegations that a counsellor you know well and have worked with is financially exploiting her clients.

In these circumstances, there must be some doubt about the credibility of such a rumour because you do not have direct personal evidence. If you think that they are unbelievable, then you may wish to let the counsellor know about the existence of such rumours so that she can choose what to do about them. If the counsellor admits to you that the rumours have an element of truth about them, you are in a similar position to the second example. If, on the other hand, you have reason to suspect the rumours might be true but the counsellor denies them then it is a matter of personal judgement about how to proceed or whether to wait and see whether your suspicions are confirmed or disproved.

Within the British Association for Counselling, it is accepted that counsellors have a responsibility for challenging any suspected malpractice by other members of the Association. The *Code of Practice* states:

> B.2.4.2. If a counsellor suspects misconduct by another counsellor which cannot be resolved or remedied after discussion with the counsellor concerned, they should implement the Complaints Procedure, doing so without breaches of confidentiality other than those necessary for investigating the complaint.

The act of reporting a fellow counsellor can seem extremely daunting and full of potential conflict and embarrassment. However, these are seldom sufficient reasons for not doing it. Far more important as the basis of your decisions is the appropriate protection of clients' rights and, ultimately, the members of the public who seek counselling.

Conclusion

The exploitation of clients raises important issues for counsellors. It is not merely a matter of harm to the clients most directly concerned but to the reputation of counselling as a whole. When I am dealing with issues on behalf of BAC which might turn into formal complaints, I am constantly reminded how hard it is for counsellors to make judgements about others and perhaps themselves. Counsellors tend to value diversity in people and relationships. When faced with clear examples of exploitation it is all too easy either to under-react by maintaining an inappropriate level of non-judgementalism or to overreact with excessive zeal. Neither of these responses tends to be helpful. It is important that exploitative practices are challenged and eliminated but, as this chapter has shown, it requires great care to assess the issues involved in specific situations and to be fair to the client and everyone else who is involved.

One issue which recurs for any counsellor considering how to respond to situations of exploitation relates to the management of confidentiality. This is the subject of the next chapter.

9 Confidentiality

Confidentiality is probably the single issue which raises the greatest number of difficulties for counsellors. The sources of these difficulties are twofold. They arise from uncertainty about what the optimum practice ought to be, and from problems experienced in implementing ethical practice. This situation is particularly anxiety-provoking for counsellors as confidentiality is so central to their work.

The importance of confidentiality in counselling

Confidentiality is considered fundamental to counselling because, by its very nature, counselling is an intimate relationship which often involves clients in divulging information about their current and past situations, as well as their opinions and innermost feelings. This can only take place in a relationship based on trust. In particular clients need to feel that whatever has been disclosed will not be used in ways which will harm them. This usually means that disclosures in counselling are made by clients on the assumption that what is said remains confidential between the counsellor and client.

In this respect there are many parallels between counselling and psychotherapy. Clients are engaged in a process in which personal truthfulness is essential but not always easily achieved. Anxiety about confidentiality would inevitably make their search for personal truthfulness much more difficult, if not impossible. Jeremy Holmes and Richard Lindley argue that psychotherapy requires confidentiality for the following reasons:

> The subject matter of the psychotherapy includes fantasies, fears and feelings which patients find very hard to acknowledge, even to themselves, let alone to anyone their therapists might choose to talk to . . . psychotherapy is a medium where the normal rules of social encounters are suspended and where it is safe to regress at times into kinds of behaviour which would be quite inappropriate in another setting. This feeling of safety requires a strong understanding that what goes on in therapy is strictly between therapist and patient.

> Because of social prejudice against people suffering from psychological distress, there can be a stigma attached to going to a therapist. This provides a good reason why not only the contents of the therapeutic relationship but also the fact of such a relationship should be regarded as a matter of confidentiality.

There are then, rather as in the case of lawyers, good reasons for believing that the principle of respecting confidentiality in therapy should be very strong indeed. Without such an assumption most psychotherapy would be impossible. (1989)

I think this line of argument is directly transferable to counselling.

Differences of view about the principle of confidentiality

Although there is considerable agreement between counsellors about the importance of confidentiality, there are significant differences of view about what this means ethically and in practice.

Some take the view that confidentiality is an absolute principle. For example, Hetty Einzig (1989) in the first edition of *Counselling and Psychotherapy – Is it for Me?*, a publication designed to help potential clients, stated: 'all counselling is totally confidential'. This view still has a strong following.

On the other hand, there is an opposing view which believes that the significance of confidentiality can be overstated at the cost of ignoring other ethical principles. This view is based on the central value of autonomy in counselling. Autonomy is particularly important to the client and involves respect for 'the client's values, personal resources and capacity for self-determination' (BAC, 1992a: 3.1). The priority of the principle of autonomy suggests that confidentiality should not be imposed on the client, even though the client may desire confidentiality, but should be the subject of negotiation. These negotiations may also have to take into account other competing ethical considerations. These include any contractual obligations the counsellor may have to the person resourcing the counselling when this is not the client, such as an employer or sponsor. It may also be considered to be in the best interests of good practice that some information about the counselling is shared in a controlled way with colleagues, or between agencies. The consequence of this view is that total confidentiality cannot be taken for granted by the client. This creates its own ethical principle which is based on the integrity of the counselling relationship. This principle is summarized by Anne Munro and others as 'the client should know where she stands in relation to confidentiality. For example if case discussion is routine within an agency, the client should be told this' (1988).

In view of the existence of these conflicting views it is worth exploring what view has been taken by BAC in its codes for counsellors and secondly, what is the legal position?

Code of Ethics and Practice for Counsellors

The first code published by BAC in 1984 was revised with regard to confidentiality in 1990 and is repeated in the 1992 edition. As someone who is involved in the drafting of the second code, I am aware that this code, which replaces the earlier one, was written with a view to clarifying the understanding of confidentiality. As a result the *Code* gives extended consideration to confidentiality within the Code of Practice. This includes statements which clearly assume (a) confidentiality is highly important; and (b) the emphasis is on ensuring that clients know the extent to which they are being offered confidentiality. For example:

B.4.1   Confidentiality is a means of providing the client with safety and privacy. For this reason any limitation on the degree of confidentiality offered is likely to diminish the usefulness of counselling.

B.4.3   Counsellors should work within the current agreement with their client about confidentiality.

B.4.6   Counsellors should take all reasonable steps to communicate clearly the extent of confidentiality they are offering to clients. This should normally be made clear in the pre-counselling information or initial contracting.

B.4.7   If counsellors include consultations with colleagues and others within the confidential relationship, this should be stated to the client at the beginning of counselling.

B.4.9   Any agreement between the counsellor and the client about confidentiality may be reviewed and changed by joint negotiations.

B.4.10 Agreements about confidentiality continue after the client's death unless there are overriding legal or ethical considerations.

The emphasis these sections place on involvement of the client in reaching agreement about confidentiality clearly implies that it cannot be assumed that counselling is totally confidential. Elsewhere in the *Code* provision is made for counsellors to be accountable to line managers, and also to engage in regular and on-going counselling-supervision. The assumption is that any discussion of the counselling in these contexts will be anonymous.

B.4.2   Counsellors treat with confidence personal information about clients whether obtained directly or indirectly or by inference. Such information includes name, address, biographical details, and other descriptions of the client's life and circumstances which might result in identification of the client.

B.4.8   Care must be taken to ensure that personally identifiable information is not transmitted through overlapping networks of confidential relationship. For this reason it is good practice to avoid identifying specific clients during counselling supervision/

consultative support and other consultations, unless there are sound reasons for doing so.

If discussions cannot be anonymous, the client's consent to them is usually required.

It is also envisaged that in exceptional circumstances where there is a well-founded risk that clients will cause serious physical harm to others or themselves, the counsellor may communicate personally identifiable information.

> B.4.4 Exceptional circumstances may arise which give the counsellor good grounds for believing that the client will cause serious physical harm to others or themselves or have harm caused to him/her. In such circumstances the client's consent to a change in the agreement about confidentiality should be sought whenever possible unless there are also good grounds for believing the client is no longer able to take responsibility for his/her own actions. Whenever possible, the decision to break confidentiality agreed between a counsellor and client should be made only after consultation with a counselling supervisor or an experienced counsellor.

Counsellors are well advised to be cautious about breaking confidentiality on the sole grounds that a client is suicidal – see later in this chapter and Chapter 6. Any breaking of confidentiality in order to protect someone from serious physical harm should be done in a carefully controlled way.

> B.4.5 Any breaking of confidentiality should be minimised both by restricting the information conveyed to that which is pertinent to the immediate situation and to those persons who can provide the help required by the client. The ethical considerations involve balancing between acting in the best interests of the client and in ways which enable clients to resume taking responsibility for their actions, a very high priority for counsellors, and the counsellor's responsibilities to the wider community.

These sections were developed on the basis of principles deduced from the values and ethics of counselling as they are understood in Britain. To this extent these sections were developed independently of the law.

Confidentiality and the law

I cannot discover any cases reported of counsellors being sued for breach of confidence. This poses some difficulties in establishing what the law requires of counsellors because courts have no precedents arising from counselling upon which to base their decisions. Therefore there must be a degree of uncertainty about how the law of confidentiality will be applied to counsellors. These circumstances make it all the more important that counsellors with specific concerns relating to the law of confidentiality seek proper advice through their lawyer, professional association or any legal helpline which may be available to them as part of their professional indemnity insurance scheme.

Nevertheless, it is possible to outline some of the basic legal principles about confidentiality and indicate how these are likely to be applied to counselling. An analysis conducted by Kenneth Cohen (1992), a solicitor with a special interest in counselling, is particularly informative.

The first and most important matter for counsellors is that confidentiality is an important principle in the law and courts will intervene to uphold legally enforceable obligations of confidence. These obligations may arise from (a) an expressed term of a contract, or (b) someone simply stating 'what I am about to tell you is in confidence', or (c) someone agreeing to accept a communication in confidence, or (d) a presumption about the nature of the relationship, for example doctor/patient, counsellor/client. As any or several of these circumstances are likely to arise in counselling, there is a strong basis for working on the assumption that counselling is a confidential relationship. The legal status of confidentiality is a two-edged sword for counsellors. There are situations where it may be helpful to counsellors seeking to protect a confidential relationship with a client against someone else's enquiries, but the law also creates responsibilities. Breaches of confidence may result in damages or injunctions being awarded against the counsellor.

However, the principle of maintaining confidentiality is not absolute in law. Only barristers and solicitors have the absolute privilege of not being required to disclose information given to them by clients. Counsellors are in a similar position to doctors and priests in that the courts expect counsellors to maintain high standards of practice about confidentiality but there are circumstances when (a) a breach of confidence may be regarded as defensible, and (b) counsellors must break confidentiality or incur legal penalties for not doing so.

When is breaking confidentiality defensible?

In law, it is defensible, but not mandatory, to break confidentiality in a number of circumstances.

The most important of these circumstances for counsellors arises when the client gives consent to the counsellor breaking confidentiality. The consent may be implied or expressed and may be open-ended or restricted to the disclosure of only part of the confidential information, or without the use of real names, or to a limited number of people. Cohen observes,

> ... it is the experience of many counsellors that where the client's express consent to appropriate disclosure is necessary, it is often possible to persuade her to give that consent. Although it may not be ideal to have to try to persuade a reluctant client to agree to disclosure, to do so will often show greater respect for her autonomy than not making the attempt. (1992)

The second situation arises because, by definition, it cannot be a breach of confidence to disclose information which is already in the public domain, so no longer secret. However, caution is required before deciding that this is the case. It is possible for everyone 'in the know' to be bound by a series of obligations of confidentiality. For example, it is possible for the counsellor, other members of a supervision group, doctors and nurses, personnel officers and others to be bound by a chain of confidentiality. There has to be some uncertainty about the point at which a court would say that the information is so widely known that it is not entitled to legal protection.

The third circumstance in which the law regards breach of confidence as defensible arises when the public interest in the protection of the confidence is outweighed by the public interest in disclosure or use. 'In the public interest' does not mean 'the public would enjoy knowing about this'. The 'public interest' is taken to mean 'the best interests of society as a whole' or 'in the national interest'. It is therefore 'for the public good'. This is essentially a matter of weighing one principle against another. Inevitably, there is a degree of uncertainty about what decision would be made by a court. The decision would be based on the circumstances of a particular case, and would include consideration of whether the disclosure was restricted to people who could best act in the public interest and whether the information was disclosed to this end. (Therefore observance of B.4.5 – see previous section – in the *Code for Counsellors* provides important legal protection for both client and counsellor.) In two instances the courts have held that psychiatrists were acting in a defensible manner when they disclosed to courts confidential information about patients who, in their opinion, constituted a danger to the public. It seems therefore that the law would grant defence to a counsellor where she discloses confidential information to prevent the client causing 'serious physical harm to others'. On the other hand disclosing confidential information to prevent clients harming themselves, except where serious mental illness is involved, is less likely to be viewed as being in the public interest (see Chapter 6). This is important for counsellors working with suicidal clients.

Cohen suggests that an application of the principle of public interest is the common practice of counsellors in disclosing anonymous information in counselling-supervision, training and research. Technically this must be a breach of confidence but, as Cohen has observed, 'it seems plausible to say that the public interest in supporting literally total confidentiality between counsellor and client is outweighed here by the public interest in the proper training and supervision of counsellors, and in the development of a public body of knowledge about counselling' (1992). The law is much more certain with regard to confidentiality about serious wrongdoing, such as fraud and crime. Even if information about serious wrongdoing is given in confidence, the public interest in the prevention and detection of crime outweighs the public interest in maintaining confidentiality. This is encapsulated in the legal maxim 'there is no confidence in iniquity'. It is therefore impossible for a client to bind the counsellor by the terms of any contract to keep confidential disclosures about serious wrongdoing. Whether the counsellor ought to disclose on ethical grounds is a matter of personal judgement. However, there is no general legal duty imposed on the counsellor to disclose criminal acts. There are no legal penalties for not providing information to the police or refusing to answer their questions. On the other hand, lying to the police can constitute an offence (see Chapter 10).

When is breaking confidentiality mandatory?

As the law generally seeks to uphold agreements about confidentiality, it is not surprising that there are very few circumstances in which counsellors may be legally obliged to break confidentiality. Whenever there is a legal obligation to break confidentiality, the law also protects the counsellor from liability for that breach. An obligation to break confidentiality may arise in the following circumstances:

1 Parliament has the power to make statutes requiring disclosure of confidential information, for example Prevention of Terrorism (Temporary Provisions) Act 1989. Section 18 makes it an offence to fail to disclose information, without reasonable excuse and as soon as reasonably practicable, which would assist the prevention or investigation of an act of terrorism connected with the affairs of Northern Ireland. It seems probable that mere existence of a confidential relationship

would not be regarded as a 'reasonable excuse' but I am unaware of a decisive authority on this point. However, it is possible to seek legal advice about a counsellor's legal duty from a solicitor without the solicitor necessarily being obliged to inform the authorities as the Law Society (1992) takes the view that the 'reasonable excuse' defence means that a solicitor is not obliged to disclose confidential or privileged information under this provision other than in wholly exceptional circumstances. The implications of the Children Act 1989 for counsellors working with young people are complex and are discussed later in this chapter.

2   A judge in court may require a counsellor, appearing as a witness, to answer questions put to her even if this means breaking confidences. Refusal to answer may constitute contempt of court. Nonetheless, a psychoanalyst has been prepared to risk such a penalty rather than break confidentiality. She wrote anonymously in *The Lancet* about her experience,

> I complied with the sub poena by attending Court, but I decided I could not answer any questions about the 'patient', and I made all arrangements, including having a barrister to plead in mitigation of sentence, for the possibility that I should be sent to prison for contempt of court. In the event, although my silence probably did constitute a contempt, the judge declared that he would not sentence me, saying it was obviously a matter of conscience. In this he was acting within the discretion the Law allows him. Though I had no legal privilege, I was in effect given the same freedom to remain silent usually allowed to priests for the secrets of the confessional. It is possible that the judge was partly moved by the idea that any evidence I could give might only be of marginal relevance to the case. (Hayman, 1965)

It is probably a wise precaution to follow this psychoanalyst's practice by ensuring that you are legally represented if you are planning to refuse to answer questions put to you in court.

3   A counsellor's notes and records cannot usually be protected from disclosure and use in proceedings if they are required by court. Stephen Jakobi and Duncan Pratt (1992) have recently summarized the complex law on this point (see also Chapter 12).

4   An obligation to disclose confidential information may also arise from the contractual terms of the counsellor's employment. For example, a counsellor may be employed on explicit conditions which require disclosure of criminal acts by clients to the counsellor's employer. In other words, what might be

a matter of discretion has become an obligation. This is a fairly typical condition for employee counsellors, particularly if the offence is against the employer. As there is potential for conflict between a counsellor's obligations to the client and the employer, this situation is worth considering in more detail.

Conflicting obligations of confidentiality

The counsellor working in private practice is least likely to experience conflicting obligations over confidentiality because the client is also the counsellor's employer. Clients who are particularly concerned about confidentiality may wish to bear this in mind. Counsellors in private practice are in the best position to be able to offer the highest levels of confidentiality. This is not to say that counsellors working in agencies cannot offer similar levels of confidentiality. Many do, but the potential for conflicting requirements of confidentiality between the client and counsellor's employer makes this a less predictable situation. There is also the likelihood of counsellors finding their own individual ways of reconciling their obligations of confidentiality to a client and the counsellor's employer.

The potential of conflicting obligations over confidentiality may arise in two different situations. In the first situation, the employer is the employer of both the counsellor and the clients, for example employee counsellors and counsellors in staff health units. Their clients are the employees of the same organization. Therefore the transmission of information about the counselling to the employer is particularly sensitive.

The Law Commission on 'Breach of Confidence' considered this situation:

A doctor or a psychologist employed in industry is faced with the demand by his employer for the disclosure of medical records relating to other employees of the firm who have frankly discussed their personal problems with him on a confidential basis and without any express or implied understanding that the information would be made available to the employer.

Assuming that no question of the public interest is involved (as it might be, for instance, if the health or safety of other employees was at stake), we think that the doctor or psychologist must preserve the confidences of those who confide in him. Of course, if he only accepts the confidence on the express or employed understanding that, pursuant to his contractual duty, he may disclose the information to the employer, this would constitute a limitation on the scope of the obligation of confidence to which he is subject. (1981)

The same principles are applicable to counsellors. A counsellor who offers counselling to employees is bound by the agreement about confidentiality made with each client. If the counsellor ignores (or is unaware of) terms in his own contract of employment which restrict the terms on which he can offer confidentiality the counsellor may be disciplined or dismissed for breach of his own contract of employment when he seeks to maintain confidentiality.

It is clearly in the interests of the employer to keep the restrictions on the counsellor's ability to offer confidentiality to a minimum if the counselling offered is to be acceptable to employees. The usual restrictions relate to issues of the safety of other employees or members of the public and criminal activity against the employer. If an employer has not incorporated these restrictions into the counsellor's contract of employment, there is no formal obligation on the counsellor to restrict the level of confidentiality offered to employees. Should issues of safety or criminal acts arise during counselling, the counsellor would have to decide whether the 'public good' would best be served by disclosure or by maintaining confidence. This puts tremendous reliance on an individual counsellor making the right decision and creates uncertainty for the client. It is therefore better for everyone concerned that an agreement be reached between the employer, counsellor and employees' representatives, usually a trade union, about the terms on which the counselling will be offered so that clients can be informed about issues of confidentiality in advance of the counselling. The existence of an agreed basis for confidentiality also means that the counsellor is not having to make decisions about confidentiality in isolation and without guidelines.

In the second situation, the employer employs a counsellor to provide a service to non-employees, for example a student counsellor works with pupils rather than employees, or a counsellor works with patients in a doctor's surgery. In these circumstances, it is sometimes argued that because the whole organization is working for the well-being of the client, there is less of a need for confidentiality to be restricted to the counsellor. It is also sometimes argued that it is desirable for other members of staff to be kept informed. I do not think this argument is valid as most people are reluctant to disclose personal information except to individuals of their choice and they do not wish to lose control of who gets to know this information afterwards. It seems therefore more realistic if counsellors seek to establish agreements which give their clients the maximum levels of confidentiality possible. However, the general principle of ensuring the compatibility of the agreement about confidentiality with the employer and what is offered to the client is important. Inconsistencies between these agreements can leave the counsellor at risk of disciplinary proceedings for failure to observe conditions of her employment.

A number of different kinds of agreements are currently in use. The most frequently used is that confidentiality will be maintained between the counsellor and client except in specified circumstances. A variation on this is that whether or not someone attended for counselling will be communicated to someone who made the actual referral but the content of what is discussed will be kept confidential between the counsellor and client.

Occasionally agreements are made on the basis of confidentiality existing between the client and a team of people or even a whole organization. Arrangements which automatically include other members of staff are exceptional in my experience. They are usually used in situations where security is an issue, such as institutions for offenders, or if young people are being counselled who lack the intelligence and understanding to give a valid legal consent (discussed later in this chapter). Even in these circumstances, formal or informal controls often exist which will have the effect of restricting what is passed on. For example, there may be specific agreement with the client and within the institution that matters not directly relating to security or the safety of other people will be kept confidential.

Counsellors working in medical settings and social services experience particular challenges over establishing good practice with regard to confidentiality. Counsellors often report that their practice of assuming that the content of the counselling is confidential between the client and counsellor is a source of conflict. When I explored this issue in relation to HIV counselling (Bond, 1991b) I became aware that the conflict was not fundamentally between a profession which is cautious about confidentiality and one which is careless or lax in its practice. The roots of the conflict lay in the working practices required to provide different kinds of services. Medical staff in particular need to be interchangeable so that a patient continues to receive treatment even if the person on duty changes. This necessitates a flow of information within a medical team and across different professional groups. Confidentiality is therefore usually restricted to a team of people or a unit. In social services, there is always the possibility of another worker needing to respond to a client, particularly should an emergency arise, so there is also the need for a pooling of information to make this possible. In contrast, counselling depends on a personal relationship being established between the counsellor and client. The counsellor is not interchangeable. The trust of the client is often directly related to the level of confidentiality on offer. For these reasons counsellors have adopted a more restrictive practice over confidentiality. The only way of reducing the conflict over confidentiality experienced by counsellors in health care and social services is to create a situation in which the differences in practice are accepted as the consequences of the requirements of different roles.

Counsellors in medical settings are particularly fortunate in having some recent legislation which, strictly speaking, applies only to human fertilization and embryology, but could be used as an example of good practice elsewhere. The Code of Practice which accompanies the Human Fertilisation and Embryology Act 1990 states: '6.24 A record should be kept of all counselling offered and whether or not the offer is accepted.' It appears this record, as distinct from the content of counselling, would be available to the clinical team. '6.25 All information obtained in the course of counselling should be kept confidential . . .' Confidential information is confidential to the person to whom it is disclosed and therefore is not freely available to the other members of the team. The code provides safeguards for giving confidential information to other team members.

> 3.24 If a member of the team has cause for concern as a result of information given to him or her in confidence, he or she should obtain the consent of the person concerned before discussing it with the rest of the team. If a member of the team receives information of such gravity that confidentiality *cannot* be maintained, he or she should use his or her own discretion, based on good professional practice, in deciding in what circumstances it should be discussed with the rest of the team.

These standards of practice could usefully be applied to other settings, both in and outside medicine.

Confidentiality of records

Confidentiality includes the protection of confidential records from disclosure. What this means legally and in practice is discussed in Chapter 12.

Confidentiality and young people

The general tendency in law has been towards giving children and young people greater rights with regard to confidentiality. The Gillick decision in the House of Lords about the rights of children under sixteen years old represents a landmark in this movement.

The case was brought by Victoria Gillick to establish her parental rights if one of her children was receiving treatment or advice about contraception and it was finally decided in the House of Lords in 1985. The result of the case was widely reported at the time as having given doctors unfettered rights to provide contraceptive advice. It is more accurate to think of it as abolishing the Victorian concept of absolute parental authority between parents and children. The powers of the parent dwindle and the powers of the child increase as the child grows in years and understanding. Lord Scarman stated '. . . parental right yields to the child's right to make his own decisions when he reaches a sufficient understanding and intelligence to be capable of making up his own mind on the matter requiring decision'.

A young person who has sufficient understanding and intelligence to give a legally valid consent is now often referred to as a 'Gillick competent child'. Deciding whether a young person is of sufficient understanding and intelligence is a matter of assessment. The assessment is important because it forms the basis for deciding whether or not parents ought to be consulted before the counselling commences. The Gillick ruling requires that children and young people should be persuaded to allow their parents to be consulted before they are given contraceptive advice or treatment. However, if the young person is of sufficient understanding and intelligence, there is no requirement that the parents are consulted. It is advisable to follow similar procedures in any counselling relationship. It follows that counsellors working with young people of sufficient understanding and intelligence are not under any duty to consult with parents in advance of counselling. Nor is there any duty to inform parents that counselling has taken place.

If the young person is assessed as not being of sufficient understanding or intelligence, it may still be permissible to give counselling without the parents' consent. The Children's Legal Centre (1992) suggests this may arise either when the parent is an alleged perpetrator of abuse or in emergencies (such as where the young person is in immediate danger, or likely to commit suicide). In these circumstances, the counsellor is likely to be more concerned about whether there is a duty to notify statutory services, particularly with regard to abuse.

In the absence of any better guidance, I think a counsellor would be well advised to assess the competence of the child by checking the child's understanding of the problem for which she is seeking assistance and of the counsellor's role, particularly with regard to confidentiality. There must be a degree of uncertainty in making these assessments and the remote possibility of being challenged in court. Nonetheless, the conscientious application of an assessment procedure which is recorded in counselling records made contemporaneously adds to the credibility of a counsellor's judgement.

Four years after the Gillick judgment much of the legislation relating to child care was consolidated into the Children Act 1989. Unfortunately this Act adds nothing further to clarify the rights of children and young people to confidential counselling but it accepts the principle of the 'Gillick competent child'. The provisions to protect children from abuse have caused some counsellors concern so they are worth considering separately.

Reporting incidents of child abuse

In order to understand the provisions of the Children Act 1989 it is important to remember the all too frequent deaths of children caused by abuse. Many of these deaths were followed by official enquiries which reported that the deaths occurred in spite of the involvement of many different workers from separate agencies with the family. Each of the workers often suspected the dangerous situation of the young person but each worker only had a partial picture of the risks. This meant that assessments of the risks were based on an incomplete knowledge of the situation. On the other hand, if the partial knowledge of each of the workers could be put together like so many pieces of a jigsaw a much more accurate assessment of the risks facing the child could be made. Therefore various government departments issued policy statements about 'Working Together' recommending co-operation and the exchange of information between agencies, particularly social service departments and the NSPCC. The Act made some of the recommended practices about inter-agency co-operation a legal obligation. However, it is one of the weaknesses of the Act that it does not explicitly take into account the ethical dilemma caused by a legal requirement to share information about a young person's allegations of abuse and a young person's request for confidentiality. This means that there is some uncertainty about the application of the Act, and counsellors who are worried about specific situations should seek legal advice.

I understand the Children Act to create different duties for counsellors, depending on the setting in which they are working. The issue which most concerns counsellors arises from S.47 of the Act, which places on local authorities a duty to investigate situations where they believe that a child is suffering, or is likely to suffer, significant harm. This duty is carried out by social service departments with responsibility for the area where the child lives or is found. Because the Act makes no provision for taking a young person's request for confidentiality, it may be that counsellors employed in social services are wise not to promise or agree to confidentiality about matters relating to abuse. The Children's Legal Centre has expressed concern about the apparent lack of any provision for respecting a child's right to confidentiality in the published policies about inter-agency co-operation. When this point of view was considered by the Cleveland Inquiry Report (HMSO, 1987) which undoubtedly influenced the drafting of the Children Act, no clear recommendation was made. Instead, the Cleveland Inquiry Report recommended that, 'Professionals should not make promises which cannot be kept to a child, and in the light of possible court proceedings should not promise a child that what was told in confidence can be kept in confidence.' Because the Act places a general duty on social services to investigate, it may be the duty of the counsellor working within the social services to instigate these investigations.

The Children Act 1989 also creates a qualified duty for some specified organizations to assist a local authority with their enquiries by providing relevant information and advice. This has implications for counsellors working in any of these organizations, which are: any local authority, local education authority, local housing authority, health authority, and any persons authorized by the Secretary of State. The duty is qualified by an exemption that no-one is obliged 'to assist a local authority where doing so would be unreasonable in all the circumstances of the case' (S.47(10)). Judging by my correspondence, many counsellors, along with other employees within these specified organizations, have not been given any guidance as to the meaning of the term 'unreasonable' or been made aware of this exception. In some instances, it would appear that they are instructed not merely to co-operate with enquiries made by social services as part of a current enquiry but to pass information to social services whether or not an enquiry is under-way. This practice is in the spirit of some policy statements about inter-agency co-operation, that procedures should be brought into action at the earliest possible stage and in respect of every allega-tion. However, to do so is beyond the statutory requirements of the Act, which appears to permit greater scope for professional judgement about when to communicate information about alleged abuse. A strict interpretation of the Act only requires the communication of information when requested in order to assist a current enquiry by social services. Counsellors working in the specified agencies may be able to use the law to argue against any automatic communication of information to social services, which is only required 'if called upon by the authority to do so' (S.47(9)).

It seems reasonable to assume that an Act which has taken into account a Law Commission and extensive consultation at many stages would have imposed a general duty on these specified agencies to take the initiative in the communication of information about abuse if this was what was intended. Instead, the Act avoids creating this general duty. It also qualifies the duty to assist the enquiries of a local authority, except where doing so would be 'unreasonable'. There has been doubt about what constitutes 'unreasonable'. The issue is not even considered in most legal commentaries on the Act. The Children's Legal Centre has received guidance that what is deemed unreasonable is a matter for local Area Child Protection Committees to determine. The Children's Legal Centre (1992) argues that a breach of a confidential relationship with a young person of sufficient understanding, without that person's consent, could be 'unreasonable'. It is apparent from my correspondence that many counsellors, particularly in education authority establishments, would wish to support this view of what is 'unreasonable'. It may be that this issue will eventually be resolved by a decision of the courts. In the mean time, counsellors working in specified authorities may wish to consult with each other in order to prepare a submission to their local Area Child Protection Agency. So far as I know, this has not yet been attempted and I would recommend that it is only done after careful preparation. The level of public concern in favour of preventing child abuse means that any committee receiving submissions which appear to limit inter-agency co-operation are likely to be extremely cautious. I think that they would need to be assured about the competence of counsellors to assess the seriousness of allegations of abuse, and the criteria used to keep something confidential and when it would be considered appropriate to override confidentiality. This may be an issue which requires further consideration at a national level, perhaps by counsellors in consultation with other professional groups including youth workers, local authority advice workers and others. In the absence of a clear policy about what constitutes 'unreasonable', it is wise to be cautious about promising clients confidentiality about child abuse if the counselling is provided within any of the specified authorities.

There are agencies which are not included within the Children Act. These are mostly voluntary organizations which may be national or local. It is particularly desirable that these agencies adopt clear policies with regard to confidentiality over child abuse so that counsellors and clients can be clear about the nature of their agreement. Those agencies who wish to offer clients high levels of confidentiality will often do so unless the child is in an immediately life-threatening situation, for example, requires immediate treatment for serious injuries, is about to be seriously injured, is suicidal, or may be injured by an attempt to escape the abuser (perhaps by jumping from a high building or running away). Some agencies may consider intervening if the abuse is taking place over a long time and the child is unable to avoid it. In all cases, it is considered good practice to keep the child informed of what the counsellor intends to do. In my view, it is important that children have places to contact where they can discuss anxieties about abuse of themselves or others and be able to expect that their request for confidentiality will be respected. Unless organizations and telephone helplines offering confidential services are readily accessible, children have to be certain that they want direct intervention from social services or others before seeking help. This must deter some children from seeking help at an early stage or when they just wish to clarify their options and share their uncertainty about what to do for the best. I am sure that all counsellors would prefer to prevent abuse whenever possible; however, it seems to me that this ethical intention needs to be balanced by a recognition that children of sufficient understanding also need access to a confidential service in which they retain a substantial degree of control over the direct actions taken on their behalf. To offer a child or young person confidential counselling and then routinely to break that confidence, even in response to something as serious as child abuse, is in itself a betrayal of trust and form of abuse. Unfortunately, my post bag suggests that many voluntary organizations are increasingly adopting a policy of routinely informing social services about allegations of abuse, often as a requirement of receiving local authority funding. Whenever this occurs, it is important that existing and new clients are informed about the limitations over confidentiality about issues involving child abuse.

Publications and research

The accepted practice amongst counsellors is: 'The use of personally identifiable material gained from clients or by the observation of counselling should be used only after the client has given consent, usually in writing, and care has been taken to ensure that consent was given freely' (B.7.1). The publication of material which is not personally identifiable does not require the consent of the client. Whether or not it is 'personally identifiable' depends on the adequacy of removing, or disguising, whatever would identify the client.

A grievance reported by the *Independent on Sunday* and referred to in Chapter 1 raises important issues. Should the counsellor take into account the possibility of the clients recognizing themselves? Even though the published account may be stripped of all the trappings of personal identity, clients may still recognize themselves. In this instance a client recognized herself in an account by a well known therapist of a session involving the client and her mother. The account was published in a national newspaper. This caused considerable distress to both the clients but particularly the mother. In addition, because a friend already knew that they had seen this therapist, that friend was also able to identify them from the scanty details contained in the article and could have learnt new information about what happened in the session. I draw attention to this instance because I think it illustrates how difficult it is to produce anonymous publications. If the counsellor is writing about his own work with clients, or about the work of a named counsellor, the risk of the case being identified is increased. Knowledge of who conducted the counselling is an important identifying feature. Also if the published account contains material not previously communicated to the client, for example, the counsellor's evaluation of the sessions, there is the risk of the client being distressed by such revelations. The likely readership of a publication is also a factor to be considered. It is easier to assess whether a client is likely to be known to the readership of a specialist professional journal or to read it herself, than to predict the readership of popular publications. For all these reasons, it is better practice to obtain the client's consent prior to publication unless the author can be really confident that clients will not be identifiable by others or themselves.

A client's duty of confidentiality?

At workshops I have often been asked whether a client is bound to keep everything that happens in the counselling confidential. Two arguments in favour of expecting clients to observe strict confidentiality are usually offered. First, total secrecy helps to mark a boundary between the counselling and the rest of the client's life. The existence of this boundary may increase the intensity of the personal experience of counselling and therefore its effectiveness. It may also prevent interference from partners and friends. Second, counsellors may be quite self-disclosing about themselves during counselling. This is an issue of particular importance for the users of the person-centred approach and related methods which require the counsellor to be self-revealing.

Although these are strong arguments I think they are countered by the adverse effects of attempting to impose confidentiality on a client. First, on ethical grounds it would be difficult to enforce without undermining the counselling by putting the counsellor in the conflicting roles of counsellor and enforcer. Second, the issue of confidentiality is complex enough for the counsellor without the need to develop parallel standards for the client. Third, most clients have considerable emotional barriers against seeking counselling because of the necessity of acknowledging their own neediness. To impose confidentiality on clients could increase the personal barriers in seeking counselling because of a widespread cultural tendency to associate secrecy with shame. Therefore a general principle of client secrecy seems inappropriate.

Occasionally it may be appropriate for the counsellor to say something in confidence to a client. Usually this would be because the counsellor is about to say something which is personally sensitive about herself and the counsellor wishes to retain control of whom she informs. For example, a counsellor with relevant personal experience who is working with a sexually abused client may wish to say something about her own experience of being sexually abused and how she overcame it. However, the counsellor needs to be aware that any attempt to enforce confidentiality on the client would raise the ethical difficulties already mentioned. Therefore counsellors do sometimes have to accept that some clients might break confidences and the counsellor is unlikely to be able to do much about it. Both client and counsellor take a risk in confiding in each other. Observance of the *Code of Practice for Counsellors* minimizes the risk to clients but counsellors are not protected in the same way. Counsellors need to assess which clients to confide in and to recognize that there is some unavoidable risk of the confidence being broken.

Inadequacies in current practice about confidentiality

What little evidence there is indicates that some counsellors may not be achieving a satisfactory standard of practice over confidentiality. A national survey of a wide range of agencies offering confidential counselling services to young people showed that there may be some inconsistency between the level of confidentiality apparently offered and the actual practice. This survey by the Children's Legal Centre created a lot of interest at the time and provoked many agencies into discussing and drafting a policy for the first time. The survey of over 100 agencies reported:

There are some agencies who do guarantee absolute confidentiality (although it is debatable whether some of them, on further questioning, would have acknowledged extreme circumstances in which even they would feel forced to breach confidentiality – what if a child comes in and shows a counsellor a bottle of deadly poison which they intend to pour into the city's water supply. . .?). Others had carefully defined exceptional circumstances. . . But a sizable number showed a worrying degree of confusion – suggesting an answer to one question that they did guarantee confidentiality, and then proceeding to indicate very wide exceptions (e.g. if client child was thought to be 'at risk'). (1989)

This is clearly unsatisfactory. The Children's Legal Centre commented that:

. . . it is vital that children and young people should have adults outside their family that they can go to for confidential advice and counselling, and that all agencies should have clear and well-publicised policies – available to the client before they use the service – indicating to what degree they will guarantee confidentiality. (1989)

Anecdotal evidence suggests that if a survey were to be conducted now the findings would not be too dissimilar. Participants at workshops and consultations on ethics have told me about situations with regard to adults where there are discrepancies between the level of confidentiality offered and what is actually delivered. At the beginning of this chapter, I referred to Hetty Einzig's published view in 1989 that 'all counselling is totally confidential'. The 1991 edition no longer makes such a claim. The word 'totally' has been removed for what I imagine to be many of the reasons mentioned in this chapter.

It is clearly in the interests of the integrity and credibility of counselling that counsellors at least ensure that clients know where they stand in relation to confidentiality in all reasonably foreseeable circumstances.

Confidentiality and the counsellor's conscience

The law permits limited discretion for counsellors over confidentiality which means that in the end many of the decisions depend on the counsellor's individual conscience and personal judgement. In this respect, their position is similar to that of doctors. The British Medical Association offers the following guidance:

A doctor, like any other citizen, is a member of society with all the responsibilities this entails. Occasions may arise in which these persuade the doctor that information acquired in the course of medical consultation must be disclosed. In line with the principles of medical secrecy, whenever possible the doctor should seek to persuade the patient to disclose the information himself, or give permission for the doctor to disclose it. Failing this, it will be for the doctor and for his own conscience to decide on this further course of action. (1981)

Should a counsellor pass on information with a client's consent? The answer must depend on the circumstances. In many situations, there may be no difficulty because of the clarity of the client's consent and the factual nature of the information involved. However, the problems increase if the counsellor is working psychodynamically or with clients' fantasy and imagery. When Anne Hayman refused to give evidence in court she was specifically asked by the judge if she would still refuse to answer questions if the 'patient' gave permission. Arguing from a psychoanalytic point of view she answered with an example,

> . . . suppose a patient had been in treatment for some time and was going through a temporary phase of admiring and depending upon me; he might therefore feel it necessary to sacrifice himself and give permission, but it might not be proper for me to act on this.

> This example involves a vital principle. Some of the United States have a law prohibiting psychiatrists from giving evidence about a patient without the patient's written permission, but this honourable attempt to protect the patient misses the essential point that he may not be aware of unconscious motives impelling him to give permission. It may take months or years to understand things said or done during analysis, and until this is achieved it would belie all our knowledge of the workings of the unconscious mind if we treated any attitude arising in the analytic situation as if it were part of ordinary social interchange. If we allow and help people to say things with the ultimate aim of helping them to understand the real meanings underlying what may well be a temporary attitude engendered by the transference, it would be the crassest dishonour and dishonesty to permit unwarranted advantage to be taken of their willingness to avail themselves of the therapeutic situation. It would be as if a physician invited a patient to undress to be examined, and then allowed the Law to see him naked and arrest him for exhibiting himself. Where no permission has been given, the rule to maintain discretion is, of course, similarly inviolable. Patients attend us on the implicit understanding that anything they reveal is subject to a special protection. Unless we explicitly state that this is not so, we are parties to a tacit agreement, and any betrayal of it only dishonours us. That the agreement may not be explicit is no excuse. Part of our work is to put into words things which are not being said. We are the responsible parties in the relationship, so surely it is we who should pay, if there is any price to be paid, because something has not been said clearly. (Hayman, 1965)

Some counsellors would share these views and would refuse to break confidentiality under these circumstances and regardless of personal cost. This is a matter of individual conscience. Such a stance is not required by the ethics of counselling where the emphasis is on honouring what has been agreed with the client and ensuring that the agreement is consistent with the many different ethical responsibilities which impinge upon the counselling relationship.

Conclusion

Confidentiality is extremely important in counselling. This has led some counsellors to regard the keeping of confidences as an absolute principle. I have agreed that this is unrealistic. Total confidentiality would prevent discussions in counselling-supervision. There may also be times when the principle of confidentiality needs to give way to a more important ethical imperative, perhaps to prevent serious physical harm to another or self-harm by the client. The law of confidence creates legally enforceable obligations for the counsellor but also recognizes that this is not an absolute obligation. There are times when a counsellor may be legally required to break a confidence, for example, by statute or in court. There are occasions when breaking confidence is regarded as legally defensible. In view of these circumstances, counsellors are wise not to offer absolute or watertight promises of confidentiality. Counsellors should be as clear as possible about the level of confidentiality they can offer a client at the start of the relationship. The basic principle is that clients should be made aware of the known limits of confidentiality likely to apply to them. However, counsellors cannot anticipate all the possible scenarios in which confidentiality might not be kept because of the exceptional nature of many of these events. Therefore I recommend that counsellors regularly review agreements about confidentiality with clients in order to ensure that what is agreed matches the current and reasonably forseeable circumstances.

10 Responsibility to oneself, colleagues and the community

Responsibilities to the client are the primary concern of the counsellor but they are not the only responsibilities. There are four other categories of responsibility identified in the *Code for Counsellors* (BAC, 1992a). Any or all of these may impinge on how the responsibility to the client is implemented or occasionally may even take priority. Each of these is considered in turn.

Oneself as counsellor

The ethical principle of autonomy is usually referred to in terms of respect for the client's capacity for self-determination. However, autonomy also applies to the counsellor. Like clients, counsellors should only enter into a counselling relationship on a voluntary basis and as a result of having made a deliberate choice to do so. The *Code* sets out a standard of care for counsellors to exercise on behalf of themselves.

> B.2.3.1 Counsellors have a responsibility to themselves and their clients to maintain their own effectiveness, resilience and ability to help clients. They are expected to monitor their own personal functioning and to seek help and/or withdraw from counselling, whether temporarily or permanently, when their personal resources are sufficiently depleted to require this.

This requirement is clearly directed towards ensuring the counsellor is competent to provide counselling and has the personal resources to do so. But behind it is an even more important principle. Counselling places considerable demands on the counsellor. There is always the risk of emotional burnout when working closely with the pain and problems of others. Counsellors have a responsibility to monitor their own responses and to protect their own well-being by avoiding excessive working and by making use of regular counselling-supervision. Counselling-supervision has a supportive role but this is only one of the tasks addressed in supervision.

Sometimes, it is useful to supplement the support offered in supervision with personal counselling.

I think these are minimum standards of self-care. The optimum standard would include periodic reviews of whether providing counselling enriches the counsellor's quality of life. A great deal is said and written about the demands on the counsellor but if the only effect is personal depletion then why continue to do it? It is important to the mental health of the counsellor that there is also personal satisfaction in providing counselling.

Indemnity insurance

The importance of indemnity insurance from the client's point of view is considered in Chapter 4. There are also gains to the counsellor in terms of peace of mind. Even though the risks of having a claim made against a counsellor appear to be relatively small, should it arise, the sums of money even in just obtaining legal advice can be quite large. Adequate insurance helps to reduce the risk that the counsellor could incur unanticipated expenditure to compensate a client, and some insurance schemes also include free legal advice.

Personal safety

Fortunately it is rare for counsellors to be physically or sexually attacked by clients but it is not unknown. If a counsellor is assaulted, some aspects of what are generally thought to be good practice add to the potential seriousness of the situation. For example, the counselling will usually take place away from other people in order to give the client confidentiality and privacy. These circumstances also make it harder for the counsellor to call for help. It is also not unusual for counselling rooms to be sited well away from busy areas to reduce extraneous noise. The same situation may arise if the counsellor is working in her own home. This means that there may be no-one about to hear cries for help. The usual practice of taking clients who are not previously known to the counsellor to maintain clarity about the nature of the relationship also creates an element of unpredictability and risk whenever a counsellor takes on a new client.

It is reasonable that counsellors should organize their work in ways to reduce the risk of assault on themselves. Counsellors who are vulnerable to assault have adopted one or both of the following strategies which can be implemented without compromising the ethics and standards of practice intended to protect the client:

● taking referrals through someone else, such as GPs, voluntary organizations or colleagues, rather than seeing clients who walk in directly off the street or respond directly to advertisements.

- making telephone contact whenever possible with clients before the first meeting. This provides a basic check on their physical location and gives the counsellor an opportunity to make a preliminary assessment.

Counsellors working with some client groups may not be able to implement any of these safety measures. For instance, counsellors who see clients with alcohol and drug problems may find the potential benefits of a referral system for the counsellor's safety are outweighed by the deterrent effect it has on clients seeking counselling. Some clients do not have telephones or do not wish to have telephone calls from a counsellor because of the risk of someone they live with discovering they are receiving counselling. For example, a client seeking counselling about an extra-marital affair or a violent partner may have good reasons not to want the counsellor to make phone calls to their home.

However, all counsellors can take a number of basic precautions once the client arrives by:

- avoiding seeing new clients, or clients where there is any risk of assault, in an empty building. It is better to have someone around who could be alerted by shouting or any unusual sounds. This is one of the advantages of counselling services that have receptionists or where counsellors share premises.
- providing the counselling rooms with telephones with outside lines. If counsellors are seeing clients in premises with a switchboard operator telephone service they may need a direct line to the public exchange when they see clients outside the usual working hours of the switchboard.
- installing an alarm or 'panic button'; which may be particularly useful if there is a high level of risk to the counsellor.
- letting someone know in advance a specific time when the counsellor will contact them and giving them instructions about what to do if the counsellor fails to make contact.

These strategies may not prevent an assault but they increase the possibility of obtaining assistance.

A sense of personal safety is important if the counsellor is to feel secure enough to work creatively with clients. Sometimes counsellors experience a sense of danger without any attack actually occurring. These feelings ought to be taken seriously and discussed in supervision. The sense of threat may arise from real danger, or a counsellor picking up a client's sense of threat to himself, or the re-stimulation of something from the counsellor's past. Whatever the cause of the sense of danger, there is no ethical requirement that the counsellor should continue to see clients who evoke such feelings. The counsellor may refer the client to another counsellor if taking reasonable steps to promote safety is insufficient to reduce the sense of danger to acceptable levels.

Clients who harass counsellors outside the counselling relationship

It is extremely rare for counsellors to be harassed by clients making nuisance phone calls, sending frequent unsolicited correspondence or making unwelcome visits to the counsellor's home. To the best of my knowledge the Standards and Ethics Sub-committee has only been contacted about two situations of this kind over the last seven years. Despite the infrequency of such incidents, they are potentially extremely distressing for the counsellor when they occur. The distress is compounded by the ethical constraints of confidentiality. Although the *Code of Practice* does not explicitly consider this kind of situation, a number of strategies consistent with the ethics of counselling have been identified. These are:

- Counselling-supervision is important in providing emotional support for the counsellor as well as reviewing potential courses of action.
- Medical and legal opinion may be sought about the client at an early stage. Providing the client's identity is not communicated, there is no significant breach of confidentiality. These consultations should take place with people who are unlikely to know the client.
- If the client is making public statements which are untrue and to the detriment of the counsellor, it may be appropriate to write to the client by recorded delivery in the following terms: (a) any repetition of the statements by the client will be taken as an indication that the client regards the issue as a matter for public debate and no longer requires confidentiality over this issue, and that should this occur (b) the counsellor will feel entitled to put her side of the story to those directly involved, and (c) the counsellor may contact solicitors, police, doctors etc. as appropriate.
- If the client persists after receiving a letter from the counsellor, then it is appropriate to consult with doctors who may be treating the client, solicitors about any action they may take on the counsellor's behalf and/or the police.
- Events which happen outside the counselling relationship or

after the counselling relationship has ended need not be treated as confidential.

One of the situations brought to the attention of the Standards and Ethics Sub-committee was resolved by the combination of a solicitor's letter and a refusal by the counsellor to enter into any further communications. All subsequent telephone calls and letters were ignored and eventually they stopped. At the time of writing these strategies have failed to resolve the other situation.

These actions would be reserved for extreme situations. Counsellors do have to accept that from time to time clients misrepresent what has happened within counselling. This most often happens when the counsellor is seeing one partner about difficulties in a relationship. Sometimes clients will attribute to the counsellor things which they are afraid to say for themselves. For example, 'My counsellor says we should separate.' I have known students tell their parents that their counsellor says they should give up their course when this has not been said by the counsellor. These situations are clearly potentially difficult, especially if the counsellor is approached by the partner or parent directly. Nonetheless, it is important that the counsellor maintains confidentiality by neither admitting nor denying what has happened in the counselling. Such incidents are on quite a different scale from a situation where the client is seeking out the counsellor's colleagues or friends, or is persistently phoning late at night, or sending letters in disguised handwriting to ensure they are opened by the counsellor.

Other counsellors

Undermining public confidence in counselling

Counselling is only possible in a relationship of trust. The public reputation of counselling can create circumstances in which it is easier or harder to establish trusting relationships. Therefore the *Code of Practice* requires:

> B.2.4.1 Counsellors should not conduct themselves in their counselling-related activities in ways which undermine public confidence in either their role as a counsellor or in the work of other counsellors.

The requirement to avoid undermining public confidence in counselling is restricted to when counsellors are engaging in 'counselling-related activities'. Exactly what this means in practice will depend on consideration of the specific circumstances. Some of the following principles have been applied in the past. 'Counselling-related activities' include circumstances when someone is:

(a) providing counselling or in a role closely associated with counselling, such as training others in counselling or counselling skills, providing supervision etc.; or

(b) explicitly using the role of counsellor as a means of establishing personal credibility and then betraying that trust to commit a crime such as fraud, assault etc. or to exploit a client; or

(c) acting unprofessionally whilst in the occupational role of counsellor, that is, employed in a post formally identified as 'counsellor'.

The seriousness of what has occurred is also relevant in deciding whether public confidence in counselling is undermined. In my opinion, a fairly robust view has to be taken. For instance, two counsellors engaged in a heated public debate would not fall into this category unless either party became personally abusive and defamed the other or violence resulted.

Whether a counsellor can bring counselling into disrepute by activities unrelated to counselling has not been discussed. For example, if someone who works as a voluntary counsellor in his own time is convicted of fraud at his place of work, would this amount to bringing counselling into disrepute?

Suspicion of misconduct by a counsellor

The *Code* places a duty on counsellors to monitor each other's standards of practice and if appropriate to use the Complaints Procedure:

> B.2.4.2.   If a counsellor suspects misconduct by another counsellor which cannot be resolved or remedied after discussion with the counsellor concerned, they should implement the Complaints Procedure, doing so without breaches of confidentiality other than those necessary for investigating the complaint.

Because BAC can only be responsible for its own membership and not for counsellors who belong to other associations or none at all, it is only possible to use the Complaints Procedure to address issues about misconduct by members of BAC. Other organizations like the British Psychological Society and the Association of Humanistic Psychology Practitioners have their own complaints procedures.

The circumstances in which the counsellor learns of the misconduct by another counsellor need to be taken into account in deciding how to respond. This is considered further in Chapter 8.

Colleagues and members of the caring professions

Accountability to others

Counsellors working on their own in private practice are free of the need to be accountable to anyone other than their client and their counselling-supervisor. However, counselling is provided within organizations involving others. In these circumstances the *Code* requires that:

> B.2.5.1 Counsellors should be accountable for their services to colleagues, employees and funding bodies as appropriate. The means of achieving this should be consistent with respecting the needs of the client outlined in B.2.2.7 [privacy], B.2.2.13 [avoiding conflicts of interests] and B.4 [confidentiality].

There have been situations in which it has seemed that counsellors have wanted to use confidentiality as a shield to protect them from appropriate accountability to colleagues. This provision is clearly stating that this is not acceptable and that counsellors ought to be prepared to be accountable for the time and any other resources used during the provision of counselling. However, the methods used in being accountable should be consistent with the ethics and standards of practice of counselling. What this means in practice is considered in detail in Chapter 13.

The counsellor's responsibility to increase colleagues' understanding

Counsellors report that the voluntary nature of counselling and the need for confidentiality are the two aspects of counselling which most frequently give rise to misunderstandings. It takes positive action by counsellors working in organizations to develop appropriate expectations of counselling.

Sometimes clients and colleagues have inappropriate expectations of the counsellor's role. The *Code for Counsellors* requires that counsellors ought to challenge such inappropriate expectations, particularly if someone making a referral is expecting a service which is not available from the counsellor but could be made available elsewhere. For example, a tutor may refer a young person with an eating disorder for counselling and assume that the counsellor will also monitor the client's weight and general health. These are inappropriate expectations. The weighing of the client and health checks would need to be provided by someone with medical or nursing qualifications. Therefore the *Code for Counsellors* states,

> B.2.5.2   Counsellors are encouraged to increase their colleagues' understanding of the counselling role. No colleague or significant member of the caring professions should be led to believe that a service is being offered by the counsellor which is not, as this may deprive the client of the offer of such a service from elsewhere.

Resolving conflicts of interest

In Chapter 9 on confidentiality, a recurring theme was the importance of counsellors based in organizations negotiating policies over confidentiality with their employers and with the possible assistance of representatives of the counselling service. Working with an agreed policy considerably reduces the possibility of conflicts of interest arising.

Other conflicts of interest can arise because of personal relationships. For example, a counsellor could experience serious conflicts of interest if she counsels the wife of a colleague about her difficulties with her husband. Conflicts of interest may arise because of policy decisions made in the agency. Some agencies find it necessary to ration the number of sessions available to clients and counsellors are required to work within limits which may not be appropriate to all clients. If the number of sessions available are unlikely to meet the client's needs then the counsellor may decide to inform the client of this or to attempt to negotiate a more flexible policy. It is impossible to anticipate all the potential conflicts of interest which can arise but the *Code for Counsellors* states:

> B.2.5.3   Counsellors should accept their part in exploring and resolving conflicts of interest between themselves, and their agencies, especially where this has implications for the client. (1992)

The wider community

Responsibilities to the wider community are sometimes defined in law. One recurrent issue which concerns counsellors is what to do if a client talks about committing or having committed serious crimes. For example:

> Sheila talks about her distress at being involved in a robbery in which someone was injured. She also mentions plans for another robbery in a week's time. What should the counsellor do?

Does the counsellor have a duty to report the crime that has been committed? There is no general duty in criminal law to report to the police or anyone else that a client has committed a crime. One exception exists with regard to a criminal law duty to report any information which would assist with the prevention or detection of acts of terrorism connected with Northern Ireland.

Alternatively, a counsellor may have a contractual duty to report a crime, arising, for example, from the counsellor's contract of employment. This would not make failure to report a criminal offence but disciplinary action or dismissal could result as part of civil proceedings for breach of contract.

There is no general duty to answer police questions about a client. A polite but clear refusal to answer is all that is required. However, to give false or misleading answers can amount to the offence of wasting police time or obstructing a police officer in the execution of his duty.

Does the counsellor have a duty to prevent crime? There is no duty under criminal law to prevent someone committing a crime outside the counselling room (with the exception of the prevention of terrorist offences connected with the affairs of Northern Ireland).

If the crime is being committed within the counselling session then the legal position is rather different. A counsellor who failed to prevent or take reasonable steps to prevent an offence in the counsellor's presence may have committed the offences of aiding and abetting, or 'counselling' (in the criminal law sense of being an accomplice to a crime). This would only arise if the counsellor's inactivity amounted to a positive encouragement. The circumstances in which a counsellor could be charged with these offences are most likely to happen when a client assaults another, uses illegal drugs or attempts suicide in the presence of the counsellor.

There is a right, but not a duty, to use such force as is reasonable in the circumstances to prevent crime. Some crimes are not serious enough to justify the use of force. Illegal drug using may come into this category. The use of more force than is reasonable is in itself a crime. Therefore the use of physical restraint to stop someone hitting someone else is usually reasonable, but the use of a weapon would not be. Because suicide is no longer a crime, there is no general right to use reasonable force to prevent suicide attempts or suicide (see Chapter 6 for further discussion of this issue).

Could the counsellor inadvertently incur liability for a client's acts? The answer is 'yes'. Kenneth Cohen offers an example of how a counsellor could commit the criminal offence of incitement.

... suppose the counsellor honestly but mistakenly believes that it is not illegal for his 18-year-old male client to engage in sexual intercourse in private with another consenting adult in private over the age of 18, and encourages and supports his client in sexual experimentation of this nature as part of his 'homework' assignment. (1992)

It is not necessary for the counsellor to know that the activity is an offence for the counsellor to be guilty of incitement. (The age of consent for homosexual acts between men is 21 years old.) The counsellor may not want his client to break the law. But if the law has been broken, the offence has been committed, although the counsellor's mistake about the law and lack of deliberate intention to incite an offence would be taken into account in sentencing. It is therefore wise to be cautious when setting the client tasks between sessions, a technique frequently used in behavioural methods of counselling. Windy Dryden cautions, 'Whatever behavioural assignment you negotiate with your client, ensure it is both legal and ethical' (1990).

A counsellor can also incur civil liability for inciting or encouraging a client to break a contract with a third party. For example, a counsellor encourages his client to change jobs without giving the contracted amount of notice to the first employer or to stop supplying goods which the client has contracted to provide. If the client carries out the act which has been encouraged, the counsellor may become jointly liable for any resulting loss to a third party. It is also possible that the counsellor could be jointly liable for a client's breach of confidence that has been incited by the counsellor.

Although I am not aware of any counsellor being prosecuted or sued for incitement of a client's wrongdoing, this is a theoretical possibility. At a workshop, Kenneth Cohen cautioned counsellors to be careful when using empathic responses with a client who is intending to commit an unlawful act. The counsellor has to choose between being empathic, which the client often interprets as encouragement, and the possibility, albeit a remote one, of incurring legal liabilities as a consequence of the client's subsequent acts.

So far I have concentrated on the counsellor's legal responsibilities to the wider community and the potential consequences of these. However, ethical dilemmas which do not necessarily involve the law can also arise. For example,

Edward uses counselling to ease his guilt about deceiving his partner about his frequent sexual relationships with other people. Sheila, the counsellor, feels increasingly concerned on behalf of his wife.

The ethics of respecting the client's autonomy and confidentiality would prevent the counsellor from communicating her concern to the wife directly. But what if Edward has a life-threatening illness with which he could infect his wife? This makes the ethical dilemma much more acute. This has arisen in HIV/AIDS counselling. The general practice has been to respect the client's control over confidential information but to work in ways which make it easier for him to tell his wife, including the offer to be present when he tells his wife. Occasionally, counsellors have told partners with the client's consent or at the client's request. Alternatively clients have, often of their own volition, chosen to abstain from doing anything which would put their partner at risk of infection until they feel able to tell them about their health problem. Some clients prefer to abstain from sex or other activities which would put their partner at risk for the rest of their lives rather than tell a partner. But what if the client deliberately and recklessly continues to put a partner at risk of infection? This would appear to be a situation in which, after consultation with the client and other experienced counsellors, the counsellor might decide it is defensible to break confidentiality to warn the partner (see Chapter 9). The seriousness of the situation for everyone involved means that the counsellor would need to be sure that there was no alternative possible course of action (see Chapter 14).

Conclusion

The management of conflicting responsibilities is particularly challenging for a counsellor. Whenever possible, it is better to anticipate what these might be and to find ways of avoiding them in advance. If the conflict of responsibilities cannot be avoided then it is important that the client knows of this so that either the contract between the counsellor and client can take them into account or the client can seek counselling elsewhere. These situations are much easier to handle prospectively rather than retrospectively.

One of the best ways to be forewarned of potential conflicts of responsibility is to discuss situations with an experienced counsellor working in a similar situation. This is one of the important functions of counselling-supervision.

11 Counselling-supervision

The emphasis on on-going and regular supervision for as long as the counsellor is providing counselling has become paramount in the British tradition. The *Code for Counsellors* (BAC, 1992a) is unequivocal.

> B.3.1 It is a breach of the ethical requirement for counsellors to practise without regular counselling supervision/consultative support.

The *Code* uses the term 'consultative support' as an alternative to 'counselling supervision'. At the time the *Code* was being written, 'consultative support' was gaining some popularity as a means of emphasizing the importance of the independence of the supervisor, i.e. consultant, and that the relationship is intended to be supportive rather than exclusively concerned with standards and accountability. The attraction of this alternative terminology rests on the avoidance of confusion which can arise from the term 'supervision'. In everyday usage, 'supervision' usually refers to the overseeing or superintending of someone's work, the emphasis being on the worker's accountability. There is therefore considerable potential for the term 'supervision' to be confused with managerial oversight. This is discussed later. My impression is that the use of the term 'consultative support' is now falling out of fashion because although it avoids confusion arising from the use of 'supervision', it too generates potential confusion over the term 'consultant', which to many people is associated with expertise and status rather than independence. The emphasis on 'support' misrepresents the range of tasks that are involved in this activity, of which support is only one. Therefore, there is still the need to find an adequate term for what counsellors refer to as 'counselling supervision'. Throughout the text in this book I have hyphenated 'counselling-supervision' to indicate the two words are closely linked and describe a single activity.

What is counselling-supervision?

The *Code for Counsellors* states:

> B.3.2 Counselling supervision/consultative support refers to a formal arrangement which enables counsellors to discuss their counselling regularly with one or more people who have an understanding of

counselling and counselling supervision/consultative support. Its purpose is to ensure the efficacy of the counsellor/client relationship. It is a confidential relationship.

As with counselling, there are different models for providing counselling-supervision which are associated with different schools of thought about counselling. It is therefore advisable for trainees and counsellors who are relatively inexperienced to seek counselling-supervision from someone who uses the same theoretical orientation in supervision that they use in counselling. Once someone is experienced in a particular model of counselling it can be stimulating to be supervised by someone with a different approach.

Further reading about different approaches to counselling-supervision

Anyone interested in learning more about the different approaches to counselling-supervision is likely to find the following writers useful. John Foskett and David Lyall (1988) describe a psychodynamic approach to supervision of people providing pastoral care. Gaie Houston (1990) writes from a humanistic tradition rooted in gestalt therapy. Robin Shohet and Joan Wilmot (1991) also write from a humanistic perspective. Dave Mearns (1991) gives a person-centred view of the experience of being a supervisor. Peter Hawkins and Robin Shohet (1989) provide an overview of supervision in the helping professions but because their work is based substantially on the supervision of social workers, it does not make the distinction between line-management supervision and independent counselling-supervision that is considered so important in counselling. Nonetheless it is useful for its process model of supervision. A useful training package combining introductory pamphlets and audio tapes on the skills for supervising and being supervised has been produced by Francesca Inskipp and Brigid Proctor (1989). It is closely related to a skills model of counselling and the work of Gerard Egan. I have found their classification of the tasks involved in counselling-supervision particularly helpful.

Why is counselling-supervision considered so essential?

1 Supervision provides a system of personal support for the counsellor. The need for supervision is emphasized in BAC's information sheet on supervision.

  By its very nature, counselling makes considerable demands upon the counsellor. Supervision helps to overcome some of the difficulties this creates. A counsellor can become over-involved, or ignore some important point, or may be confused as to what is happening with a particular client. He may have undermining doubts about his own usefulness. (BAC, 1992a)

Working with the distress and difficulties of others can affect the counsellor. For example a counsellor may seek to avoid areas which are personally painful to herself but in doing so may be frustrating any healing for the client. Peter Hawkins and Robin Shohet observed in *Supervision and the Helping Professions* 'A good supervisory relationship is the best way we know to ensure we stay open to ourselves and to our clients' (1989).

2   Providing systematic supervision and support within the usual working practice of counsellors helps to protect confidentiality. It reduces the risk of counsellors feeling the need to disclose information inappropriately in order to obtain personal support.
3   Counselling is a complex process. It is difficult to be as personally involved in a relationship as counselling requires, and at the same time to maintain a degree of objectivity. Supervision helps a counsellor to maintain both perspectives. In addition, the independence of the supervisor may enable other things to be detected of which the counsellor was previously unaware.
4   Development of the counsellor is helped by supervision. It provides an important forum for further learning.
5   An independent supervisor can draw the counsellor's attention to ethical issues and standards of practice which may have been overlooked.

The duration of counselling-supervision

In most parts of America and Europe supervision is only required during training and for a subsequent probationary period. Thereafter it is optional for the counsellor. What are the reasons for a different approach being adopted in Britain?

1   The counsellor continues to develop and change throughout her lifetime. This means an important part of the counselling relationship is continually changing and therefore needs regular review.
2   The knowledge and methods which contribute to counselling are not static. They are continually evolving through the

interaction of practitioners using different models, research and accumulated experience. This means the counsellors do not stop learning. Supervision provides regular stimulation to further learning, as well as a forum in which learning can take place.

3 Experienced and trained counsellors report that supervision continues to be useful long after training and any probationary period. The way supervision is provided may change as the counsellor's needs change. A novice counsellor may want the counselling-supervisor to provide more structure and input into the supervision than a more experienced counsellor who is more likely to structure the session for himself and want to be facilitated rather than directed.

At international conferences I am aware of a growing interest in the British use of counselling-supervision with the result that some counsellors in Europe and the United States are now seeking on-going supervision for themselves and reconsidering whether it ought to be obligatory.

The independence of the supervisor

It is established practice that the supervisor should be sufficiently independent of the counsellor to be able to create a safe forum in which matters discussed in supervision do not spill over into the counsellor's daily life. Supervision often raises issues of trust and safety for counsellors which parallel their own clients' experiences of counselling. Issues of confidentiality and privacy can be extremely important if the counsellor is to feel able to express personal vulnerability and anxieties or voice any negative feelings about the experience of providing counselling. Usually sounding off only forms a small part of counselling-supervision but it can be an important ingredient in the process of opening up situations in which the counsellor feels blocked or de-skilled in her work with her clients. Therefore it is important that the supervisor does not have other significant roles in her life. It follows that the supervisor ought not to be a sexual partner, a close friend, a business partner, or someone with whom the counsellor has frequent contact outside the counselling supervision.

Supervision and accountability to management
Confusion between counselling-supervision and accountability to management has been a constant difficulty in establishing standards of practice and communicating what counsellors mean by counselling-supervision. In the context of work and professional

standards, 'supervision' is usually taken to imply overseeing or superintending by someone who has authority over the worker. The requirement that the counselling-supervisor should be independent of the counsellor clearly makes this an inappropriate model for the supervision of counsellors.

Counsellors working in organizations with a line-management structure are particularly aware of the difficulties of establishing appropriate means of being accountable to both a manager and a counselling-supervisor. For example, social workers and youth workers are usually expected to receive supervision from their team leader. This method of providing supervision conforms to the standards of practice recommended by Peter Hawkins and Robin Shohet (1989), which integrates educative, supportive and managerial roles. However, there are distinct limitations to this approach for the counsellors. During my recent consultations with HIV counsellors working in statutory and voluntary agencies, counsellors reported difficulties arising from an expectation that they should receive supervision from line-managers. Sometimes these difficulties arose from a concern that the manager may be less experienced and/or trained in counselling than the counsellor herself. Alternatively, there may be a poor relationship between the counsellor and manager. However, even when these difficulties were not present, it was still felt that a line-manager was inappropriate to act as a sole counselling-supervisor. One participant expressed a view which was representative of many comments.

> I have the greatest respect for my manager. She is a very positive influence on my work. But there are things I can't raise with her because they are too personal, or I need to be clearer in my own mind before I voice them. This is no reflection on her as a person. It is because of our different roles in relation to each other. (Bond, 1991b)

This view is widely held by counsellors working in other settings, and is so well established that it has been adopted by BAC. The *Code of Practice for Counsellors* states:

> B.3.3   Counsellors who have line-managers owe them appropriate managerial accountability for their work. The counselling-supervisor role should be independent of the line-manager role.

This envisages that a clear distinction between issues of accountability to the agency and issues relating to work with the client will be maintained. It is anticipated that the separation of roles in this way will be the usual practice. However, as counselling is developing, counsellors themselves are being appointed to management roles and there are circumstances when the line-manager also has considerable experience of counselling and could play a constructive role in counselling-supervision. Nonetheless it is considered undesirable that the line-manager should be the exclusive source of supervision. The *Code* states: 'However, where the counselling-supervisor is also the line-manager, the counsellor should also have access to independent consultative support' (B.3.3). The requirement that counsellor-supervision should be given by someone who is independent is potentially problematic unless the boundaries between management-supervision and counselling-supervision are clearly negotiated and understood by everyone involved.

Division and balance of supervisory tasks

There are three broad themes requiring consideration of supervision within an agency. These are:

- accountability to the agency
- issues arising from the work with the client
- personal support for the counsellor.

The first theme could be the subject for discussion within managerial supervision. Similarly the last would be primarily a subject for independent counselling-supervision. The extent to which issues arising from work with the client ought to be subject to managerial supervision will depend on several variables. These include the role of the agency, the experience and/or training of the manager, and the terms on which counselling is offered to the client. For example, employee counsellors have to be extremely careful in their methods of accountability to management because the management will be the managers of both the counsellor and the employees. In these circumstances it is of greater importance that the issues arising from work with clients are discussed independently of any management-supervision. On the other hand a free-standing counselling service offered to the general community which is managed by counsellors could be more flexible in division of line-management-supervision and counselling-supervision. Nonetheless many counsellors believe it is still important to maintain a distinction between line-management accountability and independent counselling-supervision. No matter how experienced the line-manager is as a counsellor or approachable as a person, it is impossible for her to escape the inhibiting effect of her power as a manager. Good management of the supervisor's responsibilities split between the supervisee and the organization can minimize the effects of the supervisor's power within the organization on the supervisory process but it cannot eliminate them. Neither supervisee nor manager can ignore the fact that the manager also has responsibilities to provide references, make recommendations for advancement or to institute disciplinary proceedings. This inevitably circumscribes what counsellors feel able to present in supervision. It is therefore important that the counsellor also has access to supervision which is independent of the manager. However, the way the supervisory tasks are divided between a line-manager and independent counselling-supervisor might be quite different from a counsellor working in an agency where the line-management has little or no knowledge of counselling.

In my study of HIV counselling (Bond, 1991b) I suggested a framework for negotiating a division of tasks between counselling-supervision and management (Figure 11.1). This framework is adapted from the division of tasks developed by Francesca Inskipp and Brigid Proctor (1989). With some minor revisions to accommodate feedback, this framework appears applicable to counsellors working with clients in a wide variety of different circumstances. Counsellors working on their own in private practice are fortunate in not having the problems posed by a dual accountability to an agency through a line-manager and an independent counselling-supervisor. All these tasks would be undertaken by the single supervisor.

Each of the tasks has its specific function. The formative is about developing new skills. The normative is about maintaining standards. The restorative is an opportunity to receive personal support. The perspective is about stepping back and looking at the pattern of the counsellor's work and relationship with other counsellors and the providers of the other services.

It is important that a balance between the tasks is maintained so that no single one comes to predominate to the exclusion of the others. For example, if the teaching component of the formative task were to predominate, supervision would quickly become training. Too much emphasis on the restorative task could turn supervision into personal counselling. If the normative function predominates, supervision might become a seminar in ethics. If the search for perspective predominates, the counselling-supervision could be subverted into organizational analysis. None of these outcomes are considered desirable in counselling-supervision. The objective is to move from one to another. A psychodynamic approach to counselling-supervision emphasizes that it is a process designed to develop the counsellor's own 'inner supervisor'. This 'inner supervisor' needs to be an all-rounder.

Background of counselling-supervisor

It is important that the supervisor is trained and experienced in

Task	Description	Undertaken by	
		Line-Manager	Counselling Supervisor/ Consultative Support
Formative	Skill development Reflection on experience New understanding New knowledge about counselling process, client group, specific issues raised by client		
Normative	Counselling: Standards; ethics and practice Agency: Standards; ethics and practice Monitoring the quality of counselling Consideration of feedback from client		
Restorative	Dealing with personal issues and stress arising from counselling Validating achievements		
Perspective	Overview of total counselling work Relationship between counselling and other methods of clients obtaining help Relationships with counsellors and with members of other professions		

Figure 11.1 *Division of tasks between counselling-supervision and management*

counselling. Increasingly supervisors will have received training in supervision as well, as courses are becoming more widely available. BAC has also recently started a scheme for the accreditation of counselling-supervisors. At the moment only a relatively small number of people hold this accreditation but it is conceivable in the medium term there will be substantial numbers of accredited counselling-supervisors spread throughout the country.

Some counsellors working in parts of the country where counselling generally is less developed and training courses are not readily accessible report they have difficulty in finding supervisors who are both trained and experienced in counselling. In these circumstances it is better to receive supervision from someone who is trained in a closely related role and who is informed about counselling than not to receive any counselling-supervision. Alternatively, counselling-supervision may be provided within peer groups, although this is not generally thought to be desirable for newly trained counsellors as they would benefit more from supervision by someone who is more experienced than themselves. On the other hand peer supervision for experienced counsellors can be extremely effective.

Frequency of supervision

The *Code for Counsellors* states:

> B.3.4 The volume of supervision should be in proportion to the volume of counselling work undertaken and the experience of the counsellor.

It is easier to state the principle that the amount of time spent in supervision should be in proportion to the time spent counselling than it is to indicate what this means in practice. It has been an important issue in determining the accreditation of counselling practitioners.

The current minimum requirement for counselling-supervision in order to be accredited by BAC as a counsellor is one and a half hours per month. For people receiving group supervision, the total group time divided by the number of participants should equal one and a half hours or more, in other words a group of three would need to meet for four and a half hours monthly for each participant to be considered to have had one and a half hours' supervision. Any supervision provided by a line-manager would not be counted towards the required time. Only independent counselling-supervision can be counted.

The criteria for accreditation by the Association for Student Counselling (ASC) are similar. ASC requires that 'consultations should take place preferably once a fortnight and should be an integral part of the counsellor's professional work'. No further guidance is given about frequency and duration for one-to-one counselling-supervision. However, more detailed guidelines are offered for group supervision:

> Group supervision for counsellors should be weekly for at least one and a half hours and preferably in a group of no more than four, so that each counsellor can present casework once a fortnight. Each applicant

should describe in detail the organisation and structure of the group supervision process and should also include the number in the group, frequency of presentation, etc. (ASC, 1992)

As someone who has received both individual and group supervision, I wonder whether the fixed ratio between individual and group supervision adopted by both BAC and ASC is really appropriate. It seems the current formulae are based on the assumption that supervisory tasks are only taking place when someone is presenting a case. It makes no allowance for the learning and stimulation of observing others work in supervision. My experience is that in the group setting I learn a great deal from the presentation of cases by others. There have been memorable occasions when I have become aware of issues that would never have occurred to me unless someone else had raised them. I doubt that some of these issues would have been raised in my own presentations because I would not have recognized them as issues. In comparison, the process of getting access to previously unrecognized problems in one-to-one supervision is often slower. My personal view is that a truer representation of the ratio of time between one-to-one and group supervision is 3:2. In other words one and a half hours in one-to-one supervision is the equivalent of one hour in a group, and a group of three would meet for two hours in order to have the equivalent of one hour's individual supervision each. This is on the assumption that the available time is divided evenly between the participants. However, this is a personal opinion based on my own experience and not the policy currently being implemented by BAC or ASC.

Confidentiality and supervision

The *Code* states:

> B.3.5 Whenever possible, the discussion of cases within supervision/consultative support should take place without revealing the personal identity of the clients.

The reasons for this requirement are both ethical and legal. There is no practical need to reveal the client's identity during supervision as the subject matter of supervision is almost invariably concerned with the counselling process rather than the identity of the client. Indeed in the interests of confidentiality it is better to avoid disclosure. Legally, unless the client has consented to being discussed in supervision, then any discussions at all are a technical breach of confidentiality. However, Kenneth Cohen (1992) speculates that this may be defensible as being in the public interest to promote the quality of the counselling provided that discussions are anonymous. Maintaining the anonymity of clients during supervision therefore constitutes the baseline of acceptable practice. However, despite taking considerable care to ensure the anonymity of clients, it is always possible that the supervisor may recognize someone with whom she is already acquainted. This prior relationship may be unknown to the counsellor. Therefore good practice suggests that counsellors ought to inform clients about their supervision arrangements including the identity of their supervisor and negotiate how the counselling should be presented in terms of protecting or revealing the client's identity.

Conclusion

The ethics and practice of supervision parallel those of counselling in their scope. This chapter has been primarily concerned with issues which are mentioned within the *Code for Counsellors*. A much fuller explanation of the ethics and practice of the supervision of counsellors is contained in the *Code of Ethics and Practice for the Supervision of Counsellors* (BAC, 1988).

In the last resort, much of the value of counselling-supervision depends on counsellors' willingness to present their own work as truthfully as they can and without omitting the ethical and personal dilemmas they experience. The supervisor cannot observe the counselling directly and therefore must work with the supervisee's account of her own work. Brigid Proctor, writing as a supervisor, highlights the importance of the supervisee's openness.

> . . . it is a fantasy that as supervisor I can gain access by demand to what is essentially a private relationship between counsellor and client, or worker and group. In reality, the work people do with other people is predominantly 'unsupervised'. What someone brings to supervision is selective and subject to 'presentation'. What is watched or heard direct (or on video or audio tape) is always partial and influenced by the watching or hearing. I can encourage my supervisee to give me more appropriate access to her practice. I cannot control the courage, honesty, good will or perception which determine the presentation (or performance) she chooses to offer me. (1988)

12 Record-keeping

Issues around the keeping of written records by counsellors about their work with clients are becoming increasingly important. However, there is such a diversity of views held by counsellors that it is difficult to determine what constitutes good practice. At the time the code was written no clear agreement was possible about whether records ought to be kept. The *Code for Counsellors* (BAC, 1992a) avoids this particular issue by making the keeping of records optional, but if records are kept then certain safeguards are required.

> B.2.2.14 If records of counselling sessions are kept, clients should be made aware of this. At the client's request information should be given about access to these records, their availability to other people, and the degree of security with which they are kept (see B.4 [about confidentiality]).

Although this is as far as it is possible to go in making a statement about record-keeping within the *Code of Practice*, there are a number of issues associated with record-keeping which require further consideration.

Is it desirable to keep records?

The arguments in favour of record-keeping include the following:

(a) The process of writing records involves the counsellor in organizing her own thoughts and feelings. This process is in itself helpful to the counselling because it enables the counsellor to reflect systematically on what has occurred and plan for future sessions. In other words, the process of making records enhances the quality of the counselling.

(b) Records provide counsellors with an *aide mémoire* for incidental details such as the names of the people mentioned by the client and therefore leaves the counsellor free to concentrate on issues raised by the client rather than recalling the detail from one session to another.

(c) Systematic record-keeping makes any changes in the client's material over a series of sessions more apparent. The process of recall by memory inevitably involves a degree of 'rewriting' the past in terms of a perspective rooted in the present. Therefore, written records produced contemporaneously with the counselling make any changes that have occurred during the counselling more visible. This provides valuable information to the counsellor, who may choose to share this knowledge with the client when it is appropriate.

(d) Systematic record-keeping provides evidence of the degree of care taken by the counsellor in her work, which may be useful if the client makes a complaint against the counsellor to a professional body or starts any legal action against the counsellor. In the more litigious culture of the United States, it may not be surprising that Kenneth Austin has expressed the view that counsellors

> need to be aware of how your record-keeping procedures can determine the outcome of a legal case brought against you. Although such a case is unlikely to be due to inadequate record-keeping, such practice could negatively affect the outcome of your case. Some students and therapists view it as unwise to keep detailed records about their clients. However, should you be involved in a lawsuit, you are likely to be deemed as behaving unprofessionally if you have not kept adequate records. (Austin et al., 1990)

Within the UK, Kenneth Cohen has made similar observations about the desirability of record-keeping.

> From a legal point of view, they [records] could be a valuable way for a counsellor to support his version of what took place in the session if any dispute about this should arise. In particular, such notes might be valuable evidence that he had indeed discharged his duty of care towards the client. Nevertheless, it is interesting to note that the BAC *Code of Ethics and Practice for Counsellors* (1990) does not require counsellors to keep records. So, applying the rule in *Bolam* v. *Friern Hospital Management Committee*, failure to keep records might not in itself be a breach of a counsellor's legal duty of care to the client, but the context in which the counselling took place could displace this presumption. (Cohen, 1992)

A corollary of Cohen's view is that should BAC decide that record-keeping is a requirement of good practice, this will create a potential legal liability for counsellors who do not keep records.

The arguments most frequently offered against record-keeping are:

(a) There can be problems in ensuring records are both secure and really confidential. For example, some counsellors may work in situations where they cannot ensure that colleagues will honour agreements with the client about who has access to records. Also, some clients may work in circumstances where burglaries are so frequent that it is difficult to maintain secure records.

(b) Record-keeping may complicate trust-building with clients. For example, counsellors working with clients who are vulnerable to legal prosecution, such as prostitutes, illicit drug-users and others, may have to take account of their clients' fears that any records could be seized by the police or other authorities.

(c) Record-keeping is time-consuming.

(d) Some counsellors have reservations about producing records which may be demanded by clients for use outside the counselling relationship in legal actions against others (see later).

(e) In some circumstances, clients have a legal right to see records kept by their counsellor. Some counsellors, therefore, prefer not to keep records in order to prevent this eventuality (see later).

It is clear from this summary of the case for and against the keeping of records that the arguments are, on balance, in favour of record-keeping by counsellors as a general standard of good practice. However, keeping records is not yet required by BAC for an adequate level of practice and in some circumstances there may be good reasons for being cautious about keeping any records.

Security of records

The *Code for Counsellors* merely requires that clients are informed about the degree of security with which any records are kept. This sets a baseline for acceptable practice which increases the client's control of the situation by giving him information which he may wish to take into account when deciding what to disclose to the counsellor. However, the optimum level of good practice suggests that records should be kept with sufficient security to prevent them becoming known to people other than those authorized by the client. Counsellors who have taken this into account have adopted different kinds of procedures according to their circumstances.

The first line of defence against unauthorized disclosure is the physical security of the records. This would normally match the anticipated risks to the records. Locking records in a desk or filing cabinet will prevent casual inspection by anyone with access to the room in which they are kept but this is inadequate against someone willing to force an entry as most desks and filing cabinets are easily broken into. In circumstances where forced entry is reasonably foreseeable, it may be more appropriate to keep the records in a safe.

In addition to the physical security of the records, or sometimes as an alternative to it, some counsellors have adopted systems which ensure the anonymity of records. Four methods are frequently used.

1 Some counsellors use codes exclusive to them in the form of numbers, fictitious initials, or fictitious names to identify records and systematically avoid including information within the records which identify clients. This may be practical with small numbers of records but is usually impractical with larger quantities.

2 An alternative method is to keep a split system of record-keeping. For example, the personally identifiable information, such as name, address, contact numbers, names of significant others mentioned by the client, are kept on small file cards which can be readily taken away by the counsellor from where the lengthier records of sessions and other documents may be kept. As each of these cards is numbered or coded and this is the only identification on the records, someone needs access to both the card and the record to obtain significant information about the counselling. The cards on their own only indicate who is receiving counselling but not the issues raised in the counselling. The records on their own merely contain the contents of the sessions but cannot easily be linked to identifiable people.

3 Some counsellors work in settings where they are expected to make entries on agency records which are available to all authorized personnel within the agency and may even be passed on to another agency if the client seeks their services subsequently. For example, counsellors in medical settings may be expected to make an entry on the patient's health record or, in social services, on the client's case file. The best practice in these circumstances usually involves the counsellor in negotiating an agreement with both the agency and their clients which enables them to make brief entries on the agency files and to keep separately more detailed records of the counselling process and any information which the client indicates is personally sensitive. These latter records would usually be treated as highly confidential and therefore access to them may be restricted to the counsellor and/or the client. They may, in

addition, be protected by a split record system or by being locked away from other staff. The minimum standard of practice is that clients should know who has access to their records.
4 Some counsellors may keep records on computer. Although the technology of computer records is different, the principles are much the same as for paper-based records.

Access to records

The question of who ought to have access to records is frequently raised with regard to four situations. The first relates to situations where the counsellor is working in an agency where the manager or employer is seeking access to client records, the second relates to the clients' access to their own records, the third to police access to files, and the fourth to the use of records in court. It is useful to consider each of these situations separately because the ethical issues and legal considerations are different.

Access by employers
The demand for access to records by an employer is only possible when there is an employer of the counsellor. Counsellors working on their own in private practice are therefore free from this particular concern. In some circumstances this may be an important factor in the client's choice of counsellor.

Counsellors who have not clarified their employers' access to records in advance of counselling and are working without a corresponding agreement with their clients about access are likely to find themselves caught between two principles which have both ethical and legal implications. The usual principle is that records made on materials provided by an employer or in the employer's time belong to that employer. However, the principles and law of confidentiality (see Chapter 9) suggest that there are restrictions on how the employer exercises that ownership. To break a confidence could create legal liabilities for the counsellor. Therefore, counsellors should be cautious about giving employers access to confidential information. In order to avoid conflicting responsibilities to the client and employer a prudent counsellor will have established clear guidelines which are known to both employer and client about who, other than the client, will have access to records of counselling.

Access by clients
In certain circumstances, clients have a statutory right of access to their records. The Data Protection Act 1984 entitles individuals to

be informed about records kept about them which are stored on computer. It also gives the person who is the subject of the data certain rights to inspect the records about himself or herself. The data holder should withhold from disclosure parts of the information from which another person could be identified, unless that person's consent is given. The law recognizes some exceptions to this right.

Recently clients' statutory rights of access to their own records have been expanded to include some forms of written records. Counsellors working within social services are required by the Access to Personal Files Act 1987 to give clients access to their own files. Parts of the files from which another person could be identified should be withheld unless that person's consent is given.

Similarly the Access to Health Records Act 1990 gives individuals right of access to health records made after 1 November 1991. The Act defines a health record as a record which:

> consists of information relating to the physical or mental health of an individual who can be identified from that information, or from that and other information in the possession of the holder of the record; and has been made by or on behalf of a health professional in connection with the care of that individual . . .

The definition of health professional includes registered medical practitioners, registered nurses, clinical psychologists, dentists, opticians, chiropodists, dietitians and different types of therapists. It is clear from the definition that the Act extends beyond work within the National Health Service and, for example, includes occupational health practitioners. It is less clear whether it includes counsellors who are not already included within the listed categories such as, for example, a counsellor who is also a registered nurse or clinical psychologist. In the absence of any legal precedents, BAC is advising counsellors to work on the basis that counsellors who contribute to medical records or make records within health settings should work on the assumption that the client may have access to these records. The Act contains a number of procedural requirements including that applications to see the records must be made in writing, the time limits within which access must be provided, and the circumstances in which a maximum fee (currently £10) may be charged. The Act specifically excludes the following:

- access to records after the patient's death where a note has been included in the file, at the patient's request, that access should not be given;
- access to any part of a record which would disclose information likely to cause serious harm to the patient or another;

• access to any part of a record which would disclose information relating to or provided by an individual who can be identified by that information (unless that individual has consented to the application or is a health professional involved in that patient's care);

• access to any record made before 1 November 1991.

If the patient disagrees with the record because it contains inaccurate information, that is, 'incorrect, misleading or incomplete', the record may be corrected or a note of the dispute may be entered in the record if the holder of the record does not accept that there is an inaccuracy. This Act applies to all the UK.

The provisions of this Act have been given in some detail because they indicate what may be good practice when clients request access to counselling records which are not included within a statutory right of access. In deciding whether to grant access, I would suggest that a number of considerations are useful. One of the guiding principles ought to be whether others, for example team members, have access to the records, albeit on a confidential basis. This would increase the grounds for giving the client access in order to check the accuracy of what is being communicated to others. On the other hand, if the records are merely the counsellor's personal working notes which are never seen by anyone else, they may remain more justifiably private. The timing of access may also be an important consideration. The counsellor may judge that access to records ought to be delayed to avoid disruption to the counselling. For example, notes about projections and transferences may be withheld until these have been worked through. Alternatively, the counsellor may hold the view that any access may damage the therapeutic process. Some counsellors within the psychodynamic tradition have expressed concern that any access to records may disrupt the client's transference and therefore destroy one of their major therapeutic methods.

Counsellors following a person-centred tradition may be concerned that their notes may be too revealing of their own feelings towards a client. If the records are not covered by a statutory right to access the counsellor has discretion in when and whether to give a client access to them.

The use of counsellors' records in court
What if one of your clients asks you to supply a report to help him in a legal action against someone else?

For example:

Michelle has given birth to a severely handicapped child and is bringing an action for medical negligence. You, as the counsellor, are asked to provide a report about your client's feelings towards the child. The lawyers acting for the medical staff seek access to the therapy notes you based your report upon.

This in broad terms was the situation which Stephen Jakobi and Duncan Pratt (1992), as lawyers acting for the Psychologist Protection Society, were asked to consider. In my experience counsellors are also sometimes asked to provide reports following motor accidents and in marital disputes.

Many counsellors are understandably reluctant to provide reports, appear as witnesses or supply case records on behalf of clients. To do so could be seen as a confusion of roles, with the counsellor being drawn into acting on behalf of a client rather than working towards the client acting autonomously. Counsellors may also feel that writing reports for courts is not part of their role and that they have not been trained in how to write them, in comparison to doctors and social workers who are usually more experienced in court work. So far as I can tell, there is no way a client can compel a counsellor to produce a report on his or her behalf. The choice is the counsellor's. However, if you refuse to provide a report, the client can compel you to appear as a witness and to bring documents, including case notes, by issuing a witness summons. A court may set aside the summons if it is considered that you have no relevant evidence to give or the summons is oppressive, fishing, or speculative. Alternatively, the client can make an application to the High Court, supported by an Affidavit, describing the documents and showing their relevance. The High Court may set strict conditions on the use of the documents. For example, their circulation may be restricted to legal advisers, medical or other professional advisers. These are two methods by which a client could force a counsellor into disclosing case notes if the counsellor refuses to write a report. On the other hand, agreeing to write a report would not necessarily prevent the case notes being required. As in the example, the opposing side can insist on seeing the records which informed the writing of the report. A judge may agree to having parts of the record withheld because they are not important or because of the degree of harm that might be done to a patient, for instance, in revealing intense feelings about parents who were unaware of them. You can ask for a judge's assistance about whether you can be excused answering particular questions for these reasons, but it will be at the judge's discretion whether the request is granted.

If you are asked to write a report on behalf of a client, Jakobi and Pratt recommend that a number of precautions are taken:

1 The request for a report is likely to be made by the solicitors acting for the client. Technically, this can be treated as the client's consent to disclosure. However, it is sensible to see the client to ensure that he realizes that the production of the report could lead to a requirement to disclosure of case records to the other party; that you may need to include sensitive information in the report; and that the client really is consenting to the production of the report in full knowledge of what is entailed.

2 If a counsellor is asked to disclose records in addition to the report, this request should be refused unless either the client consents, or a court order is made.

3 If disclosure could cause serious harm to the client, then you should inform his or her solicitor so that an adequate explanation can be given requiring disclosure. Again, through the client's solicitor it may be possible to limit disclosure to matters which are highly relevant to the case or to restrict who sees the counselling records, such as to a relevant expert. Alternatively, there may be other ways of obtaining the same information, perhaps by an expert examining the client independently.

4 Sometimes it is possible to request that an expert be appointed to examine the documents rather than have them considered in full to the open court.

5 If limitations on the disclosure of documents have been agreed, no reference should be made to the excluded material in court. Any limitations on disclosure cease to have effect once the excluded material is referred to or read out in open court. You will need to bear this in mind if you are called to give evidence.

Once a client is engaged in litigation, a counsellor's notes are vulnerable to disclosure and use in proceedings. It is only in the most exceptional circumstances that you will be able to prevent disclosure. For a more detailed explanation of the law, I recommend reading the article by Stephen Jakobi and Duncan Pratt (1992) or seeking legal advice.

Access by the police

The law places counsellors' records in a special category which excludes them from the usual search warrant, and substitutes a more demanding procedure before the police can obtain access to them. A search warrant must be signed by a circuit judge instead of a magistrate. This requirement of the Police and Criminal

Evidence Act 1984 is particularly interesting because it makes several specific references to counselling in its definition of 'personal records'. Personal records are defined in section 12 as:

> . . . documentary and other records concerning an individual (whether living or dead) who can be identified from them and relating:
> (a) to his physical or mental health;
> (b) to spiritual counselling or assistance given or to be given to him; or
> (c) to counselling or assistance given or to be given to him for his personal welfare, by any voluntary organisation or by any individual who –
> > (i)   by reason of his office or occupation has responsibilities for his personal welfare;
> > or
> > (ii) by reason of an order of a court has responsibilities for his supervision.

Counsellors' records therefore belong in the same categories as doctors', vicars', social workers' and probation officers', regardless of whether the counselling is paid or voluntary. Even if a circuit judge has signed a warrant, it is possible to go to the High Court to reverse this decision. In a recent case, the High Court ruled that an Old Bailey judge acted outside his powers when he ordered the Royal London Hospital to disclose someone's medical records to help a murder investigation. The precise reasons for this have not yet been reported but the case demonstrates the possibility of counsellors resisting disclosing records to the police. An exception to this requirement for a warrant may arise if the police are searching for documents in order to detect or prevent terrorism under the current Prevention of Terrorism (Temporary Provisions) Act. However, despite the sweeping powers seemingly given to the police under this legislation, they are required to exercise their powers 'reasonably'. What this means is complex and I recommend that a solicitor's advice should be sought whenever counsellors are aware that they are holding information which relates to terrorism.

The contents of counselling records

Relatively little appears to have been written in British literature about what ought to be included in a counsellor's records. This is in contrast with what is happening in the United States.

Kenneth Austin and others (1990) reviewed the American literature on record-keeping in their book on confronting malpractice. I have compiled from this review, and particularly Schutz (1982), a list of the items counsellors in the United States would be encouraged to keep as part of their records:

- written and signed consents to all treatment
- written and signed consents to all passing of confidential information
- all appointments including non-attendance by client
- treatment contracts (if used)
- up-to-date record of content of sessions with client
- up-to-date record of counsellor's reasoning behind decisions about significant interventions and general strategies
- consultations with anyone else about the client
- copies of any correspondence from the client or relating to work with client
- any instructions given to the client and whether or not the client acted on these.

In the American context Soisson and others (1987) suggest that certain things ought *not* to be included in records, such as 'emotional statements and other personal opinions. Information about illegal behaviour, sexual practices or other sensitive information which may embarrass or harm the client or others are rarely appropriate for the record.' Their view is that 'records should document the decision and treatment processes and the patient's response to treatment'. The title of the article, in which they make these recommendations, 'Thorough Record Keeping: A Good Defense', indicates that they are very much concerned with the use of records in the legal process.

This is probably good advice in Britain if you are working with clients where there is a significant possibility of the counselling records being used in a legal dispute. You may also wish to take into account the possibility of your client having the right to see her own records. Although these must be important factors in influencing what you decide to exclude from your records, I think it is important not to become so defensive that the primary purpose of the records, to assist you in providing counselling, is lost. I would include reference to my own feelings and creative speculations but would be careful to separate these from the more factual record of the content.

The format of counselling records

Very little has been written about how best to structure counselling records. Gaie Houston (1990) recommends keeping the records in two sections. The first section contains useful background information about the client and the contractual terms you have agreed between you. She suggests these headings:

1   NAME [probably coded] AND MEANS OF REFERRAL.
2   PRESENT CIRCUMSTANCES [Mrs A is 28, living since she was 18 with Claud. Works at Boots.]
3   HISTORY [Leave plenty of room to put in facts about her life and her ways of dealing with its events. You can add as the weeks go by. Noting the date can be informative here.]
4   REASON FOR SEEING ME [Has changed jobs three times in the last few months, and thinks she is unreasonably difficult with everyone at work, though she gets on perfectly, her word, with family and Claud.]
5   MY HUNCHES [She said strongly out of the blue that she was not thinking of leaving work and having a baby. I guess she is. Longer-term work probably needs to be about her daring to acknowledge her own needs, and admit the humanness of close family, and therefore self.]
6   TIMES AND PAYMENTS [Tuesdays at 11 am, with 3-week break at Easter when she will be abroad. One month paid in advance, next payment due . . .]

One way of establishing the contractual relationship with a client is to send her a letter after the first session which includes what you have agreed between you. This letter could be attached to this section, as could copies of any subsequent correspondence.

The second part of the records would be the record of the actual counselling sessions. Gaie Houston suggests separating the factual account of what happened from your own personal responses and evaluations by using several vertical columns. The factual account of whether your client arrived on time, what was said etc., can be put down in a left-hand column. The commentary can be written in a column to the right. I think there is a lot to commend this approach. My own system is slightly different but has evolved out of a need to separate the background information from the session notes and within those notes to separate factual reporting from my observations and speculations. The system I have used is shown in Figures 12.1 and 12.2. At times when I have been seeing lots of clients, or when time is at a premium, I have used pre-printed forms. The code numbers are only required if the two parts of the records are being kept separately. However, if split records are being kept it is advisable to store any correspondence away from the second part of the record as correspondence usually contains information which would identify clients and defeat the purpose of creating the split records.

In situations where the counsellor believes there is a real risk of records being seen by unauthorized people, the security of the part of the record containing personal identification is particularly important. If the security of this part of the record cannot be

```
┌─────────────────────────────────────────────────────────────────┐
│                                                                   │
│   Name: ..........................................................│
│                                                                   │
│   Address: .......................................................│
│                                                                   │
│   Contact tel nos: ...............................................│
│                                                                   │
│   Summary of counselling contract (e.g. frequency, duration, review│
│   periods, confidentiality, fees, etc.): .........................│
│                                                                   │
│   ................................................................│
│                                                                   │
│   ................................................................│
│                                                                   │
│   Reason for wanting counselling: ................................│
│                                                                   │
│   ................................................................│
│                                                                   │
│   ................................................................│
│                                                                   │
│   Significant names, relationships and places mentioned by client: .....│
│                                                                   │
│   ................................................................│
│                                                                   │
│   ................................................................│
│                                                                   │
│   Correspondence (attached) .................... Code no.*: ......│
│                                                                   │
│   * For split records only                                        │
│                                                                   │
└─────────────────────────────────────────────────────────────────┘
```

Figure 12.1 *Card for background information*

guaranteed, it is better to omit any reference to the 'Reason for wanting counselling' and to keep any correspondence separately from both parts of the records. This would limit the information gained by unauthorized access to the background information card to the identity of a client without giving any clues to the issues being considered in counselling.

Use of records in counselling-supervision

Some supervisors insist on counsellors keeping records and using these in counselling-supervision. The process of writing notes helps the counsellor to sort his various responses to the counselling session and therefore helps the counsellor to focus attention on important issues. It is agreed that this makes for a much better

---

Date: .... Time/duration .... Code no.:* ....

Content: Summary of client's narrative, behaviour, feelings and counsellor's interventions ....

....

Process: Any comments made by client about process, counsellor's observations and/or speculations about the process ....

....

Notes for next session: e.g. any agreement about what client or counsellor would do between sessions, issues to be raised during the session or for the counsellor to be aware of ....

....

Issues for counselling supervision: ....

....

Notes about any correspondence or telephone conversations: ....

....

* For split records only

Figure 12.2   *Card for record of session*

supervision session. This view is not universal but it is gaining ground.

How long should records be retained?

This is a difficult question to answer. In straightforward circumstances, where there are no other legal or professional considerations, the records could be destroyed any time after the end of the counselling relationship. One year's retention might be appropriate where the contact had been lengthy and there is the possibility of the client returning.

However, where there are unresolved issues which might result in a complaint against a counsellor to a professional body or legal proceedings in which the records might be required, a much longer period is required before the records should be destroyed. In the absence of any better guideline, three years corresponds to the maximum time within which someone may start a legal action for personal injury. The time starts from when the injury occurred or when someone could reasonably have known about the injury.

If any legal action involving a client is a possibility, it is prudent to obtain legal advice about how long the records should be kept, as the expiry time for initiating legal action varies according to the type of case.

Conclusion

Although it is not regarded as essential to good practice to keep records of counselling, the arguments are weighted on the side of keeping them. They are part of a systematic and professional approach to counselling. In my opinion, clients deserve this amount of care.

13 Monitoring counselling

Counsellors appear to be divided in their experience of monitoring their own delivery of services. Counsellors working on their own in private practice have not been caught up in the new management strategies that have had so much impact on counsellors working in all kinds of organizations. In private practice, a combination of counselling-supervision, on-going professional development through attending courses and/or involvement in professional associations and watching for fluctuations in numbers of people wanting counselling has often proved adequate as a package of strategies for on-going monitoring. When I first started counselling in public sector organizations in the 1970s, these were considered adequate methods for monitoring counselling services in organizational settings, with the additional requirement of some form of accountability to management. If a mutual respect and trust existed between an individual counsellor and the management, then the requirements of accountability could be nominal or virtually nonexistent. Sometimes I look back to those times with fond memories, but times have moved on. Just as counselling has developed over the past two decades, so have management techniques. Counsellors working for private sector organizations, in the public sector and in voluntary organizations are all under pressure to find better strategies to show that resources allocated to counselling are being well used. Some counsellors who have not been willing to participate in greater accountability through the active monitoring of their services have found that they have lost funding. Therefore, most counsellors in organizations now accept the reality of higher expectations about how they monitor their services. Some even welcome greater accountability as a way of enhancing recognition of the contributions a good counselling service can make. This is now my view.

However, the problem of how to monitor a counselling service and to communicate the results to other people in the organization without compromising confidentiality and privacy is a considerable challenge to the ingenuity of counsellors. I think most people involved in this process of developing strategies for monitoring counselling feel there is still more to learn and further new strategies will emerge. Nonetheless, within the current state of the art, it is possible to identify strategies which are consistent with counselling standards and ethics, particularly when the monitoring is carried out by the counsellor and then reported to others. It has been much more problematic to find ways of co-operating with monitoring and inspections conducted by someone from outside the counselling service. It is clear that independent assessments of a counselling service are useful to both the counsellors and the organization. They have additional credibility because they are independent of the service provider and are therefore thought to be less influenced by vested interests. However, independent inspections pose acute problems over confidentiality and privacy, particularly if as part of an inspection someone wants to sit in and observe a client and counsellor working together or to have access to files. This has proved to be an ethical and legal minefield but it is one where it is becoming possible to see a way forward after several years of what has felt like an uneasy standoff between irreconcilable forces. Therefore, in this chapter I shall deal with the issues associated with counsellors conducting their own evaluations first, as I think I can make observations with a reasonable degree of certainty. I shall then outline the issues arising from assessments conducted by people from outside the counselling service and the current understanding of how these issues may be resolved.

Self-monitoring by counsellors

There are two major strategies currently being used to monitor all kinds of services. These are service audit and quality assurance. I will look at each of these because they provide methods of monitoring which counsellors can operate themselves and therefore minimize some of the ethical difficulties of monitoring being conducted by someone else. In my experience, counsellors who have been pro-active and taken the initiative by establishing these monitoring procedures adapted to their own circumstances have been much less likely to experience the imposition of external inspections.

Service audit

Service audits aim to identify who uses a service and how resources are allocated within that service. The method used is systematic data collection and analysis. Much of this information is statistical and therefore can usually be provided by methods which protect the anonymity of clients, particularly if the counsellor (or receptionist) maintains a running numerical log of service use according to pre-determined categories. Two broad categories of information are usually collected. The first is socio-demographic and categorizes service users according to variables such as age, gender, marital/relationship status, educational attainment, occupation, ethnic origin or geographical location. The choice of variables is important and will be determined by the setting of the service. A counselling service used by the general public might want to use the categories just mentioned. On the other hand, a counselling service within an organization might be more interested in which parts of the organization make greatest use of the counselling service. This can raise problems of confidentiality because even from bare statistical data it can be possible to deduce the identity of a particular individual if the categories relate to small numbers of readily identifiable people. For example, it would be ethically dangerous if an employment assistance programme providing counsellors for a manufacturer included a category 'secretarial' if there were only a small number of secretaries on the staff. It would be better ethically (but perhaps less informative statistically) to include categories of small numbers in with others, e.g. 'office-based staff' or 'secretarial and management'. An alternative system of categories may be more appropriate to student counselling. For example, it may be highly informative to know the proportions of clients living in residences and those living out, or whether they are full-time or part-time, or the category of course being attended. Information of this kind can be very useful for predicting future demands on the service or for identifying short-falls in the service delivery.

The second broad category of information collected is about the range of problems and issues presented for counselling. Again, this is valuable information because it may reveal significant clustering of problems within particular client groups which may be most appropriately dealt with by a counselling service or perhaps prevented by some other strategy. For example, it would be appropriate for an educational establishment to review the assessment procedures for some groups of students if these were found to be disproportionately stressful compared to other student groups. On the other hand, the counselling service may be an invaluable safety net for students who are stressed by assessment procedures for personal reasons rather than by the way these procedures are organized.

Provided that care is taken over the way these statistics are gathered and disseminated, they can often be used as the basis of an annual report about a counselling service and, as these accumulate, it becomes possible to identify broader trends and issues which help in longer term planning.

Quality assurance

Quality assurance aims to monitor the quality of the service that is delivered by setting standards and comparing these with actual performance when services are delivered. Again, it is a management strategy which is useful to counsellors. One of the ways quality assurance can be implemented is by creating a 'quality circle' in which counselling practitioners devise their own standards and evaluate how far these are achieved. It is often less costly of time and resources to measure practicalities such as time taken between someone requesting counselling and actually being seen, and whether appointments run to time, etc. Such practicalities are important and can easily be overlooked. However, in order to enhance the quality of the counselling actually given to clients, I believe it is important to look at what actually happens in sessions. In this respect, counsellors are more fortunately placed than many others of the caring professions, including some psychotherapists who do not have a system of on-going supervision. The ethical requirement that counsellors receive counselling-supervision means that there is a resource already available which can be incorporated into the quality assurance process. For example, it would be possible to undertake a review of work with clients and to agree some target standards with a counselling-supervisor and then to evaluate how far these are met. In terms of establishing what actually happens in sessions, as opposed to what the counsellor subjectively experiences as happening, it can be useful to include listening to tape recordings of sessions, provided the client's identity is protected and the recording is made with the client's full consent.

Quality assurance is primarily concerned with direct services to clients but other factors may also be taken into account including strategies adopted nationally by counsellors in order to improve the quality of service to clients. These include the use of on-going training, quality of presentations at counselling-supervision and the counsellors' opportunities for their own personal development. Personally, when I see quality assurance assessments of counselling services, I like to see these indicators taken into account as they have an important influence on actual counselling practice. They may be indirect evidence of what actually happens between counsellor and client but they are direct evidence of the counsellor's, and their organization's, commitment to maintaining a quality counselling service.

Monitoring of counselling by others

I have already shown that counsellors can do a great deal themselves to monitor the services they provide in ways which are systematic and show appropriate accountability to managers, funders and even the general public. However, it is reasonable that from time to time someone with a legitimate interest in the management of a counselling service will want and need some more direct evidence from their own first-hand experience or by the use of an independent assessor. This can pose substantial ethical problems around confidentiality and privacy. This is a growing concern for counsellors in both the private and public sectors of the economy and so far as I can tell will become more of an issue as the trend towards a 'contract culture' becomes more widespread across organizations. One of the purposes of contracts is to clarify responsibilities for service delivery and therefore to facilitate the monitoring or auditing of service delivery. It is a strategy to sharpen the focus on accountability for resources used. The increasing use of this management strategy has caused an increase in the number of people writing to BAC to ask how they should respond to requests from managers, inspectors and external consultants to be able to observe the counsellor at work with their clients. Alternatively, people have been concerned about requests or instructions to permit auditors access to case records in order to conduct a service audit. Although the increase in numbers of counsellors caught up in this trend is recent, the issue is an old one with a particular history in higher education. I think it will be useful to explore something of this history as a case study to serve as a pointer to how the issue might be resolved in other settings such as health services, employee counselling and voluntary organizations.

HMIs' powers to inspect student counsellors

Since the mid 1980s, Her Majesty's Inspectors (HMIs) of education have been in discussion and ultimately in disagreement with the Association for Student Counselling (ASC) about whether they have the power to insist that they should sit in with a counsellor working with a client to observe the quality of the work. This has not been a problem in Scotland, where I am told the Inspectorate accept that direct observation raises serious ethical concerns and prefer to use other methods to inspect counselling services. The experience in England and Wales has been very different, where HMIs have routinely asked to be able to sit in with counsellors and clients subject to the client's consent. They have maintained that their powers enable them to insist on direct observation of counsellors working with clients, even if the counsellor considers it inappropriate. ASC has regarded this view as unacceptable. For many years, an awkward standoff has been maintained by both sides while negotiations towards an agreed joint policy have been taking place. These negotiations broke down a few years ago when it was reported that a senior HMI claimed that they have the power to enforce whatever they think fit and cited a passage from BAC's 1990 *Code of Ethics and Practice for Counsellors* as evidence of their right to observe counselling directly, subject to the client's consent. The passage referred to states,

> B.2.2.7   Clients should be offered privacy for counselling sessions. The client should not be observed by anyone other than their counsellor(s) without having given his/her informed consent. This also applies to audio/video taping of counselling sessions.

The negotiators on behalf of ASC were understandably dismayed at having all their hard work seemingly undermined by a section in BAC's *Code*. This resulted in a formal motion at BAC's AGM in 1991 asking that the Standards and Ethics Sub-committee review the wording of this section of the *Code* with a view to clarifying and strengthening the powers of counsellors when an inspector insists on a right to observe a live counselling session.

The first task of the Standards and Ethics Sub-committee was to establish what legal entitlements and constraints operate in this kind of situation. Legal advice had been consistently clear about the importance of the client's consent to someone sitting in to observe. If someone observed the counselling without the client's consent this would constitute breach of confidence and the client could seek a court order to prevent it or sue for damages. It was much less clear how far the counsellor's professional judgement about whether to ask a client to consent could be taken into account. There was a view expressed by experienced senior managers in education that counsellors could be ordered to seek a client's consent under the terms of the counsellors' contracts of employment. Failure to comply could result in disciplinary procedures and perhaps dismissal. It was also said that this could apply to counsellors working in other settings. In the negotiations with HMIs, an additional factor had to be taken into account. There are specific statutory powers given to HMIs conducting inspections. S. 77 of the Education Act 1944 states that a person who wilfully obstructs any person authorized to inspect an educational institution shall be guilty of an offence which could result in a fine or up to three months' imprisonment or a combination of both.

On the other hand, it was succinctly argued by Roger Casemore, a senior manager in an educational authority and former chairperson of BAC, and by others, that under administrative law the Inspectorate were required to exercise their powers subject to the constraints and the test of 'reasonableness'. It was argued that it was manifestly unreasonable to insist on direct observation with all the difficulties this raises about confidentiality and consent when there are reasonable alternative methods of inspection which would produce more accurate results and without compromising confidentiality. Unfortunately, 'reasonableness' in a legal context carries a meaning which is not the same as its everyday meaning and therefore this highly rational argument may not be legally enforceable. Nonetheless, it is worth summarizing the concerns about the usefulness of direct observation as a means of assessing the quality of a counselling service because they would apply wherever this method of assessment is proposed. The objections to direct observation are:

1   The presence of an observer changes the way the client interacts with the counsellor and therefore invalidates what is observed.
2   The act of observation undermines the counsellor's ethic and practice of offering the client privacy and confidentiality.
3   There are real difficulties in determining whether clients are in a position to give or refuse consent due to their dependence on the counsellor or the institution with which the counselling is provided, for example, a young person at school, a redundant worker on an out-placement counselling service.
4   The observer may not be suitably qualified or experienced to assess what is observed.
5   There are better alternative methods of conducting assessments of quality which are more reliable.

The Standards and Ethics Sub-committee was unable to find any way of resolving the conflict of views between the inspectorate and the counsellors. Therefore, BAC sought legal opinion from John Friel, Barrister, which was given in January 1993. The main points made in the legal opinion are:

1   Inspection of schools is now based on section 55 of the Further and Higher Education Act 1992 which makes it the responsibility of HMIs and the local education authorities. Section 70 of the new Act creates a new system for further and higher education which requires that each Council of Further and Higher Education sets in place a system for assessing the quality of education provided.

2   The confidentiality of the counsellor/client relationship is as strong as that between doctor and patient.

3   Subject to exceptions which this opinion was not asked to address (such as in respect of the confidentiality of confessions of crime), there is no right to override such confidentiality without the client's consent unless there is an express statutory power to do so. The Act does not contain such a power.

4   Inspectors, whether HMIs, or appointed by a local education authority or a Council of Further and Higher Education have no legal basis to insist on observing counselling sessions without the client's consent, and any attempt to do so could be prevented by applying to the courts for judicial review. Counsellors who permitted such observation would be in breach of BAC's rules.

5   The Inspectorate have no right to insist that a request for the client's consent be made against the counsellor's professional judgement. It is a misunderstanding of paragraph B2.2.7 of the *Code of Ethics and Practice for Counsellors* – which is quoted in full at the beginning of this section – that it gives the Inspectorate any such right. At most, this section allows a counsellor who agrees that such an observation is appropriate to request a client to give consent to observation of a session by an HMI.

What does this legal opinion mean to counsellors? First, it is important to realize that it is a legal opinion and is therefore less authoritative than if it was a judgment given in court. Nevertheless, it is an unequivocal legal opinion and is therefore a reasonable basis for further decisions unless or until it is qualified or contradicted by a decision of the courts. More specifically, counsellors in education subject to inspections under the system first established by the Education Act 1944 or the new systems established under the Further and Higher Education Act 1992 have much better grounds for defending their entitlement to use their judgement about whether or not to ask a client whether he consents to being observed.

The legal importance of confidentiality has implications for counsellors working in establishments outside education which are not covered by the two Acts already mentioned. It will take some time to work out what these are and may require additional legal opinions. In the meantime, I would encourage any counsellor faced with a similar request from a third party, such as a manager, auditor, inspector or independent consultant, to do the following:

1   Ask whether the request is based on a statutory power to inspect.

2   If the answer is 'no', explain that observation of counselling is an intrusion on the client's legal right to confidentiality and is only possible if, in your professional judgement, it is appropriate to ask whether the client is willing to be observed and the client consents to waive her right to confidentiality. Provided you are a member of BAC you can point to the *Code for Counsellors* to justify this view. You may wish to suggest that there are more reliable ways of assessing a counselling service including the methods mentioned below. If an agreement still proves impossible, seek legal advice.

3   If the answer is 'yes', ask for details of the statutory power, in particular the name of the act, its year and the relevant sections or schedules. Seek legal advice about whether the legislation gives express powers to override a client's wishes about confidentiality.

The Association for Student Counselling has given careful consideration to finding more reliable alternative methods of inspection for HMIs. These could be equally applicable to other assessors.

(a)   Access to appointments book in order to assess the flexibility within the service, ability to deal with urgent cases, balance between short-term and long-term work (if appointment books contain initials only, or code for each client, there is little problem with confidentiality).

(b)   Diary or log of one month's work for each counsellor (coding or numbering clients) showing range of work.

(c)   HMI to have access to team meetings.

(d)   Possibility for HMI to meet a range of clients who have come to the end of counselling (with counsellor's and client's consent).

(e)   HMI to have access to general student and staff body and to senior management to identify perception of the service.

(f)   HMI to have access to a range of case notes (having due regard to confidentiality) including a statement of therapeutic aims for each of these clients and an assessment of how far these are being met; these should also demonstrate the depth and repertoire of the counselling skills. If there are difficulties in presenting certain cases because of the specific nature of confidential issues (e.g. could identify individuals), then this needs to be explicit and reasons given.

(g)   Presentation of written case-study with the informed consent of a client. All means of identifying the client would have to be deleted or altered.

(h)   Presentation of taped sessions (audio or video) where this is a normal method of working to the counsellor and client.

(i)   Presentation of taped sessions (audio or video) with client's informed consent.

(j) Direct observation of a supervision session.

(ASC, 1991)

During the consultations for good practice in HIV counselling (Bond, 1991b) the additional method of using video/sound recordings was also considered appropriate provided the client's identity is protected and the recording has been made with the client's consent. Again it would be a matter for the counsellor's own professional judgement whether it would be appropriate to seek a client's consent.

One of the consequences of the legal opinion is that BAC could change the wording of its code. It is too early to say whether this will happen. As most counsellors working in organizational settings are members of BAC, it is important that they keep up-to-date on this issue.

Conclusion

It will be clear from this chapter that counsellors working in organizations are increasingly likely to be expected to monitor the counselling services they provide. Whenever possible, it is ethically desirable that counsellors are actively involved in conducting their own monitoring as this reduces the potential for dilemmas over privacy and confidentiality.

The disagreement about the powers of HMIs to inspect counselling services in schools and some colleges shows how complex some of these dilemmas can be. Perhaps more important, it shows how compatible counsellors' concerns about confidentiality are with the law. This is an example of the working through of a dilemma about ethics and standards at an organizational level. I doubt if an individual or even an organization much smaller than BAC would have had the resources and authority to have got to the point where this issue appears to be moving towards a satisfactory solution. In my experience, this has been an exceptionally difficult issue to resolve. Fortunately, most dilemmas can be resolved by counsellors as individuals in consultation with a counselling-supervisor. The next chapter provides a systematic model for this kind of ethical problem-solving.

PART IV THE WHOLE PICTURE

14 Ethical problem-solving

Whenever you are confronted with a problem or dilemma about ethical standards, it is useful to approach the problem in a systematic way. This maximizes the likelihood of reaching a solution about which you can have confidence that it is the best possible outcome. This chapter contains a six-step process which is a development of an ethical problem-solving model derived from American sources (Paradise and Siegelwaks, 1982; Austin and others, 1990). It is intended to act as a basic framework and to stimulate you to consider a wide range of possibilities before making a decision.

Produce a brief description of the problem or dilemma

Making sure that you can produce a short spoken or written description of the main elements of your ethical dilemma is doubly useful. Sometimes the process of doing this reduces confusion to the extent that the problem disappears. On the other hand, if the problem still remains, you are much better placed to seek assistance and to be clear about what are the main issues to be considered. When I find it difficult to define a problem clearly, I know it is something which I need to discuss with my counselling-supervisor(s) or another experienced counsellor. It is very difficult to make much progress until the problem can be expressed clearly. It may be that some of the later steps will cause me to revise my description of the main issues but a short and clear statement about what these appear to be is a good starting point.

Whose dilemma is it anyway?

This is a basic question which often casts a sharp light on the darkest of ethical problems in counselling. Counselling is an activity which requires careful monitoring of boundaries of responsibility in order to ensure that these are not becoming blurred. In Chapter 5, I suggested that a useful way of approaching boundary issues is to start from the position that the counsellor is responsible for the methods used and the client for the outcome of the counselling. Often this general principle is very clarifying but it is important to check that the specific dilemma is not a rare exception to the rule that clients carry a high level of responsibility for the way they use counselling in their own lives: for example, the principles of autonomy and confidentiality are overridden by some other ethical concern, perhaps the protection of children from abuse.

The following scenarios are examples of issues about ethics and standards classified according to boundaries of responsibility.

- Client's own ethical dilemma:

  Sheila decides she cannot face telling her partner that she has stronger feelings of attraction for someone else. She makes the decision to lie to her partner about the time she is spending with her new lover.

  Trevor is feeling guilty about money he has embezzled from his employer. He had intended to pay it back but he has lost the money through gambling. He knows it puts the future of the business at risk. Should he tell his employer? (If the counselling is taking place in the work setting, it is likely that this would become a dilemma shared by counsellor and client.)

- Counsellor's own ethical dilemma:

  Zoe is very wealthy and, having fallen out with all her close family, has decided that she wants to make a will bequeathing all her possessions to you as her counsellor. You suspect that this is a manipulation to win your support for Zoe's side in a family dispute. You also know that if you accept the bequest, it is likely that it will be suggested that you used your position of influence to persuade Zoe to make you a beneficiary. On the other hand, £100,000 or thereabouts would be very useful.

  Frances has been talking in counselling sessions about her difficulties with someone who is already well known to you. Do you tell Frances that you know the person she is talking about and risk inhibiting her, or do you stay silent?

  Rachel has sought counselling from the student counselling service about whether to leave a course before its completion.

As the counsellor, you know that if one more student leaves this course it will be closed and the remaining students will be transferred to other courses. For one of your other very vulnerable clients, this could be disastrous as she sees this course as a lifeline. It could also have serious consequences for other students and staff.

The organization which employs you as a counsellor wishes to impose a restriction on the number of sessions you can offer to any one client. You know that the maximum number of permitted sessions is unrealistically low for a majority of clients you see for counselling. What should you say to new clients who might be affected by the proposed policy? What should you do about the proposed policy?

● Ethical dilemma shared by counsellor and client:

Bill is unbearably stressed by his work but his partner and children need the money. He is feeling guilty about letting them down and therefore he decides to lie to his wife and says that you, as his counsellor, have said that he should give up work. To add credibility to his deception he tells his wife that you are willing to see her and to explain your recommendation. Bill's wife has arranged an interview with you.

Susan seeks counselling about an eating disorder. She states that she is not receiving counselling or therapy from anyone else. You agree to be her counsellor. Several sessions later, Susan admits to having lied about not having another therapist. She had a prior agreement to work exclusively with someone else. She does not want to stop seeing you or the other therapist and values her work with you. She feels unable to discuss seeing you with the other therapist.

One of the reasons for deciding at this stage who holds responsibility for the dilemma is that it may make all the subsequent steps in this model unnecessary. If the client has the sole responsibility for the dilemma, it is most appropriate to explain the issue to him and help him make his own decision. Where there is joint responsibility, some clarification and negotiation with the client is usually indicated. The stages which follow are particularly appropriate for the resolution of dilemmas which are primarily the counsellor's responsibility. On the other hand, the model is flexible enough to be shared, wholly or partially, with some clients in order to help them decide issues which are their own responsibility or joint responsibilities with the counsellor.

Consider all available ethical principles and guidelines

The aim of this stage is to become better informed about possible ways of resolving the ethical dilemma. The main codes of standards and ethics of use to counsellors in Britain are published by the British Association for Counselling, British Psychological Society and British Association for Sexual and Marital Therapy. The guidelines produced for specific professional groups by the United Kingdom Central Council for Nursing, Midwifery and Health Visiting, the British Association for Social Workers, the General Medical Council and others sometimes offer general insights for all counsellors but are highly relevant to counsellors working in related roles. Some counselling services have developed their own codes which can be very informative.

Some ethical issues cannot be decided without consideration of the law. Up-to-date publications may be useful but if the matter is complex or there is uncertainty about the law, I strongly recommend seeking legal advice from a solicitor. The general questions you may want answered are:

1 What actions are prohibited by law?
2 What actions are required to be performed by law?
3 What are the people involved, including yourself, entitled to by law?

In the absence of any relevant guidelines or decisive legal advice, you may find yourself considering the issue from the general ethical principles outlined in Chapter 3.

1 Beneficence – what will achieve the greatest good?
2 Non-maleficence – what will cause least harm?
3 Justice – what will be fairest?
4 Respect for autonomy – what maximizes the opportunities for everyone involved to implement their choices?

In counselling the fourth principle is especially important and will often prove decisive, particularly if it is possible to act in ways which are consistent with client autonomy and also satisfy one or more of the other principles.

At the end of this stage you would hope to be clearer about the goals which are ethically desirable. This will give you an orientation and some criteria for choosing between possible courses of action.

Identify all possible courses of action

This stage is an opportunity to brainstorm all the possible courses of action open to you which will achieve the ethical goals you identified in the earlier stage. Some courses of action will seem highly probable ways of resolving the dilemma. Others may seem silly. However, it is better not to discard the ideas which seem silly too readily because sometimes they contain the basis for an original approach or new insight.

Select the best course of action

A former chairperson of the American Association for Counseling and Development (Holly A. Stadler, 1986 a and b) has proposed three tests for a chosen course of action.

- Universality
  - Could my chosen course of action be recommended to others?
  - Would I condone my proposed course of action if it was done by someone else?
- Publicity
  - Could I explain my chosen course of action to other counsellors?
  - Would I be willing to have my actions and rationale exposed to scrutiny in a public forum, e.g. at a workshop, in a professional journal, newspaper or on radio/TV?
- Justice
  - Would I do the same for other clients in a similar situation?
  - Would I do the same if the client was well known or influential?

If you find yourself answering 'no' to any of these questions, you may need to reconsider your chosen outcome. A final step in identifying the best course of action may be checking whether the resources are available to implement what is proposed.

The aim of this stage is to make an informed choice between all the possible courses of action identified in stage 4. The consideration of guidelines and the law in the previous stage will be useful but may not be decisive. Therefore a practical set of questions is very useful.

Evaluate the outcome

After you have implemented your course of action, it is useful to evaluate it in order to learn from the experience and to prepare yourself for any similar situations in the future.

- Was the outcome as you hoped?
- Had you considered all relevant factors with the result that no new factors emerged after you implemented your chosen course of action?
- Would you do the same again in similar circumstances?

Examples of ethical problem-solving

I have chosen two issues as examples of how this model of ethical problem-solving might work in practice. The first raises the issues of dual relationships. The second poses what participants in training workshops often consider to be one of the most difficult ethical dilemmas which could confront a counsellor. I am offering both these as examples of how the model works rather than suggesting that my conclusions are necessarily right. You may use the same model but come to different conclusions.

Example 1

You are approached by Pam, the teenage daughter of a friend, who asks you to offer her counselling. You hardly know Pam but it is apparent that she is emotionally troubled and she has dropped hints about not eating properly. Pam is insistent that from her point of view you are ideal as a counsellor. You are neither too much a stranger nor too close. She turns down any suggestion of seeing anyone else. It has taken her months to pluck up the courage to speak to you. You check with her mother, who is your friend. She is supportive of the idea and offers to pay whatever is your usual fee. You feel her friendship matters to you.

The first step is to produce a brief description of the dilemma. The main elements, in order of importance, are:

1 divided loyalties if you take on Pam as a client between putting her interests as a client first and your friendship with her mother. What if Pam's difficulties involve her relationship with her mother or perhaps abuse within the family?;
2 the management of confidentiality vis-à-vis the mother, your friend. You suspect that neither Pam nor her mother

understands some, of the potential complications of what is proposed;

3 the payment for counselling by someone other than the client when there is uncertainty about that person's role in the client's problems. This could be considered once the other issues are resolved.

The second step is to consider whose dilemma it is. As it is presented, Pam and her mother are in agreement and the onus is on you to accept or reject the role of counselling Pam.

The third step is to consider all the available codes and guidelines. The BAC *Code of Ethics and Practice for Counsellors* (1992a) requires that:

> B.2.2.13 Counsellors should avoid unnecessary conflicts of interest and are expected to make explicit to the client any relevant conflicts of interest.

This raises the question of whether the potential conflicts of interest are avoidable. The possibility of referral has been considered but this is unacceptable to Pam. There is the additional requirement to explain the conflicts of interest to Pam, and perhaps secondarily her mother. What is the nature of the conflict of interest? It is a potential dual relationship with Pam as 'counsellor' and 'mother's friend' simultaneously. A secondary issue is the potential dual relationship with Pam's mother as 'daughter's counsellor' and 'friend'. There is almost nothing published about dual relationships in British literature but it has been the subject of recent publications in the United States. Barbara Herlihy and Gerald Corey (1992) argue against the automatic prohibition of all dual relationships and suggest a decision-making model (Figure 14.1) for dual relationships.

There are no apparent legal constraints. Therefore the next step is to consider all possible courses of action.

Potential courses of action include:

- Refuse to take Pam on as client stating reasons.
- Offer a 'white lie' for not taking Pam on, say, too busy, don't work with teenagers, etc.
- Agree to see Pam but only once she understands the potential conflicts of interest and has explored how she wants you to deal with any issues relating to her mother.
- Agree to see Pam but for as long as you are seeing Pam to minimize contact with her mother and have a clear agreement with both Pam and her mother about confidentiality and what may be communicated.

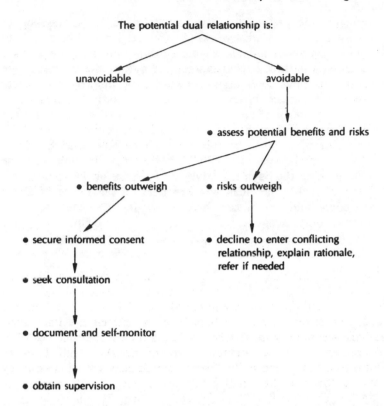

The potential dual relationship is:

unavoidable   avoidable

• assess potential benefits and risks

• benefits outweigh   • risks outweigh

• secure informed consent   • decline to enter conflicting
                                      relationship, explain rationale,
                                      refer if needed

• seek consultation

• document and self-monitor

• obtain supervision

Figure 14.1 *Decision-making model for dual relationships (Herlihy and Corey, 1992)*

- Accept risk of losing a friend by seeing Pam.
- See Pam for a fixed period with review at which the possibility of referral or continuation can be considered.

The final stage is to choose a possible course of action. The choice will depend on the exact circumstances of the situation and your assessment of the possibility of maintaining clear boundaries and the likelihood of being able to help Pam. If I were faced with this dilemma, I would prefer to decline this dual relationship on ethical grounds. It is likely that Pamela will have issues relating to her mother which she will need to explore and resolve for herself in the process of overcoming her eating disorder. My existing friendship with her mother is likely to complicate this process for both Pam and me. If I took on any role, it would be to assist Pam in finding a source of help which she considers acceptable and perhaps offering to be present to introduce Pam to her counsellor or therapist before they start working together. I would be willing to be quite firm about the ethical undesirability of taking on the role of counsellor in these circumstances, and quite active in giving Pam information which could assist her search for an alternative source of help. In these circumstances, I would not charge any fees so the subsidiary problem of fees would not arise. However, this is often an issue when seeing young people so I will consider it.

The issue of payment of fees by someone other than the client is often a tricky issue, especially if a client's relationship with the person making the payment might be an issue in the counselling. It is possible that the client will experience a sense of guilt about using counselling to explore difficulties with the benefactor, and therefore may avoid this subject. The counsellor may also experience similar inhibitions. Therefore this arrangement may be contrary to B.2.2.2 of the *Code for Counsellors*, which places a responsibility on the counsellor 'for working in ways which promote the client's control over his/her own life . . .'. Several alternatives exist:

- reducing fees to a level where client can afford direct payment;
- client making contribution to fees paid by someone else;
- suggesting that the money for fees be given as a gift to client who takes responsibility for managing payment to counsellor.

Any of these arrangements would be preferable to direct payment by the mother, which might further confuse an already difficult set of dual relationships. My own preference is to reduce fees to a level the client can afford directly. This provides the best way of placing the client in control of the counselling relationship. However, if this is not feasible, I prefer the client to make a contribution to the fees and to take responsibility for managing the payment of fees.

Example 2

A client tells you in confidence that he has a sexually transmittable disease which is untreatable and which may be fatal. He is taking no precautions to protect his regular sexual partner and has not informed the partner of his medical condition.

The dilemma which faces the counsellor is whether to maintain confidentiality or to act to protect the partner.

This situation is one which is of particular concern to counsellors of people with HIV. The dilemma is particularly acute because of the widespread fear of HIV and prejudice against people with HIV, which mean that any action to protect the partner may expose the client to additional risks of social rejection or worse.

The second step is to decide who has responsibility for the dilemma. In this example, the primary responsibility is the client's. The counsellor's potential responsibility arises from being in possession of information which could be used to protect someone from serious physical harm.

The third step of identifying ethical goals reveals a great deal of common ground between a range of professions which may experience this dilemma. The BAC *Code of Ethics and Practice for Counsellors* states:

> B.4.4 Exceptional circumstances may arise which give the counsellor good grounds for believing that the client will cause serious physical harm to others. . . . . In such circumstances the client's consent to a change in the agreement about confidentiality should be sought whenever possible unless there are also good grounds for believing the client is no longer able to take responsibility for his/her own actions. Whenever possible, the decision to break confidentiality should be made only after consultation with a counselling supervisor or an experienced counsellor.

The *Code* therefore envisages the counsellor has an option to warn the partner, subject to certain safeguards, but does not impose a duty to do so. Codes of other professions who might encounter this dilemma come to similar conclusions.

The United Kingdom Central Council for Nursing, Midwifery and Health Visiting requires that its registered practitioners should 'protect all confidential information concerning patients and clients obtained in the course of professional practice and make disclosures only with consent, where required by the order of a court or when you can justify disclosure in the wider public interest' (UKCC, 1992). The ethical guidelines provided by the General Medical Council (1991) and the British Medical Association (1988) with regard to HIV infection require a similarly cautious approach to breaches of confidentiality with the emphasis on obtaining the client's consent.

Guidance on Partner Notification for HIV Infection issued by the Department of Health (1992) points out the common law duty of confidentiality and the additional statutory duties with regard to venereal diseases which may apply to health workers. The guidance also points out the need to recognize that confidentiality 'helps to protect public health. Without confidentiality patients with sexually transmitted diseases, including HIV infection, may be unwilling to come forward for diagnosis, treatment and counselling.' The emphasis in this guidance is on avoiding undue pressure on clients or patients to notify partners or to agreeing to someone else doing it on the client's behalf. A person with HIV should be encouraged to inform sexual partners (and drug injecting partners) but 'should be counselled in an unbiased way and not put under undue pressure'.

These are guidelines for workers who have a major responsibility for HIV treatment and prevention, and are based on considerable experience of this work. Therefore it is arguably quite reasonable that a counsellor working in other settings would choose to adopt this standard of practice.

At the next step, all possible courses of action identified might include:

- encouraging client to inform partner;
- helping client to prepare for how to inform partner by teaching skills or rehearsing how to tell;
- offering to be present when partner is informed;
- encouraging client to modify sexual or other behaviour to reduce risk of infection of partner, e.g. safer sex, or abstinence.

In my experience, in most circumstances the situation will be resolved by the appropriate selection of one of these strategies. If the situation is not resolved, the counsellor may feel that he has done all that can be done ethically. I have not yet encountered a situation where a client persists in placing a partner at risk without the partner being told of my client's HIV infection. I anticipate that I would feel that I had done everything I could ethically, although I would continue to feel concerned about what I would see as an unsatisfactory outcome. I would express my concerns to the client so that he is not under the misapprehension that I am in agreement with his actions. I would hope that this would encourage my client to reconsider alternative courses of action. If this intervention was unsuccessful, I would persist in trying to find a way in which the client is willing to improve the situation. However, this situation has not arisen in my own work, and is reported as being very rare in actual practice. Nonetheless, it is a situation which is often posed in ethical workshops as creating the most acute ethical dilemmas for the counsellor, therefore it is worth considering and arriving at your own decision. In reality, clients who are determined not to consider the consequences of their actions for a partner usually do not seek counselling, or conceal the true nature of the situation from the counsellor by pretending the partner has been informed or other precautions have been taken. Fortunately for counsellors, clients who communicate their concern about the implications of their own HIV infection for their partners are also most likely to want to take responsibility for finding an ethical way of resolving their dilemma, particularly if they can be offered adequate support when the partner is informed. One of the consequences of respect for a client's autonomy and careful practice of confidentiality is sometimes living with disquieting knowledge about the risks to other people and feeling unable to do anything about it.

Conclusion

Ethical dilemmas occur on a daily basis in counselling. Dilemmas of the level of difficulty posed by the examples in this chapter are relatively rare. Most are more likely to be of the order of considering whether to refer a client, choosing what to discuss in counselling-supervision or how to respond to a client, including whether to touch. They are all complex situations which demand thought, knowledge, feeling and a considerable amount of courage to make and sustain decisions. Michael Carroll (1993) has likened the process of resolving ethical dilemmas to general problem-solving and argues that it is a process in which counsellors can become more skilled with training. The model of ethical problem-solving I have offered is not definitive, but it is intended to be useful in everyday counselling.

15 Epilogue

Counsellors in Britain have been remarkably rapid in their progress towards publishing their understanding of counselling standards and ethics. It took the American Counseling Association, formerly known as the American Association for Counseling and Development and originally the American Personnel and Guidance Association, eleven years to reach the point of approving a first formal code of ethics (Gibson and Pope, 1993). In comparison, the British Association for Counselling agreed its first code in seven years. Both organizations were motivated to produce their codes for similar reasons. The creation of a code of ethics and standards is seen as fundamental to the identity of counselling as a credible activity. Some counsellors would wish to emphasize the need for ethical guidelines as essential to professionalization and this has undoubtedly been a motivating factor amongst some salaried counsellors. However, in Britain a great deal of counselling is provided on a voluntary basis and all counsellors, whether paid or not, have supported the need to develop high professional standards in order to protect the public. As we have seen, the process of developing a coherent set of ethical standards is not easy and often involves a process of re-assessment in the light of experience. On both sides of the Atlantic, codes of practice have required periodic revision and I anticipate that this will continue. However, I think it is very likely that future changes will be in the details rather than the broad framework of counselling standards and ethics. This broad framework has been influential in the content of each of the chapters of this book and is worth summarizing.

Respect for client autonomy

Respect for the client's autonomy is a fundamental principle in counselling. Indeed the whole process of counselling is working towards increasing the client's autonomy. It is a process of enabling the client to take more control of her own life. Exactly how this commitment to the client's autonomy is expressed will depend on the issues presented by the client. It may involve working on difficulties in a current situation or resolving some aspect of a historical relationship or event. Sometimes the issues which confront clients are primarily emotional, on other occasions they are essentially practical. There is an enormous variety of circumstances in which counsellors are expected to show respect for a client's autonomy. I often think that counselling is most simply explained as giving someone a safe space in order to enable that person to work out issues to his or her own satisfaction. The way the counsellor intervenes to establish the space and to assist the client to reach her own conclusions will be due to a combination of the counsellor's personality and theoretical orientation. The overall aim will be to assist the client towards a greater capacity for autonomous action.

However, the principle of respect for the client's autonomy is not absolute. There are limitations on how far it is ethically desirable to respect someone's autonomy. Two examples have recurred throughout several chapters. The first relates to the issue of whether someone has the capacity to act autonomously. This is particularly relevant in the case of young people. Does the young person have the intelligence and maturity to make the judgements involved in taking responsibility for herself? Taking responsibility for oneself includes the possibility of making mistakes. Therefore the question is not about whether the client is capable of making the decisions in her best interests. The client may make decisions which ultimately turn out to be personally disadvantageous. The question is, does the client have the capacity to make decisions, regardless of whether they are personally beneficial or disadvantageous? What this means for working with young people is discussed in Chapter 9. The same issue arises in another set of circumstances when someone is feeling suicidal. If the principle of respect for someone's autonomous acts, whether these are personally beneficial or disadvantageous, is accepted, then certain consequences follow. The suicidal client has to be considered from the viewpoint of whether she has the capacity to make an autonomous judgement. When this issue has been considered in law, the courts have set different standards for adults and young people. I have made a number of suggestions in Chapter 6. However, I believe this issue is still not as well understood as it could be and requires considerably more debate amongst counsellors before a consensus can be achieved.

The principle of autonomy is also qualified by the extent to which respect for one person's autonomy may be to the detriment of someone else's. The classic example arises when a client plans to cause serious physical harm to someone else. What should the counsellor do? In these circumstances, the counsellor may assess that there is a need to warn the person at risk of serious physical harm even though this frustrates the client's autonomous actions. Needless to say, this course of action would be reserved for what are likely to be the most exceptional circumstances.

Traditionally, respect for a client's autonomy is the bedrock upon which the counselling relationship is founded. Counsellors strive to maintain this respect and restrict limitations on that respect to situations where:

- the client lacks the personal capacity to act autonomously and/or
- a client's autonomous actions threaten the autonomy of someone else to the extent of causing serious physical harm.

Much of the subsequent elaboration of standards of practice is an elaboration of the implications of maximizing client autonomy. For example, contracting may serve many purposes. Ethically, it is a way of showing respect to the client's autonomy from the outset of the relationship by actively involving a client in the negotiation of the basis of the relationship. Therapeutically, it reinforces the message that the client's own internal locus of control is fundamental. Legally, making a contract with fee-paying clients is a wise precaution. Similarly, giving clients access to their counsellor's notes reinforces the client's sense of personal autonomy as well as being a legal requirement in some circumstances, see Chapter 12. The counsellor's avoidance of conflicts of interest or damaging dual relationships is also ultimately about protection of the client's autonomy.

The principle of confidentiality

A counsellor's practice of confidentiality is closely associated with considerations of client autonomy. Confidentiality acts like a fence round the space created for the client's autonomous actions. The fence is important to the clients' safety and creates the circumstances in which clients can look at issues which otherwise would be kept to themselves. The fence also marks a boundary of responsibility. Care over confidentiality reinforces the client's sense of responsibility for the outcome of the counselling. Therefore confidentiality is extremely important in counselling. Care over confidentiality is a practical way of signalling respect for a client's autonomy.

The exceptions to the principle of confidentiality closely parallel those of autonomy. The first relates to the capacity of a client to enter into a confidential relationship either because he lacks the intelligence and maturity or because he is too mentally or emotionally disturbed to understand the implications of a confidential relationship. This latter is particularly relevant to suicidal clients. I do not believe that merely being suicidal is sufficient grounds to justify breaches of confidentiality. The second main ethical reason for considering a breach of confidentiality arises when this principle is overridden by an even more important ethical concern such as the prevention of serious harm to someone. These exceptions parallel the law. In addition, some situations may arise where the counsellor is legally obliged to disclose confidential information. These situations are explored more fully in Chapter 9.

The management of confidentiality by the counsellor presents a number of challenges. At the start of the counselling relationship a client is entitled to be informed about any limitations on the confidentiality being offered. For counsellors working in organizations this may require some prior negotiation with the counsellor's employer. In some situations, statutory requirements, for example a duty to report child abuse, may need to be explained to the client. The exact limitations on confidentiality may vary from counsellor to counsellor and between clients. The ethical and legal complexity of confidentiality is explored in Chapter 9. It seems to me that it is pointless and probably impossible to foresee all the circumstances which might require a breach of confidentiality. By their very nature, many of these situations are exceptional and unexpected. Therefore, it is best to check with a client if she has any particular needs with regard to confidentiality at the start of the counselling and to negotiate an agreement within any known relevant constraints on the counsellor's ability to offer confidentiality. Any reasonable foreseeable circumstances should also be taken into account. For instance, it may be appropriate to discuss confidentiality over suicidal intentions with some clients but not others, depending on the client's state of mind and reason for seeking counselling. The initial agreement can be reviewed periodically as the counselling progresses to ensure that it takes into account any changes in the known and reasonable foreseeable circumstances. As a general rule, the communication of confidential information should take place only after the client's consent has been sought. Any exception to this principle should be very exceptional.

During the writing of this book, I have become much more aware of how important the principles of autonomy and confidentiality are in counselling. They are sometimes described as fundamental values. This is true, but it is only the beginning of the story. They are more than values which permeate consequences. I am convinced that skilled practice in the management of issues about autonomy and confidentiality enhances the therapeutic impact of the counselling because it helps to establish clear boundaries of responsibility between the counsellor and client.

Conversely, poor practice can undermine the counselling by creating confusion and inappropriate expectations.

Ensuring the quality of the counselling provided

I started this book with examples from the national press where the quality of therapy was experienced by clients as sub-standard and in some instances downright unethical. The impact of these experiences was nearly always to erode the clients' own sense of their autonomy. All the examples showed the vulnerability of someone seeking help from counsellors or other closely related roles. It is therefore extremely important to clients to be sure that they are receiving counselling which is of reasonable quality. Ultimately, it is also in the interests of all counsellors to ensure the good quality of counselling available to the public because this is essential to the credibility of counselling and therefore the continuity of new people seeking counsellors' services. The process of ensuring the quality of counselling is complex and requires attention at two ends of the spectrum of standards.

At the positive end of the spectrum of practice, the main concern is to identify and maintain good standards of practice. These are not static and are subject to revision and refinement based on experience. The main strategies adopted by counsellors are:

- on-going counselling supervision;
- basic training and a commitment to on-going training and personal development;
- accreditation of counsellors, trainers and counselling-supervisors;
- the monitoring of the provision of counselling services;
- research.

At the lower end of the spectrum of standards, there is a need to identify where the level falls below what is acceptable and becomes malpractice. The boundary is usually identified within the context of hearing formal complaints. Most reputable counselling organizations either have their own complaints procedure or use those of national organizations like BAC. Aggrieved clients are also entitled to use the courts if they believe there is the possibility of legal sanctions or compensation.

Between the baseline of acceptable practice and up to the best practice there exists a range of standards which accommodates both the newly trained and inexperienced practitioner and the well-respected practitioner with a national or international reputation. One of the tasks of ensuring the quality of counselling available is trying to create a dynamic which encourages more of the counselling to be at the upper end of the range of standards than at the lower end. It seems highly probable that a national registration scheme for counsellors has an important contribution to make. If a national registration scheme is established, as seems likely in the next few years, it will give members of the public a much clearer indication of quality assurance than has been possible in the past. It is likely that the media will encourage the use of registered counsellors and it will be in everyone's interests to ensure that minimum standards are followed or that clients have access to a grievance procedure which includes the possibility of removing the counsellor from the register. Almost certainly, this will start as a voluntary scheme but ultimately it might become statutory.

Counsellor autonomy

The priority given to client autonomy does imply a willingness on the part of the counsellor to relinquish control over the outcome for the client. It means taking cues from the client. Sometimes this will involve following where the client leads. Sometimes it will involve carefully leading in a direction the client has chosen. In Chapter 5 I discussed the implications of metaphors of counselling for the client's autonomy. I preferred the metaphor of the counsellor as educator rather than healer. Another metaphor comes to mind. As teenagers, a friend and I were taught rock-climbing in the Lake District by a mountain guide. The choice of where we went was made by my friend and me, albeit sometimes after negotiation if the guide felt the place we chose was unsuitable or unlikely to achieve our objectives. I have no doubt that had we chosen to override his advice he would still have come with us and allowed us to learn from the experience. When we were climbing there were times when he stood behind and watched me ascend, often very slowly and incompetently because I am not a natural climber. Often my exhilaration would turn to fear and sometimes panic. All the time he provided a degree of safety by managing the climbing rope which prevented serious injury when I fell off. He also provided encouragement. From these experiences I learnt a great deal about myself which has been very useful. I will never be a competent rock-climber because I lack physical agility and balance in comparison to my friend or the guide. Nonetheless I learnt about fear and about trust. The guide was there out of his own autonomous wishes. He had found a way of sharing what he valued without imposing his experience and views on others. No doubt he must have been frustrated by my incompetence but I never doubted that when everything was taken into consideration he wanted to be with us. I think this is how it needs to be with counsellors. It needs to be our autonomous choice to counsel. The counsellor's personal values and source of satisfaction need to be consistent with working in a situation in which someone else's autonomy is the primary concern. The commitment to the client's autonomy needs to be strong enough to cope with the moments of boredom, frustration, fears for oneself, and uncertainty which are inherent in counselling. The integrity of the counselling relationship is at stake unless the counsellor's own autonomy is compatible with a fundamental respect for the client's autonomy. Without this integrity, the client is vulnerable to deliberate or unintentional exploitation.

Conclusion

The quality of the relationship between the client and counsellor is fundamental to counselling. Different models of counselling describe the essential ingredients of this relationship in different ways. Other volumes in the Counselling in Action series are a testimony to the diversity and creativity of counsellors and their chosen methods. The function of the standards and ethics of counselling is to provide a framework within which the essential counselling relationship can flourish regardless of the actual model of counselling which is being used. To date, the emphasis of training in counselling has been directed towards teaching a specific approach to counselling, in which often standards and ethics are implicit. This has been my practice as a trainer and certainly was typical when I was training in the 1970s. However, I no longer believe that this is adequate. An American study has shown that the recognition of ethical dilemmas and the ability to resolve them improves with training (Gawthop and Uhlemann, 1992). This is a good enough reason to make training in standards and ethics a formal part of every counselling course. There will be gains to clients in a greater sense of personal safety. Counsellors will also benefit because a sound understanding of standards and ethics is something which can unite counsellors of many different orientations.

One of the questions I asked at the start of this book was 'Why be ethical?' I attempted to give several good reasons why counsellors should be ethical. But there is a sense in which the question is nonsense. It presupposes that it is possible to be unethical and counsel at the same time, in other words, that standards and ethics can somehow be separated from counselling. I do not believe this to be the case. Standards and ethics are the essential core of counselling and without these the relationship is not counselling.

Over the last decade, I have observed a considerable growth of interest in the standards and ethics of counselling. I welcome this growth in interest. Standards and ethics are too important to be merely implicit. They need to be explicitly considered and evaluated particularly as the issues are not always simple. Like many counsellors, I feel I have learnt from the public debate about standards and ethics. I hope this book will provoke further debate. Even more important, standards and ethics are only meaningful if they are put into practice. I hope that the ideas in this book will be of practical use to counsellors in their everyday work with clients.

APPENDICES

1 Code of Ethics and Practice for Counsellors

1   *Status of this Code*

1.1   In response to the experience of members of BAC, this code is a revision of the 1984 code.

2   *Introduction*

2.1   The purpose of this code is to establish and maintain standards for counsellors who are members of BAC, and to inform and protect members of the public seeking and using their services.

2.2   All members of this Association are required to abide by existing codes appropriate to them. They thereby accept a common frame of reference within which to manage their responsibilities to clients, colleagues, members of this Association and the wider community. Whilst this code cannot resolve all ethical and practice related issues, it aims to provide a framework for addressing ethical issues and to encourage optimum levels of practice. Counsellors will need to judge which parts of this code apply to particular situations. They may have to decide between conflicting responsibilities.

2.3   This Association has a Complaints Procedure which can lead to the expulsion of members for breaches of its Codes of Ethics & Practice.

3   *The Nature of Counselling*

3.1   The overall aim of counselling is to provide an opportunity for the client to work towards living in a more satisfying and resourceful way. The term 'counselling' includes work with individuals, pairs or groups of people, often, but not always, referred to as 'clients'. The objectives of particular counselling relationships will vary according to the client's needs. Counselling may be concerned with developmental issues, addressing and resolving specific problems, making decisions, coping with crisis, developing personal insight and knowledge, working through feelings of inner conflict or improving relationships with others. The counsellor's role is to facilitate the client's work in ways which respect the client's values, personal resources and capacity for self-determination.

3.2 Only when both the user and the recipient explicitly agree to enter into a counselling relationship does it become 'counselling' rather than the use of 'counselling skills'.

3.3 It is not possible to make a generally accepted distinction between counselling and psychotherapy. There are well founded traditions which use the terms interchangeably and others which distinguish them. Regardless of the theoretical approaches preferred by individual counsellors, there are ethical issues which are common to all counselling situations.

4 The Structure of this Code

This code has been divided into two parts. The Code of Ethics outlines the fundamental values of counselling and a number of general principles arising from these. The Code of Practice applies these principles to the counselling situation.

A Code of Ethics

A.1 Counselling is a non-exploitative activity. Its basic values are integrity, impartiality, and respect. Counsellors should take the same degree of care to work ethically whether the counselling is paid or voluntary.

A.2 *Client Safety:*
All reasonable steps should be taken to ensure the client's safety during counselling.

A.3 *Clear Contracts:*
The terms on which counselling is being offered should be made clear to clients before counselling commences. Subsequent revisions of these terms should be agreed in advance of any change.

A.4 *Competence:*
Counsellors shall take all reasonable steps to monitor

and develop their own competence and to work within the limits of that competence. This includes having appropriate and on-going counselling supervision/ consultative support.

B   Code of Practice

B.1   *Introduction:*
This code applies these values and ethical principles to more specific situations which may arise in the practice of counselling.

B.2   *Issues of Responsibility:*
B.2.1   The counsellor–client relationship is the foremost ethical concern, but it does not exist in social isolation. For this reason, the counsellors' responsibilities to the client, to themselves, colleagues, other members of the Association and members of the wider community are listed under separate headings.

B.2.2   To the Client:

Client Safety
2.2.1   Counsellors should take all reasonable steps to ensure that the client suffers neither physical nor psychological harm during counselling.
2.2.2   Counsellors do not normally give advice.

Client Autonomy
2.2.3   Counsellors are responsible for working in ways which promote the client's control over his/her own life, and respect the client's ability to make decisions and change in the light of his/her own beliefs and values.
2.2.4   Counsellors do not normally act on behalf of their clients. If they do, it will be only at the express request of the client, or else in the exceptional circumstances detailed in B.4.
2.2.5   Counsellors are responsible for setting and monitoring boundaries between the counselling relationship and any other kind of relationship, and making this explicit to the client.
2.2.6   Counsellors must not exploit clients financially, sexually, emotionally, or in any other way. Engaging in sexual activity with current clients or within 12 weeks of

the end of the counselling relationship is unethical. If the counselling relationship has been over an extended period of time or been working in-depth, a much longer 'cooling-off' period is required and a lifetime prohibition on future sexual relationships with the client may be more appropriate. [Author's note: The ethical standards about sex with former clients is currently being reconsidered and that part of this section is likely to be revised in September 1993 or 1994.]

2.2.7   Clients should be offered privacy for counselling sessions. The client should not be observed by anyone other than their counsellor(s) without having given his/her informed consent. This also applies to audio/video taping of counselling sessions.

Pre-Counselling Information

2.2.8   Any publicity material and all written and oral information should reflect accurately the nature of the service on offer, and the training, qualifications and relevant experience of the counsellor (see also B.6).

2.2.9   Counsellors should take all reasonable steps to honour undertakings offered in their pre-counselling information.

Contracting

2.2.10   Clear contracting enhances and shows respect for the client's autonomy.

2.2.11   Counsellors are responsible for communicating the terms on which counselling is being offered, including availability, the degree of confidentiality offered, and their expectations of clients regarding fees, cancelled appointments and any other significant matters. The communication of terms and any negotiations over these should be concluded before the client incurs any financial liability.

2.2.12   It is the client's choice whether or not to participate in counselling. Reasonable steps should be taken in the course of the counselling relationship to ensure that the client is given an opportunity to review the terms on which counselling is being offered and the methods of counselling being used.

2.2.13   Counsellors should avoid unnecessary conflicts of interest and are expected to make explicit to the client any relevant conflicts of interest.

2.2.14   If records of counselling sessions are kept, clients should be made aware of this. At the client's request information should be given about access to these records, their availability to other people, and the degree of security with which they are kept (see B.4).

2.2.15   Counsellors have a responsibility to establish with clients what other therapeutic or helping relationships are current. Counsellors should gain the client's permission before conferring with other professional workers.

2.2.16   Counsellors should be aware that computer-based records are subject to statutory regulations under the Data Protection Act 1984. From time to time the government introduces changes in the regulations concerning the client's right of access to his/her own records. Current regulations have implications for counsellors working in social service and health care settings.

Counsellor Competence

2.2.17   Counsellors should monitor actively the limitations of their own competence through counselling supervision/consultative support, and by seeking the views of their clients and other counsellors. Counsellors should work within their own known limits.

2.2.18   Counsellors should not counsel when their functioning is impaired due to personal or emotional difficulties, illness, disability, alcohol, drugs or for any other reason.

2.2.19   It is an indication of the competence of counsellors when they recognise their inability to counsel a client or clients and make appropriate referrals.

B.2.3   To Self as Counsellor:

2.3.1   Counsellors have a responsibility to themselves and their clients to maintain their own effectiveness, resilience and ability to help clients. They are expected to monitor their own personal functioning and to seek help and/or withdraw from counselling, whether temporarily or permanently, when their personal resources are sufficiently depleted to require this (see also B.3).

2.3.2   Counsellors should have received adequate basic training before commencing counselling, and should maintain on-going professional development.

2.3.3   Counsellors are encouraged to review periodically their need for professional indemnity insurance and to take out such a policy when appropriate.

2.3.4	Counsellors should take all reasonable steps to ensure their own physical safety.
B.2.4	To other Counsellors:
2.4.1	Counsellors should not conduct themselves in their counselling-related activities in ways which undermine public confidence in either their role as a counsellor or in the work of other counsellors.
2.4.2	If a counsellor suspects misconduct by another counsellor which cannot be resolved or remedied after discussion with the counsellor concerned, they should implement the Complaints Procedure, doing so without breaches of confidentiality other than those necessary for investigating the complaint (see B.9).
B.2.5	To Colleagues and Members of the Caring Professions:
2.5.1	Counsellors should be accountable for their services to colleagues, employers and funding bodies as appropriate. The means of achieving this should be consistent with respecting the needs of the client outlined in B.2.2.7, B.2.2.13 and B.4.
2.5.2	Counsellors are encouraged to increase their colleagues' understanding of the counselling role. No colleague or significant member of the caring professions should be led to believe that a service is being offered by the counsellor which is not, as this may deprive the client of the offer of such a service from elsewhere.
2.5.3	Counsellors should accept their part in exploring and resolving conflicts of interest between themselves and their agencies, especially where this has implications for the client (see also B.2.2.13).
B.2.6	To the Wider Community:
	Law
2.6.1	Counsellors should work within the law.
2.6.2	Counsellors should take all reasonable steps to be aware of current legislation affecting the work of the counsellor. A counsellor's ignorance of the law is no defence against legal liability or penalty including inciting or 'counselling', which has a specific legal sense, the commission of offences by clients.

Social Context
2.6.3　Counsellors will take all reasonable steps to take account of the client's social context.

B.3　*Counselling Supervision/Consultative Support:*
B.3.1　It is a breach of the ethical requirement for counsellors to practise without regular counselling supervision/consultative support.

B.3.2　Counselling supervision/consultative support refers to a formal arrangement which enables counsellors to discuss their counselling regularly with one or more people who have an understanding of counselling and counselling supervision/consultative support. Its purpose is to ensure the efficacy of the counsellor–client relationship. It is a confidential relationship (see also B.4).

B.3.3　Counsellors who have line managers owe them appropriate managerial accountability for their work. The counselling supervisor role should be independent of the line manager role. However where the counselling supervisor is also the line manager, the counsellor should also have access to independent consultative support.

B.3.4　The volume of supervision should be in proportion to the volume of counselling work undertaken and the experience of the counsellor.

B.3.5　Whenever possible, the discussion of cases within supervision/consultative support should take place without revealing the personal identity of the client.

B.3.6　The ethics and practice of counselling supervision/consultative support are outlined further in their own specific code: the Code of Ethics for the Supervision of Counsellors (see also B.9).

B.4　*Confidentiality: Clients, Colleagues and Others:*
B.4.1　Confidentiality is a means of providing the client with safety and privacy. For this reason any limitation on the degree of confidentiality offered is likely to diminish the usefulness of counselling.

B.4.2　Counsellors treat with confidence personal information about clients, whether obtained directly or indirectly or by inference. Such information includes name, address, biographical details, and other descriptions of the client's life and circumstances which might result in identification of the client.

B.4.3   Counsellors should work within the current agreement with their client about confidentiality.

B.4.4   Exceptional circumstances may arise which give the counsellor good grounds for believing that the client will cause serious physical harm to others or themselves, or have harm caused to him/her. In such circumstances the client's consent to a change in the agreement about confidentiality should be sought whenever possible unless there are also good grounds for believing the client is no longer able to take responsibility for his/her own actions. Whenever possible, the decision to break confidentiality agreed between a counsellor and client should be made only after consultation with a counselling supervisor or an experienced counsellor.

B.4.5   Any breaking of confidentiality should be minimised both by restricting the information conveyed to that which is pertinent to the immediate situation and to those persons who can provide the help required by the client. The ethical considerations involve balancing between acting in the best interests of the client and in ways which enable clients to resume taking responsibility for their actions, a very high priority for counsellors, and the counsellor's responsibilities to the wider community (see B.2.2.7 and B.4.4).

B.4.6   Counsellors should take all responsible steps to communicate clearly the extent of the confidentiality they are offering to clients. This should normally be made clear in the pre-counselling information or initial contracting.

B.4.7   If counsellors include consultations with colleagues and others within the confidential relationship, this should be stated to the client at the beginning of counselling.

B.4.8   Care must be taken to ensure that personally identifiable information is not transmitted through overlapping networks of confidential relationship. For this reason, it is good practice to avoid identifying specific clients during counselling supervision/consultative support and other consultations, unless there are sound reasons for doing so (see also B.2.2.14 and B.4.2).

B.4.9   Any agreement between the counsellor and client about confidentiality may be reviewed and changed by joint negotiations.

B.4.10 Agreements about confidentiality continue after the client's death unless there are overriding legal or ethical considerations.

B.4.11   Counsellors hold different views about whether or not a client expressing serious suicidal intentions forms sufficient grounds for breaking confidentiality. Counsellors should consider their own views and practice and communicate them to clients and any significant others where appropriate (see also B.2.5.2).

B.4.12   Special care is required when writing about specific counselling situations for case studies, reports or publication. It is important that the author either has the client's informed consent, or effectively disguises the client's identity.

B.4.13   Any discussion between the counsellor and others should be purposeful and not trivialising.

B.5   Confidentiality in the Legal Process:

B.5.1   Generally speaking, there is no legal duty to give information spontaneously or on request until instructed to do so by a court. Refusal to answer police questions is not an offence, although lying could be. In general terms, the only circumstances in which the police can require an answer about a client, and when refusal to answer would be an offence, relate to the prevention of terrorism. It is good practice to ask police personnel to clarify their legal right to an answer before refusing to give one.

B.5.2   Withholding information about a crime that one knows has been committed or is about to be committed is not an offence, save exceptionally. Anyone hearing of terrorist activities should immediately take legal advice.

B.5.3   There is no legal obligation to answer a solicitor's enquiry or to make a statement for the purpose of legal proceedings, unless ordered to do so by a court.

B.5.4   There is no legal obligation to attend court at the request of parties involved in a case, or at the request of their lawyers, until a witness summons or subpoena is issued to require attendance to answer questions or produce documents.

B.5.5   Once in the witness box, there is a duty to answer questions when instructed to do so by the court. Refusal to answer could be punished as contempt of court unless there are legal grounds for not doing so. (It has been held that communications between the counsellor and client during an attempt at 'reconciliation' in matrimonial cases are privileged and thus do not require disclosure unless the client waives this privilege. This does not seem to apply to other kinds of cases.)

B.5.6 The police have powers to seize confidential files if they have obtained a warrant from a circuit judge. Obstructing the police from taking them in these circumstances may be an offence.

B.5.7 Counsellors should seek legal advice and/or contact this Association if they are in any doubt about their legal rights and obligations before acting in ways which conflict with their agreement with clients who are directly affected (see also B.2.6.1).

B.6 Advertising/ Public Statements:

B.6.1 When announcing counselling services, counsellors should limit the information to name, relevant qualifications, address, telephone number, hours available, and a brief listing of the services offered.

B.6.2 All such announcements should be accurate in every particular.

B.6.3 Counsellors should distinguish between membership of this Association and accredited practitioner status in their public statements. In particular, the former should not be used to imply the latter.

B.6.4 Counsellors should not display an affiliation with an organisation in a manner which falsely implies the sponsorship or verification of that organisation.

B.7 Research:

B.7.1 The use of personally identifiable material gained from clients or by the observation of counselling should be used only after the client has given consent, usually in writing, and care has been taken to ensure that consent was given freely.

B.7.2 Counsellors conducting research should use their data accurately and restrict their conclusions to those compatible with their methodology.

B.8 Resolving Conflicts between Ethical Priorities:

B.8.1 Counsellors will, from time to time, find themselves caught between conflicting ethical principles. In these circumstances, they are urged to consider the particular situation in which they find themselves and to discuss the situation with their counselling supervisor and/or other experienced counsellors. Even after conscientious consideration of the salient issues, some ethical dilemmas cannot be resolved easily or wholly satisfactorily.

B.8.2   Ethical issues may arise which have not yet been given full consideration. The Standards and Ethics Subcommittee of this Association is interested in hearing of the ethical difficulties of counsellors, as this helps to inform discussion regarding good practice.

B.9   *The Availability of other Codes and Guidelines Relating to Counselling:*

B.9.1   The following codes and procedures have been passed by the Annual General Meetings of the British Association for Counselling.

Code of Ethics & Practice for Counselling Skills applies to members who would not regard themselves as counsellors, but who use counselling skills to support other roles.

Code of Ethics & Practice for the Supervision of Counsellors exists to guide members offering supervision to counsellors and to help counsellors seeking supervision.

Code of Ethics & Practice for Trainers exists to guide members offering training to counsellors, and to help members of the public seeking counselling training.

Complaints Procedure exists to guide members of BAC and their clients resolving complaints about breaches of the Codes of Ethics & Practice.

Copies and other guidelines and information sheets relevant to maintaining ethical standards of practice can be obtained from the BAC office, 1 Regent Place, Rugby CV21 2PJ.

Guidelines also available:
Telephone Helplines: Guidelines for Good Practice is intended to establish standards for people working on telephone helplines (sponsored by British Telecom). Single copies available from: BSS, PO Box 7, London, W3 6XJ.

2 Useful names and addresses

Professional associations

Association of Humanistic Psychology
Practitioners (AHPP)
14 Mornington Grove
London E3 4NS

British Association for Counselling
1 Regent Place
Rugby CV21 2PS

British Association for Sexual and
Marital Therapy (BASMT)
Box 62
Sheffield 10

British Psychological Society (BPS)
48 Princess Road East
Leicester LE1 7DR

Relate Marriage Guidance
Herbert Gray College
Little Church Street
Rugby CV21 3AP

United Kingdom Council for
Psychotherapy (UKCP)
Regent College
Inner Circle
Regents Park
London NW1 4NS

Professional indemnity insurance for counsellors

Bartlett and Co
Broadway Hall
Horsforth
Leeds LS18 4RS

Bartlett offers discounts to members
of the British Association for
Counselling and the British
Psychological Society.

Devitt Insurance Services Ltd
Central House
32–66 High Street
Stratford
London E15 2PF

Messrs Harvey Pettitt & Partners
187 Upper Street
London N1 2RQ

M. and A. Murray
Psychologist Protection Society (PPS)
Standalone House
Kincardine
Alloa FK10 4NX

Specialist information

For general and specialist advice
about legal and financial entitlements
and obligations:

Citizens Advice Bureau – for local
services see telephone directory.

For information and advice about
law and policy affecting children and
young people in England and Wales:

The Childrens Legal Centre
PO 3314
London N1 2WA

For those working with bereaved
families, INQUEST offers advice,
support and information on coroners'
inquests following deaths in police or
prison custody, or in psychiatric
institutions.

INQUEST
Ground Floor
Alexandra National House
330 Seven Sisters Road
Finsbury Park
London N4 2PJ

For information about local services,
the law and policy, and training about
mental health:

MIND
National Association for Mental
  Health
22 Harley Street
London W1N 2ED

**Support and information for clients
exploited by counsellors, therapists
and other caring professionals**

Abuse in Therapy Support Network
c/o Women's Support Project
871 Springfield Road
Glasgow G31 4HZ

(Please send stamped addressed
envelope. Welcomes enquiries from
men and women. Runs women only
group.)

Prevention of Professional Abuse
  Network (POPAN)
Flat 1
20 Daleham Gardens
London NW3 5DA
(Please send stamped addressed
envelope with a small contribution
with correspondence if possible as the
project is currently unfunded. All
enquiries are welcome although there
may be a delay in replying at times.)

Bibliography

Allen, R.E. (1990), *The Concise Oxford Dictionary of Current English*, Oxford University Press, Oxford.

American Association for Counseling and Development (1988), *Ethical Standards of the American Association for Counseling and Development*, AACD, Virginia, USA.

Argyle, Michael (ed.) (1981), *Social Skills and Health*, Methuen, London.

Association for Student Counselling (1991), *HMI Inspection of Counselling Services*, ASC, Rugby.

Association for Student Counselling (1992), *Requirements for Accreditation*, ASC, Rugby.

Austin, Kenneth M., Moline, Mary E. and Williams, George T. (1990), *Confronting Malpractice – Legal and Ethical Dilemmas in Psychotherapy*, Sage, Newbury Park, USA.

Bancroft, John (1983), *Human Sexuality and its Problems*, Churchill Livingstone, Edinburgh.

Bartlett & Co Ltd (1992) 'Unpublished correspondence with Roger Litton', Bartlett & Co Ltd, Leeds.

Bond, Tim (1991a), 'Sex and Suicide in the Development of Counselling', *Changes, An International Journal of Psychology and Psychotherapy*, 9(4): 284–93.

Bond, Tim (1991b), *HIV Counselling – Report on National Survey and Consultation 1990*, BAC, Rugby. Second edn (1992), BAC, Rugby/Daniels, Cambridge.

Brammer, Laurence M. and Shostrum, Everett L. (1982), *Therapeutic Psychology – Fundamentals of Counselling and Psychotherapy*, Prentice-Hall, New Jersey.

British Association for Counselling (1984), *Code of Ethics and Practice for Counsellors*, BAC, Rugby.

British Association for Counselling (1985), *Counselling: Definition of Terms in Use with Expansion and Rationale*, BAC, Rugby.

British Association for Counselling (1988), *Code of Ethics and Practice for the Supervision of Counsellors*, BAC, Rugby.

British Association for Counselling (1989), *Code of Ethics and Practice for Counselling Skills*, BAC, Rugby.

British Association for Counselling (1990), *Information Sheet 8 – Supervision*, BAC, Rugby.

British Association for Counselling (1991), *Companies Act 1991 – Memorandum of Association of the British Association for Counselling*, BAC, Rugby.

British Association for Counselling (1992a), *Code of Ethics and Practice for Counsellors*, BAC, Rugby, which contains a revised section B.2.2.6 and is otherwise the same as the *Code of Ethics and Practice for Counsellors* (1990), BAC, Rugby.

British Association for Counselling (1992b), *Complaints Procedure*, BAC, Rugby.

British Medical Association (1981), *Handbook on Medical Ethics*, BMA, London.

British Medical Association Foundation for AIDS (1988), *HIV Infection and AIDS: ethical considerations for the medical profession*, BMA, London.

British Psychological Society (1991), *Code of Conduct, Ethical Principles and Guidelines*, BPS, Leicester.

Brooke, Rosalind (1972), *Information and Advice Guidance*, The Social Administration Research Trust, G. Bell and Sons, London.

Burnard, Philip (1989), *Counselling Skills for Health Professionals*, Chapman and Hall, London.

Burnard, Philip (1992), *Perceptions of AIDS Counselling*, Avebury, Aldershot.

Carroll, Michael, (1993) 'Ethical Issues in Organisational Counselling', unpublished paper, Roehampton Institute, London.

Casement, Patrick (1985), *On Learning from the Patient*, Tavistock Publications/Routledge, London.

Children's Legal Centre (1989), 'A Child's Right to Confidentiality?' *Childright*, 57: 7–10.

Children's Legal Centre (1992), *Working with Young People – Legal Responsibility and Liability*, Children's Legal Centre, London.

Cohen, Kenneth (1992), 'Some Legal Issues in Counselling and Psychotherapy', *British Journal of Guidance and Counselling*, 20(1): 10–26.

Consumers' Association (1991), 'Psychotherapy', *Which? way to Health*, December 1991: 212–15.

Culley, Sue (1991), *Integrative Counselling Skills in Action*, Sage Publications, London.

Department of Health (1992), Guidance on Partner Notification for HIV Infection, Department of Health, London, PL/CO(92)5, Appendix 3.

Deuzen-Smith, Emmy van (1988), *Existential Counselling in Practice*, Sage, London.

Dexter, Graham (1991), *Counselling Network*, York and Scarborough College of Midwifery and Nursing Counselling Network, York.

Dryden, Windy (1985), *Therapists' Dilemmas*, Open University Press, Milton Keynes.

Dryden, Windy (1990), *Rational–Emotive Counselling in Action*, Sage Publications, London.

Einzig, Hetty (1989), *Counselling and Psychotherapy – Is it for Me?*, BAC, Rugby.

Eldrid, John (1988), *Caring for the Suicidal*, Constable, London.

Foskett, John and Lyall, David (1988), *Helping the Helpers – Supervision and Pastoral Care*, SPCK, London.

Foss, Brian (1986), Review of Accreditation Scheme of the British Association for Counselling, unpublished paper, BAC, Rugby.

Friel, John (1993) *In the Matter of the Powers of Her Majesty's Inspector of Schools to Inspect Counselling in Polytechnics, Colleges of Further Education etc*, Legal opinion obtained by British Association for Counselling.

Gawthop, J.C. and Uhlemann, M.R. (1992), 'Effects of the Problem–solving Approach to Ethics Training', *Professional Psychology: Research and Practice*, 23(1): 38–42.

General Medical Council (1991) *HIV Infection and AIDS: The Ethical Considerations*, GMA, London.

Gibson, William T. and Pope, Kenneth S. (1993), 'The Ethics of Counselling: A National Survey of Certified Counsellors', *Journal of Counselling and Development*, 71: 330–6.

Gillon, Raanan (1985), 'Autonomy and consent' in Lockwood, Michael (ed.), *Moral Dilemmas in Modern Medicine*, Oxford University Press, Oxford, pp.111–25.

Grant, Linda (1992), 'Counselling: a solution or a problem?', *Independent on Sunday*, 19 April 1992: 22–3 and 26 April 1992: 20.

Guardian Law Reports (1992), 'Re. J. (a minor) (Medical Treatment)', *The Guardian*, London, 22 July.

Gummere, Richard M. (1988), 'The Counsellor as Prophet: Frank Parsons 1854–1908' in *Journal of Counselling and Development*, May, 66: 402–5.

Halmos, Paul (1978), *The Faith of Counsellors*, Constable, London.

Hawkins, Peter and Shohet, Robin (1989), *Supervision in the Helping Professions*, Open University Press, Milton Keynes.

Hawton, Keith and Catalan, Jose (1987), *Attempted Suicide – A Practical Guide to its Nature and Management*, Oxford University Press, Oxford.

Hayman, Anne (1965), 'Psychoanalyst Subpoenaed', *The Lancet*, 16 October: 785–6.

Herlihy, Barbara and Corey, Gerald (1992), *Dual Relationships*, American Association for Counseling and Development, Alexandria, USA.

Her Majesty's Inspectorate (1988), *Careers Education and Guidance from 5 to 16*, Department of Education and Science, HMSO, London.

Heron, John (1990), *Helping the Client – A Creative Practical Guide* (revised version of *Six Category Intervention Analyses*, 1975, 1986, 1989, previously published by University of Surrey), Sage Publications, London.

Heyd, David and Bloch, Sidney (1991), 'The Ethics of Suicide', in Bloch, Sidney and Chodoff, Paul (eds), *Psychiatric Ethics*, Oxford University Press, Oxford.

Hiltner, S. (1949), *Pastoral Counseling*, Abingdon, Nashville, TN.

HMSO (1987), *Report of the Inquiry into Child Abuse in Cleveland*, HMSO, London, Cmnd 412.

Holmes, Jeremy and Lindley, Richard (1989), *The Values of Psychotherapy*, Oxford University Press, Oxford.

Hooper, Douglas (1988), 'Invited Editorial – "York 1988"', *Counselling – Journal of the British Association for Counselling*, November, 66: 1–2.

Houston, Gaie (1990), *Supervision and Counselling*, The Rochester Foundation, London.

Hoxter, Hans (1991), *The Nature of Counselling*, International Round Table for the Advancement of Counselling (IRTAC), London.

Human Fertilisation and Embryology Authority (1991), *Code of Practice*, HFEA, London.

Human Fertilisation and Embryology Authority (1992), *Code of Practice*, HFEA, London.

Independent Law Report (1992), 'Re T – Court of Appeal', *The Independent*, London, 31 July.

Inskipp, Francesca (1986), *Counselling: The Trainer's Handbook*, National Extension College, Cambridge.

Inskipp, Francesca and Proctor, Brigid (1989), *Skills for Supervising and Being Supervised*, Alexia Publications, St Leonard's on Sea, East Sussex.

Jacobs, Michael (1988), *Psychodynamic Counselling in Action*, Sage Publications, London.

Jakobi, Stephen and Pratt, Duncan (1992), 'Therapy note and the Law', *The Psychologist*, May: 219–21.

Laing, R.D. (1967), *The Politics of Experience and The Bird of Paradise*, Penguin, Harmondsworth.

Law Commission (1981), *Breach of Confidence*, HMSO, London, Cmnd. 8388.

Law Society (1992), Guide to Professional Conduct of Solicitors' Law Society, London.

Leissner, Aryeh (1969), 'Family Advice Service', *British Hospital Journal and Service Review*, 17 January: 120.

Mays, J., Forder, A. and Keidan, O. (1975), *Penelope Hall's Social Services of England and Wales*, Routledge and Kegan Paul, London.

Mearns, David (1991), 'On Being a Supervisor', in Dryden, Windy and Thorne, Brian (eds), *Training and Supervision for Counselling in Action*, Sage Publications, London.

Megranahan, Michael (1989), *Counselling – A Practical Guide for Employers*, Institute of Personnel Management, London.

Miller, Alice (1990), *Thou Shalt Not Be Aware – Society's Betrayal of the Child*, Pluto Press, London.

Munro, Anne, Manthei, Bob and Small, John (1988), *Counselling: The Skills of Problem-Solving*, Longman, Auckland, New Zealand, and Routledge, London.

Murgatroyd, Stephen (1985), *Counselling and Helping*, British Psychological Society, Leicester, and Methuen, London.

Musgrave, Arthur (1991), *What is Good Advice Work?*, NAYPCAS Discussion Paper, Youth Access, Leicester.

National Association of Citizens' Advice Bureaux (1990), 'Quality of Advice: NACAB Membership Scheme Requirements', 3(1), *National Homelessness Advice Service – Guidance on CAB Minimum Housing Advice Standards*, National Citizens Advice Bureaux, London.

Paradise, L.V. and Siegelwaks, B. (1982), 'Ethical training for group leaders' in *Journal for Specialists in Groupwork*, 7(3): 162–6.

Pope, K.S. (1988), 'How clients are harmed by sexual contact with mental health professionals: The syndrome and its prevalence', *Journal of Counselling and Development*, 67: 222–6.

Pope, K.S. and Bouhoutsos, J.C. (1986), *Sexual intimacy between therapists and patients*, Praeger Press, New York.

Pope, K.S. and Vasquez, M.J.T. (1991), *Ethics in psychotherapy and counseling – A practical guide for psychologists*, Jossey-Bass, San Francisco.

Proctor, Brigid (1988), 'Supervision: A Co-operative Exercise in Accountability', in Marken, Mary and Payne, Malcolm (eds.), *Enabling and Ensuring Supervision in Practice*, National Youth Bureau, UK.

Reiter-Theil, Stella, Eich Holger and Reiter, Ludwig (1991), 'Informed Consent in Family Therapy – Necessary Discourse and Practice', *Changes, Journal of the Psychology and Psychotherapy Association*, 9(2): 91–100.

Rogers, Carl (1980), *A Way of Being*, Houghton Mifflin, Boston, USA.

Rogers, W.V.H. (1989), *Winfield and Jolowicz on Tort*, Sweet and Maxwell, London.

Rowan, John (1983), *The Reality Game – A guide to humanistic counselling and therapy*, Routledge and Kegan Paul, London.

Rowan, John (1988), 'Counselling and the Psychology of Furniture', *Counselling, Journal of the British Association for Counselling*, Rugby, 64: 21–45 and reprinted in (1992), *Breakthroughs and Integration in Psychotherapy*, Whurr, London.

Russell, Janice (1993), *Out of Bounds – Sexual Exploitation in Counselling and Therapy*, Sage Publications, London.

Russell, Janice, Dexter, Graham and Bond, Tim (1992), *A Report on Differentiation between Advice, Guidance, Befriending, Counselling Skills and Counselling*, British Association for Counselling, Rugby and Department of Employment, London.

Rutter, Peter (1989), *Sex in the Forbidden Zone*, Mandala, London.

Schutz, B.M. (1982), *Legal Liability to Psychotherapy*, Jossey-Bass, San Francisco.

Shohet, Robin and Wilmot, Joan (1991), 'The Key Issue in the Supervision of Counsellors: The Supervisory Relationship', in Dryden, Windy and Thorne, Brian, *Training and Supervision for Counselling in Action*, Sage Publications, London.

Smith, J.C. and Hogan, Brian (1992), *Criminal Law*, Butterworths, London.

Soisson, E., Vandecreek, L. and Knapp, S. (1987), 'Thorough Record Keeping: A Good Defense', *Professional Psychology: Research and Practice*, 18(5): 498-502.

Stadler, Holly A. (1986a), *Confidentiality: The Professional's Dilemma – Participant Manual*, American Association for Counseling and Development, Alexandria, Virginia, USA.

Stadler, Holly A. (1986b), 'Making hard choices: Clarifying controversial ethical issues', *Counseling and Human Development*, 19(1): 1-10.

Sugarman, Léonie (1992), 'Ethical Issues in Counselling at Work', *British Journal of Guidance and Counselling*, 20(1): 64-74.

Sykes, J.B. (1982), *The Concise Oxford Dictionary of Current English*, Oxford University Press, Oxford.

Szasz, Thomas (1986), 'The case against suicide prevention', *American Psychologist*, 41: 806-12.

Thorne, Brian (1984), 'Person-centred Therapy' in Dryden, Windy (ed.), *Individual Therapy in Britain*, Harper and Row, London.

Thorne, Brian (1992), 'Psychotherapy and Counselling: The Quest for Differences, *Counselling, Journal of the British Association for Counselling*, Rugby, 3(4): 244-8.

Thorne, Brian and Mearns, David (1988), *Person-Centred Counselling in Action*, Sage Publications, London.

Times Law Reports (1992), Nichols v. Rushton, *The Times*, London, 19 June.

UKCC (1992), *Code of Professional Conduct*, United Kingdom Central Council for Nursing, Midwifery and Health Visitors, London.

Wise, C. (1951), *Pastoral Counseling: Its Theory and Practice*, Harper & Bros, New York.

Woolfe, R., Murgatroyd, S. and Rhys, S. (1987), *Guidance and counselling in adult and continuing education: a developmental perspective*, Open University Press, Milton Keynes.

Zytowski, D. (1985), 'Frank, Frank! Where are you now that we need you?' *Counselling Psychologist*, 13: 129-35.

Index